A MOBILE CENTURY?

Transport and Mobility Series

Edited by
Professor Brian Graham, Director, Academy for Irish Cultural Heritages,
University of Ulster, UK and Richard Knowles, Reader in Geography, University
of Salford, UK, on behalf of the Royal Geographical Society (with the Institute of
British Geographers) Transport Geography Research Group (TGRG)

The inception of this series marks a major resurgence of geographical research into transport and mobility. Reflecting the critical importance of the dynamic relationships between transport and socio-spatial change, this work includes research on:

The impacts of liberalisation, privatisation, competition and globalisation on transport policies, networks and strategies;

Traffic generation and diversion and the economic impacts of large-scale infrastructure projects such as the Channel Tunnel;

The assessment of environmental sustainability concerns about increasing mobility, dispersal of activity sites and the dependence of transport on fossil fuels and its associated air pollution;

Transport, gender and welfare issues;

The relationships between transport and leisure;

Congestion and capacity constraints in transport systems.

This monograph series complements the international, quarterly research journal, *Journal of Transport Geography* (launched in 1993) and *Modern Transport Geography* (eds Brian Hoyle and Richard Knowles, 2nd ed 1998 on behalf of the TGRG). Together, these three outlets act as a forum for cutting-edge research into transport and mobility, and for innovative and decisive debates on the formulation and repercussions of transport policy making.

Also in the Series

Rethinking Urban Transport After Modernism
Lessons from South Africa
David Dewar and Fabio Todeschini
ISBN 0 7546 4169 4

A Mobile Century?
Changes in Everyday Mobility in Britain in the Twentieth Century

COLIN G. POOLEY
Lancaster University, UK

JEAN TURNBULL
Lancaster University, UK

MAGS ADAMS
University of Salford, UK

ASHGATE

Published by
Ashgate Publishing Limited
Wey Court East
Union Road
Farnham
Surrey, GU9 7PT
England

Ashgate Publishing Company
110 Cherry Street
Suite 3-1
Burlington
VT 05401-3818
USA

Ashgate website: http://www.ashgate.com

British Library Cataloguing in Publication Data
Pooley, Colin G.
 A mobile century? : changes in everyday mobility in Britain
 in the twentieth century. - (Transport and mobility series)
 1.Local transit - Great Britain - History - 20th century
 2.Transportation - Great Britain - History - 20th century
 3.Commuting - Great Britain 4.Travel - Social aspects -
 Great Britain 5.Great Britain - Social conditions - 20th
 century
 I.Title. II.Turnbull, Jean III.Adams, Mags
 388.4'0941'0904

Library of Congress Control Number: 2005927751

ISBN 978-0-7546-4181-0

Transfered to Digital Printing in 2012

MIX
Paper from
responsible sources
FSC
www.fsc.org   FSC® C013985

Printed in the United Kingdom by Henry Ling Limited,
at the Dorset Press, Dorchester, DT1 1HD

Contents

List of Figures

List of Tables

List of Text Boxes

Preface

This book has emerged from two research projects that have together spanned much of the last decade. The first project, on the journey to work in Britain in the twentieth century, funded by The Leverhulme Trust (1996-1999), grew out of previous work by Pooley and Turnbull on migration and mobility in Britain since the eighteenth century. Although this research focused primarily on residential migration, it also touched on changes in the journey to work subsequent to relocation and led us to examine the ways in which the relationships between residential migration and everyday mobility have altered over time. The journey to work project allowed us to focus specifically on these themes during the twentieth century. The second project, on everyday mobility in Britain since the 1940s, funded by the ESRC (2000-2004) expanded our mobility research by focusing on all aspects of everyday mobility, especially the ways in which the daily mobility of children has changed over the past 60 years. In both projects we utilised and refined techniques of longitudinal data collection first developed in the migration research.

When starting this research we expected to record substantial changes in the amount and characteristics of everyday mobility since 1900. The main purpose of the projects was to examine the ways in which such changes impacted on people's lives. In practice, although some aspects of mobility have altered substantially, the most striking aspect of the data has been the degree to which, for many people, the pattern and process of everyday mobility has remained much the same for most of the twentieth century. We have thus found ourselves explaining stability rather than change and we have begun to question some established theories and assumptions about mobility in the recent past. Although not the primary purpose of the projects the research has also allowed us to relate our data on mobility change to contemporary debates about transport planning and urban sustainability.

Much of the material presented in this book is not being made available for the first time. We have presented numerous conference papers on our research and have published some ten articles in academic journals arising from different aspects of the projects. However, what this volume does do is to integrate the material in a way that has not been achieved before and to relate it to a broader context of both theoretical literature and practical transport planning. In so doing we hope to have strengthened the key messages of the research and to have communicated them to an audience beyond the small group of like-minded academics who are likely to read journal articles.

We have inevitably accumulated a large number of debts during the process of this research. Hopefully, all those who have assisted us are formally acknowledged elsewhere. If anyone has been missed we apologise and extend our grateful thanks. We have been particularly fortunate in that the research environment at Lancaster University has been especially stimulating and supportive for research on mobility. The Centre for Mobilities Research (CeMoRe), founded by John Urry, draws together academics from many different disciplines with a common interest in mobility in all its manifestations. We have learned much from seminars and other activities within CeMoRe and thank our colleagues for their interest in our work. The imperfections in the research remain, of course, entirely our own responsibility.

As with all research we complete this volume feeling that there remain many things that we do not fully understand about mobility change in the past. Due to the ephemeral and personal nature of much mobility we may never have satisfactory answers to all the questions raised. However, we hope that our research at least stimulates further interest in everyday mobility and begins to raise questions that others may go on to explore.

Colin G. Pooley
Jean Turnbull
Mags Adams
Lancaster, January 2005

Acknowledgements

We wish to thank everyone who has assisted us with the research upon which this book is based. Particular thanks to:

The Leverhulme Trust and the ESRC for funding the research.
All the respondents who completed questionnaires and agreed to be interviewed. This research could not have been completed without them, though due to a guarantee of anonymity they cannot be thanked individually.
Staff and students at the schools and colleges we contacted who assisted with recruitment of respondents.
Cait Griffith for coding and data entry.
Geraldine Byrne for transcription of tapes.
Dr Sue Owen for additional research assistance.
Siân Pooley for additional research assistance and proof reading.
Emma Joughin for additional research assistance.
Chris Beacock for help with the design of recruitment material and questionnaires.
Simon Chew (Cartographic Unit, Department of Geography, Lancaster University) for all the figures in the book.
Gemma Davies for assistance with GIS and, especially production of the figures in Chapter 5.
Mr. G. Brady (Greater Glasgow Passenger Transport Authority) for access to archives on public transport in Glasgow.
Steve Jenkins for assistance with the Access database.
The editors and staff at Ashgate who have dealt with production of the book.

Chapter 1

The Significance of Travel and Mobility

Introduction

Most people spend a substantial part of their life engaged in travel of some kind or another. Apart from those too infirm to move from their bed or chair, daily mobility is, and has always been, the normal experience for people in all cultures and time periods. The attraction of travel, and of writing about travel, is well embedded in English literature, exemplified by the works of authors including Defoe, Cobbett, Priestley and, more recently, the popular writings of authors such as Hunter Davies and Bill Bryson. But such travel writing represents only a small portion of the sum total of everyday mobility that occurs. Most people can travel only occasionally over long distances and rarely have the luxury (or even inclination) to meander slowly and write about their experiences. However, everyday journeys – to school, to work, to visit friends and relatives, to shop, for leisure and pleasure – all form part of the fabric that constructs our everyday existence. Without such trips life as we recognise it would not be possible and, to some extent, our very identities are constructed through the everyday mobility that we undertake.

It is usually assumed that levels of mobility have increased over time and that, in the twenty-first century, our ability to travel from place to place has reached an unprecedented level. For instance, data from the National Travel Survey show that in 2003 people in Britain each travelled on average 10,944km during the year, an increase of 34.2 per cent since 1972/3, and during the same period the mean trip length increased from 7.6km to 11.1km. However, such figures can be misleading, and although it is undoubtedly true that the possibility for high levels of mobility, and for faster and more frequent mobility over long distances, is now much greater than ever before, this does not mean that everyone necessarily travels further or more frequently than they did in the past. Indeed, the same data show that the number of trips undertaken each year has changed little since the 1970s (National Statistics, 2003). Nor does it mean that the basic structure of mobility, its causes and consequences, has changed radically. Thus, although the availability of low-cost airlines has increased opportunities for long-distance travel, most people will do this only once or twice each year and many people never have (or take) this opportunity. Constraints of income, work, family or simply a lack of desire to travel mean that for many people frequent long distance journeys are neither possible nor attractive. Thus, it can be suggested that, for many, everyday mobility consists mainly of local travel connected to essential everyday tasks and that this aspect of mobility has changed little over time.

Thus, one key argument of this book is that although the changes that have taken place in British (and global) economy, technology, society and culture over the twentieth century have increased mobility opportunities, and might be expected to have dramatically changed levels of everyday mobility for most people, in practice the amount of change has been relatively small. In other words, the book will construct an argument for relative stability within a changing structural context, arguing that at the individual and family levels the factors that influence mobility decisions are essentially personal and relatively stable over time. The argument advanced in this book is thus countering, or at least qualifying, much of the literature on travel and transport in the twentieth century that assumes high and increasing levels of everyday mobility (Thrift, 1995; Cairncross, 1997; Schaffer and Victor, 1997; Adams, 1999; Urry, 2000). The main reason why such assumptions have not been challenged previously is the lack of data on long-run trends in everyday mobility. In the absence of firm evidence broad structural trends in society and economy, linked to theories of social and spatial change, have been used to infer mobility change. This book presents new evidence relating to everyday mobility in Britain over the past century and for the first time allows some of the theoretical assumptions to be tested. The argument advanced does not deny that massive change has taken place, but it suggests that the impact of such changes on individual mobility can be exaggerated, and that considering the extent of structural change the degree of stability that has occurred is remarkable.

What is Mobility?

It is necessary to begin by defining precisely what we mean by mobility as both academic studies and everyday usage deploy the term loosely. The Oxford English Dictionary definition simply construes the word as pertaining to movement, which can clearly encompass a very wide range of meanings. There is no simple division between different categories of human movement, and concepts of mobility can best be understood as part of a mobility continuum (Figure 1.1). Residential migration sits at one end of the spectrum, where an individual changes their usual place of residence and intends to remain in that location for the foreseeable future. Such migration can itself occur on a variety of scales, with differing impacts, ranging from international migration across national boundaries to short distance moves from one street to another within the same urban area. Whereas in the former case migration requires a complete readjustment of all aspects of everyday life (work, school, friends) and the daily mobility associated with these activities, in the latter case a residential move requires only minor adjustments to everyday living patterns and associated travel (Pooley and Turnbull, 1998).

For some people circulation between two or more homes is normal, thus blurring the distinction between daily mobility and residential migration. There are many examples of this phenomenon though its incidence has probably increased during the twentieth century. Thus agricultural or building workers may move around the country following the availability of employment, service personnel

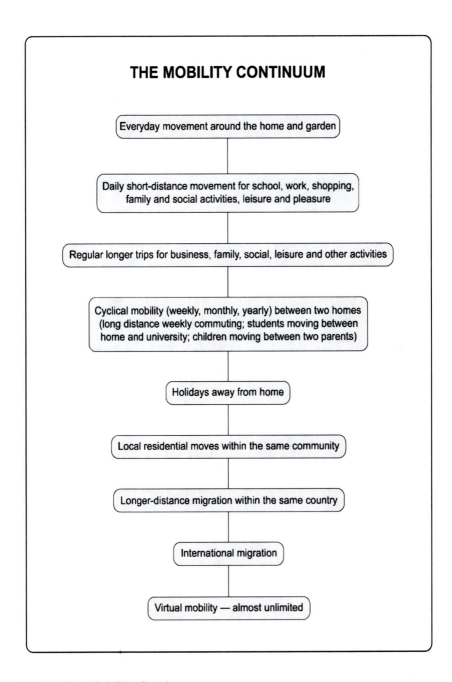

Figure 1.1 The Mobility Continuum

may be moved frequently between bases, students in higher education live in one place during term time and another during vacations and children brought up in the context of family break-up may spend part of the week with one parent and part with another. In these cases the division between residential migration and daily mobility becomes blurred as, for some, moving between homes becomes almost a daily experience.

Daily mobility sits at the opposite end of the mobility spectrum to long-distance residential migration. This category of movement encompasses all the travel that is undertaken to sustain the normal routine of daily life. Thus it includes travel to work or to school, travel for leisure and pleasure (including holidays), travel to shop and obtain other services (for instance health care) and travel to visit relatives or friends. Although most of this travel is frequent, short-term, often regular and usually over short distances within one urban area, at times it can entail long journeys and/or temporary residence away from home. Thus, for some, the journey to work can take up several hours in the day. If an individual lives for part of the week in a location that is different from his/her normal home, then this aspect of daily mobility merges into the category of population circulation cited above. At the micro-scale we are all involved in daily movement around our home and for some, for instance those with restricted mobility, this may form the majority mobility experience.

One change that has occurred is the development of new opportunities for virtual mobility. Whereas in the past most activities and transactions required people to move physically to meet and undertake (for example) work or leisure activities together, new computer communications developed over the last two decades have allowed people to interact without physical movement. Thus some people can work at home yet retain close contact with their office, it is possible to have almost instant communication with relatives on the other side of the globe, many goods and services can be bought over the internet without having to visit a shop or office, on-line education can be provided for children in remote communities and information about distant places can be gained without having to travel. At least some of the activities that previously required mobility can now be undertaken at home. This has two possible effects. On the one hand the development of computer-based communication systems can be seen as part of the globalisation process that encourages increased flows of goods, people, capital and ideas around the globe, whilst on the other hand the ability to work, shop and interact with friends from home may act to reduce spatial mobility, thus counteracting assumed trends of increased mobility over time (Kitchin, 1998; Dodge and Kitchin, 2000; Janelle and Hodge, 2000).

All the different aspects of mobility outlined above also have implications for the links between mobility and identity. If it is assumed that the ability to undertake everyday mobility is one of a number of processes that construct our everyday lives, then it also contributes to the production of individual and group identities. Where we travel, how we travel, who we travel with, what we travel for and how often we travel all impinge on the constructions of the self and on identity with people and places. For instance, daily commuting by train brings you into contact with a community of people with shared travel experiences. The routine of commuting may be reinforced by habits such as always choosing the same seat in a particular carriage. Conversations and friendships based around the journey to work can reinforce a sense of identity and, when transport systems fail, commuters with a common experience of delay and travel misery are likely to be keen to share experiences and commiserate with each other's plight (Urry, 2000). In extreme examples, for instance following a serious rail accident, survivors and their relatives may join together to form action or support groups to seek compensation or prosecution of those they consider to blame. Some of these themes are explored in more detail in Chapter 2: for the moment it is sufficient to stress that concepts of mobility are varied, and that the experience of mobility can contribute significantly to shaping individual lives.

Following from the above discussion, it is necessary to define mobility more precisely for the purposes of this study. Research reported in this book has focused on what we have termed everyday mobility, with life history data about mobility collected from a wide range of respondents through a combination of questionnaires and in-depth interviews or oral histories. Everyday mobility is defined as all travel from home undertaken on a temporary basis. This includes frequent and regular trips such as the journey to school or to work; less regular but still frequent trips to visit friends or relatives, to shop, for sport and for other leisure activities including children's play; and trips undertaken only once or twice a year such as holidays and visits to distant relatives. Although most everyday mobility does not entail a night away from home, some can, but all such trips are temporary and relatively short term. The study does not include most types of population circulation, nor adults who routinely lived in two places (though some children in the study split their time between two parents who lived apart). Residential migration is also excluded, although the interaction between daily mobility and residential migration is briefly explored in Chapter 4. Details of data collection and precisely how the different types of mobility were defined are given in Chapter 3.

The Dimensions of Everyday Mobility

Mobility is a complex process and interacts with a wide range of factors. These are central to this study and in combination they begin to explain the ways in which the mobility process changed over time. Four of the variables under consideration are internal to the family or the individual under study: age, gender, socio-economic group (income) and family structure (and, for children, parity within the family). All these factors can influence opportunities for and the experience of mobility. Three factors are mainly (though not entirely) external to the traveller and reflect structural constraints: the prevailing transport technology, the urban structure and transport networks that exist in a given place. Though largely external, these factors can be mediated by individual circumstances. For instance, access to new transport technologies may be influenced by age, gender or income, and decisions about where to live in a town may influence access to transport networks. First, each of these factors is considered in more detail and then the interactions between them are explored.

Age is clearly a major influence on both mobility opportunities and experiences. In all time periods it is likely that the mobility of children will have been different from that of adults, and it can also be suggested that the mobility of children will have changed significantly over time as concepts of childhood have altered, and as fears about the dangers faced by children travelling alone have increased. In this study the mobility of children is explored by focusing on two age groups: those aged 10/11 and those aged 17/18. It can be suggested that each of these groups will have had different degrees of independence and control over their own mobility, and that the nature and extent of this control may have varied both over time and between different groups of the population. In the present, and in the recent past, the safety of children on the streets or when travelling, and the implications of mobility constraints for children's play, have become significant research areas (Hillman, Adams and Whitelegg, 1990; Valentine and McKendrick, 1997). Some of this literature is explored in more detail in later chapters. However, we know little about how children's travel behaviour has changed over the past century.

The relationship between gender and mobility is also well documented. Feminist geographers, in particular, have explored the ways in which mobility may be constrained for at least some women (Tivers, 1985; Valentine, 1989; Pain, 1997; McDowell, 1999). A number of factors are important: lack of time due to the multiple roles that many women perform; lack of access to private transport; inconvenient and inaccessible public transport for people travelling with small children; fear of travelling alone. The role of gender in producing particular travel constraints and outcomes is explored in each section of this study and the data collected are structured to produce approximately equal numbers of female and male respondents. It can also be suggested that gender constraints will have changed over time as the position of women within society has altered. Most obviously, it may be argued that the increased emancipation of women during the twentieth century – with more women engaged in higher education, participating in the workforce, learning to drive and having access to their own car – will have lessened the mobility gap between women and men. However, it can also be proposed that although in the past women may have been more constrained one effect of those restrictions was that women were less likely to travel alone. Thus women's fear of travelling, and the limits that this imposes, may have increased over time.

It is equally obvious that mobility opportunities are structured by income and, by implication, by class or socio-economic status. Most mobility requires some combination of time and money and those on higher incomes, and with more control of their own time, are most likely to have had the greatest opportunity to travel. The impact of socio-economic factors on life chances is well documented for both the past and the present with, for instance, a clear health divide between the rich and poor within Britain. This trend is consistent over time and the gap between rich and poor shows no sign of narrowing (Dorling, 1997; Smith, Dorling and Shaw, 2001). In this study occupational and related data are briefly used to explore the impact of socio-economic factors on mobility. Whilst evidence from other studies suggests that the impact of income differentials on quality of life has changed little over time, it can be suggested that the relationship between mobility and income has been affected by other factors, not least the rapid change in transport technologies over the twentieth century. Whereas in the early-twentieth century all but the very rich were constrained to use relatively cheap and simple forms of transport (walking, cycling, trams, buses) for short trips within an urban area, the diffusion of the private car to more families has both widened mobility opportunities for some whilst increasing the mobility divide between those that do and do not have access to a private car. Such factors also, clearly, interact with age and gender: many women on low incomes may be doubly disadvantaged.

Family size, structure and composition can also have an important bearing on mobility, though this is a theme that has been explored much less fully in the literature (Anderson, 1985; Kok, 1997). For instance, it can be argued that a child growing up in an extended family with aunts or grandparents around will have different opportunities for mobility compared to a child living with a lone parent. However, it can also be suggested that the ways in which such a relationship works are complex. For some children an extended family could increase mobility because of the availability of adults to accompany the child on journeys (for instance for sport or leisure activities), however it could also be suggested that the presence of adults could reduce a child's freedom. The girl or boy growing up with just one parent may have less supervision and be given more opportunity for independent travel. Likewise, an eldest child may be given added responsibility to look after a young sibling when travelling to school or to the shops, whilst an only child could either have restricted mobility due to lack of someone to travel with or, possibly, greater independence. In this study these themes are explored by recording the family structure in which respondents were located and by relating mobility experiences – particularly travel companions – to these circumstances. In terms of change over time, it can be suggested that the combination of reduced family size, the dispersion of family members, and the impact of increasing separation and divorce will have had significant impacts on the ways in which family structures impinge upon mobility.

The external or structural factors that influence mobility have been subject to the most obvious changes over time. The impact of new transport technologies on both intra-urban and inter-urban transport have revolutionised travel opportunities for many. The broad picture is clear. In the early-twentieth century most people walked or travelled by bus or tram. A few rich families had a private carriage or motorcar. By the 1920s the bicycle was beginning to revolutionise private transport for some, the motorbus was beginning to replace the tram, but the car was still the preserve of the rich. From the 1950s access to the private motorcar increased rapidly and use of public transport, cycling and walking all declined in most cities (Dyos and Aldcroft, 1969; Thrift, 1990; Pooley, 2003). This study examines not only changes in the mode of transport used for different types of journey, but also explores the reasons why people used particular forms of transport. For instance, was the choice of a particular travel mode constrained by access to private transport or by the public transport systems available, or was there also an element of individual choice. If the latter was the case, how did the decision making process for individual travellers change over time?

Finally, the structure of an urban area, and where an individual lived in relation to that urban structure, also affected mobility opportunities. For instance residence close to a suburban railway station, tram line or bus stop provided travel possibilities that were not so convenient for someone living elsewhere in a city. It is well documented that during the twentieth century the structure of British urban areas, including the provision of transport infrastructure, changed rapidly. Not only were new suburbs, roads and public transport systems constructed, but also the pattern of travel changed as for many people home and work became increasingly separated. Thus complex cross-city journeys were increasingly generated, placing new demands on the urban transport infrastructure (Buchanan, 1963; Daniels, 1970; 1980; Daniels and Warnes, 1983). It can be suggested that changes in urban structure over the twentieth century produced a number of potential mobility differentials. For instance, differences between cities in terms of changing transport infrastructure could produce significant variations in urban travel behaviour from place to place, whilst the development of new suburbs without access to public transport could produce localities that experienced mobility deprivation. In this study these themes are explored in detail in the context of four contrasting urban areas: London, Manchester/Salford, Glasgow and Lancaster/Morecambe. Due to its size and complexity the experience of mobility in London has always been distinctive; Manchester and Glasgow were both large urban areas well away from the influence of London; and Lancaster/Morecambe represents a much smaller urban area in northern England. More details of the transport infrastructure in the four cities are given in Chapter 2. To enable change over time to be studied, as far as possible, all respondents used in the studies were resident in the same urban area throughout the survey period, thus controlling for structural differences between urban areas.

Of course, the six factors outlined briefly above were all interconnected, with mobility opportunities and decisions structured by the combined effects of personal, familial and structural factors. The ways in which some of these factors interacted to produce particular sets of travel behaviour can be illustrated from the everyday mobility of one individual, an adolescent girl living in London in the 1930s (Pooley, 1999; 2004). R left her home in Londonderry (Northern Ireland) at the age of 18 (in 1938) and moved to London to work as a typist for the Inland Revenue. Her life in London was thus unencumbered by other family members, but her mobility in the city was structured by a complex set of factors that reflected her age, gender, income and living arrangements. During her first year in London, when she was getting to know the city (and before the outbreak of war which had an obvious, though limited, impact on daily travel), R's mobility was focused on a combination of routine trips to work, church, shop and to undertake leisure activities, combined with more purposeful journeys to explore parts of London that she had not yet seen. During this period she lived in a hostel with other girls of a similar age and these, together with some work colleagues, formed her travelling companions, though when necessary she was also quite comfortable travelling alone. Her journeys included travel by tube, bus and on foot and she quickly seemed to be at ease when negotiating London's busy transport network, though on occasions she did make mistakes. The spatial extent of her travels was mostly constrained to areas through which she passed regularly on her daily routine, with only occasional forays elsewhere, and she often used the excuse of visits from her family to explore new territory. This unexceptional travel history demonstrates the way in which a single 18 year old female familiarised herself with a strange city, negotiated complex transport systems and quickly established a travel routine that gave her both freedom and a sense of security. In doing this the constraints of age, gender, income, location, living arrangements and access to transport all interacted to produce a distinctive but unremarkable pattern of urban travel. This case study is explored in more detail in Chapter 4.

The Significance of Mobility

In studies of population and society it is easy to neglect the commonplace and to overemphasise the rare and dramatic. Thus in studies of population movement the relocation of refugees and asylum seekers, and other large scale and long distance movements, have received extensive attention (Castles and Miller, 1993; Black and Robinson, 1993; King, 1995). In contrast short distance residential moves, and especially everyday mobility, have been relatively neglected. Although these are the sorts of moves that most people make most of the time, it is often assumed that their impact and significance is limited. However, it is contended that mundane and almost invisible activities (such as everyday mobility) can and do have real significance for both the individuals involved and for wider society. Figure 1.2 suggests some of the ways in which everyday mobility is connected to and has meaning for individuals, families, economy, society, culture and environment.

At an individual level many people, especially in large cities such as London, spend a large part of each day commuting or travelling around the city for other reasons. The personal costs in terms of time, stress and inconvenience of traffic congestion are considerable. These costs also have implications for families as parents with long commuting journeys see less of each other, and of their children, and may feel that work and travel force them to neglect family responsibilities. Traffic congestion has further costs for the economy in terms of a tired and frustrated workforce and in relation to missed delivery deadlines. Everyday travel clogs up the city and the economic costs can be considerable. The environmental costs associated with high levels of daily travel, especially by car, are well known. Levels of air pollution in urban areas frequently reach potentially harmful levels in summer, with consequent impact on human health. Moreover, pollution from vehicles can cause damage to buildings and is a major contributor to greenhouse gases associated with global climate change. The political implications of high volumes of daily mobility are equally obvious. Despite numerous policy documents there has been a failure by successive British governments to deliver a

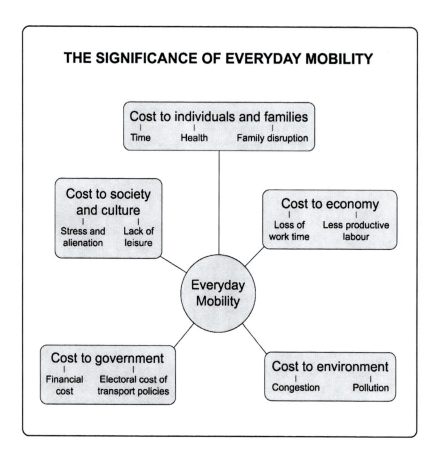

Figure 1.2 The Significance of Everyday Mobility

sustainable transport policy for urban areas. That this is politically important, and that it can be achieved, is demonstrated by the success of road charging in London and of similar schemes elsewhere in continental Europe. It can also be suggested that increasing expectations of quick and easy travel are creating societal and cultural change that may not be sustainable. If people's travel expectations are not met, then this can lead to frustration and anger. Incidents of road rage are just one example of this trend (Whitelegg, 1997; Adams, 1999; Black, 2001; Docherty and Shaw, 2003).

These themes are placed in a broader theoretical context in Chapter 2, and are explored in more detail at relevant points throughout the book. For the moment it is sufficient to emphasise that although relatively mundane journeys such as travel to school, to work, for leisure and pleasure may not have the obvious impact of large-scale refugee movements, their combined significance at both an individual and societal level is considerable. It can also be suggested that these significances will have changed over time, both as the volume and complexity of journeys have increased, and as political and societal awareness of the costs (personal, economic, environmental) of daily travel have heightened. Where appropriate, this study examines how the implications of everyday travel have changed over time, and also assesses changes in the ways that policy makers have responded to perceived travel and traffic problems in the urban areas under study.

Structure of the Book

The aims of this study are thus to examine and explain changes in everyday mobility in Britain over the twentieth century. This will be achieved by focusing mainly on four urban areas and by using original oral testimonies collected from some 250 respondents. These data are interpreted within the context of both theoretical and empirical literature on mobility and travel, and attention is directed especially to the ways in which the mobility experience has changed in relation to age, gender, occupation, family structure, transport infrastructure and urban form. One argument that runs through the book is that the obvious changes in travel and transport over the past century have too often obscured an underlying stability of everyday mobility experience. The remainder of the book is structured around the following ten chapters.

First, (in Chapter 2) we examine a range of theoretical and empirical material that has explored travel behaviour and mobility change in Britain and elsewhere to establish the intellectual landscape within which the study is set. Particular attention is focused on the links between mobility and identity. The chapter also provides an overview of transport change in the urban areas under study. Chapter 3 focuses on the problems of obtaining adequate data on long-run trends in mobility, and explains in detail how the data on which this study is based were collected. Chapter 4 paints the broad picture of mobility change in Britain, drawing on both existing census and survey data, and results from new research, to outline mobility change in Britain over the past century. Chapters 5 to 8 then focus in detail on four different sets of mobility experience: travelling to school, the journey to work, children's play and travelling for pleasure. In each case the experience of change as experienced by respondents in the four study areas is explored and set within a broader context. Chapters 9 and 10 examine in more detail two of the main sets of factors that structure everyday travel: the links between mobility, the family and the life course; and the impact of new transport technology on the experience of everyday mobility. Finally, Chapter 11 explores the lessons of history, assessing the implications of past mobility change for transport policy in the twenty-first century.

The book thus presents original research on everyday mobility over the past century, links this to relevant social and spatial theory, and draws out some implications for future transport policy. In doing so, we hope to both stimulate further interest in, and research on, the neglected history of mobility, and to demonstrate that an understanding of past mobility processes and experiences may shed new light on present-day conditions and help to formulate future transport and travel policy.

Chapter 2

Mobility and Society

Introduction

Some degree of personal mobility is fundamental to the operation of all societies but, as briefly outlined in Chapter 1, it can be suggested that the role and significance of mobility within society has changed significantly over the twentieth century. Such claims relate to arguments for increased globalisation of and complexity within economy and society, with easier and more frequent movement of people, goods, services and ideas around the world, and increased access to fast and individualistic forms of transport for everyday mobility (Urry, 2003). Indeed, Urry (2000) has argued that increased mobility is a defining characteristic of twenty-first century society, and as such could become an organising principle of Sociology. There appears to be increased global interest in adopting a 'mobilities' perspective to social research. This research agenda is defined clearly by the introductory statement on the web site of Lancaster University's Centre for Mobilities Research. The scope of mobilites research is defined as: 'both the large-scale movements of people, objects, capital and information across the world, as well as the more local processes of daily transportation, movement through public space, and the travel of material things within everyday life' and the significance of mobility within society is further justified as follows:

> Technological, social and cultural developments in public and private transportation, mobile communications, information storage and retrieval, surveillance systems and 'intelligent environments', are rapidly changing the nature of travel and of communications conducted at-a-distance. As mobile connectivity begins to occur in new ways across a wide range of cyber-devices and integrated places, so we need better theorisation and research, especially to examine the interdependencies between changes in physical movement and in electronic communications and especially in their increasing convergence. These changes are having many effects. The human body is transformed, as it is enhanced by communication devices and likely to be 'on the move'. Changes also transform the nature of 'local' communities and of the commitments people may feel to the 'nation'. And the global order is increasingly criss-crossed by tourists, workers, terrorists, students, migrants, asylum-seekers, scientists/scholars, family members, business people and so on. Such multiple and intersecting mobilities seem to produce a more 'networked' patterning of economic and social life.

This chapter cannot review all the disparate literature relating to mobility studies encompassed by the above definition, but instead focuses briefly on what we identify as six discourses of mobility that have received considerable coverage in the literature and which also have especial relevance for the empirical study of everyday mobility in North-west England reported in this volume. The focus is very much on mobility within the developed world, especially Britain and Europe. Although some of the trends identified may have salience for other parts of the globe their impacts and the ways in which they affect people's everyday lives are often very different (and in most cases under-researched). Having identified these key themes, which will be returned to at various times during succeeding chapters, we focus on one of the key variables that has influenced mobility at the local level over the past century: the development of, and changes in access to, new transport technologies. Following a brief review of key developments at a national level, attention is focused on changes in transport infrastructure in the four case study towns (London, Glasgow, Manchester/Salford, Lancaster/Morecambe) both to identify key issues at the local level, and to use particular case studies to illustrate national trends.

Six Discourses of Mobility

Mobility has implications for most aspects of economy, culture and society and the six themes discussed here represent only one of many possible configurations of the significance of mobility in the developed world. However, together, they identify some of the key ways in which mobility is embedded in modern society and some of the aspects of society that may be affected by mobility change.

First, and most basically, everyday mobility enables people to go about their everyday life. Whether it is travelling to school, to work, to shop, to visit friends or relatives, or journeys for play, recreation and leisure, these are the aspects of mobility that constitute modern human existence. The mundane, or everyday, has received increased attention from academics in recent years, recognising that those things that we do routinely and take for granted can take on real significance and meaning both for individuals and for wider society. For most people some form of mobility is the flux that makes everyday life possible. Although for most people, for most of the time, this involves physical movement, technologies that allow virtual mobilities increasingly allow transactions and other activities to be undertaken without leaving the home. Thus, even for the housebound, mobility in its broadest sense is a crucial part of everyday life. Whilst it is tempting to focus on special events, long-distance journeys and global processes, it is important to remember that despite the processes of globalisation, most people's everyday contacts and journeys are within a given neighbourhood or locality, and that on most days nothing exceptional happens. It is these everyday events and experiences that we have most control over and which constitute and give meaning to our everyday lives (de Certeau, 1984; Eyles, 1989; Holloway and Hubbard, 2001).

Second, and linked to the above, the everyday mobilities that are a necessary part of life also create the spaces in which we live, meet people, carry out transactions and develop identities. These spaces through which people move on an everyday basis, construct the communities (real or virtual) of which they are part and thus provide added meaning to everyday life. These themes have been examined from many different perspectives. In the 1960s Wolpert developed the concept of 'action space' as the area with which people were familiar, through which they moved on a regular basis, and which influenced migration decisions (Wolpert, 1965). Hagerstrand introduced the concept of time-space pathways, exploring the constraints that affected patterns of everyday life in local neighbourhoods and represented through time-space prisms of everyday activity (Hagerstrand, 1975; Carlstein, Parkes and Thrift, 1978). Others have focused on the ways in which movement through space helps to create place identities and to construct divisions between those in different areas (Sibley, 1995). Thus mobility both constructs communities and place identities and produces territoriality and potential conflicts between those from different areas. Of most relevance to this research are those experienced by children (Skelton and Valentine, 1998; Holloway and Valentine, 2000; Aitken, 2001).

Third, it can be suggested that mobility is more than the mechanism through which mundane tasks are carried out and by which we become familiar with and attached to particular localities. Movement can itself become a performance through which we make statements about ourselves and acquire status. There are many examples of this (de Certeau, 1984; Urry, 2000). For instance, from the eighteenth-century flaneur to twenty-first century street gangs, being visible as both an onlooker and an object of attention has been a central aspect of everyday street culture. Bull (2000) clearly articulates the significance of the street for certain groups in his study of 'soundscapes' that investigates the ways in which music is associated with movement around the urban area in some contemporary youth culture. More generally, Bourdieu's (1984) much-used concept of 'habitus', that describes the class-oriented, unintentional ways in which we express our identity, must have a spatial component in that where we are seen and what we do becomes an important aspect of class-based identities. Featherstone et al (2004) examine yet another aspect of the ways in which movement may equate with performance, exploring the concept of 'automobility'. It is argued that the car has become not only an essential means of travelling to undertake everyday tasks, but also an expression of personal identity as individuals customise their car, choose particular brands to suit their aspirations and personality and use the cocoon of the automobile to cushion themselves from the outside world. Thus how we move, be it on foot, by bicycle, car or train, may become a statement of class, identity, personality, environmental values and wealth (amongst other things), as well as a practical means of simply completing everyday tasks.

A fourth discourse of mobility focuses on the increase in personal travel, especially by car, in modern society and sees it as a problem that potentially threatens contemporary urban life. The car causes urban congestion, traffic accidents, and pollution and, it can be argued, rather than facilitating everyday life it is actually the cause of major inefficiencies in the urban economy caused by traffic jams, road accidents and the stress of having to cope with modern traffic conditions (Whitelegg, 1997; 2003; Dora and Phillips, 2001). Mobility can be problematised in at least three related ways. First, and most obviously, certain mechanised forms of mobility (road traffic, air travel) consume large quantities of fuel resources, cause wide-spread pollution and disturbance through emissions and noise, and contribute to mortality, injury and ill-health through accidents and the impact of pollutants on human health. Second, it can be argued that as society increasingly requires, and people come to expect, greater mobility (both locally and over long distances) then the adverse effects outlined above will be multiplied. Thus the problem is not only related to a particular technology, but is also due to changed mobility expectations and requirements. Third, it can be suggested that mobility change also heightens inequalities, with those who are unable to participate in and gain the advantages of increased personal mobility experiencing greater social exclusion. Thus those unable to travel freely may be restricted in where they can work, where their children can go to school, where they can travel for leisure and how frequently they can visit friends (Lucas et al, 2002; Hine and Mitchell, 2003).

In contrast to the assumptions of increased mobility implicit in the above themes, a fifth discourse of mobility focuses on concepts of risk and the ways in which, for some at least, mobility may be increasingly restricted. It has been suggested that we now live in a 'risk society' (Beck, 1992; Adam et al 2000), in which uncertainty is a key factor influencing people's lives and decisions. Whether in fact the twenty-first century is actually more risky than earlier periods is debatable. Certainly in the past there were, for most people in the developed world, heightened risks from disease, unregulated work places, poverty and malnutrition. Today these have been replaced by new, and in some ways more remote, risks such as global terrorism and the impact of climate change; but whatever the reality it can be suggested that perceptions of risk have altered. The mobility of children has been especially affected by these changed perceptions. Parents are increasingly fearful of risks to children from traffic, unregulated places and, especially, strangers. It has been suggested that these fears, real or imagined, have led to children being increasingly restricted in their everyday action spaces, with less opportunity to play outside. This can have consequential impacts on child health and on the ability of children to learn to negotiate the urban environment (Hillman et al, 1990; Valentine and McKendrick, 1997; Furedi, 2001). It can thus be suggested that rather than mobility universally increasing, whilst mobility expectations and opportunities may have increased for many, for others in society there may be greater constraints related to changed perceptions of the risks that mobility may bring. Although such fears are mostly focused on children, other research has shown that women and the elderly may also be restricting their movements because of fear of crime and assault (Valentine, 1989; Pain, 2000; 2001).

During the twentieth century there was a significant increase in leisure time for most people which, linked to rising real incomes, led to a massive increase in tourism (Pearce, 1995; Shaw and Williams, 1998; 2004). A final discourse of mobility focuses on leisure and tourism and the role of mobility in both facilitating and constructing this process. Increased access to the private car, cheap air travel and easily-booked package holidays have allowed unprecedented numbers of people (in the developed world at least) to travel widely for tourism and leisure. Thus one implication of mobility change is simply the globalisation of tourism and the increased ability of people to holiday, often more than once a year, in exotic places. However, the links between tourism and mobility are subtler than this. As Urry (2002) argues tourism is, at least in part, about the 'tourist gaze', with the experience of looking at places a key aspect of the tourist experience. Thus the process of travel, the view from the car, train or plane and the experience of passing through new places becomes of itself a leisure activity. In one sense there is nothing new in this (Schivelbusch, 1986). Eighteenth and nineteenth-century travellers did exactly the same things, and often recorded their experiences (Gregory, 1995; McEwan, 1996), but what is new is that the ability to travel through and to new places is now much more ubiquitous.

These six discourses of mobility to some extent underpin the arguments put forward in the empirical analysis presented in this book. In the following chapters, by focusing first on all types of mobility and then on movement for specific purposes, we explore the ways in which movement for mundane everyday activities has changed in selected British urban areas over the past 60 years and suggest the implications that this has for urban communities and wider society. We examine changes in the way that people, especially children, felt about their experience of mobility, focusing particularly on children's play and the ways in which the experience of playing in the urban environment has changed over time. We also assess the extent to which there have been changes in risk perception that have affected where and how freely children can play out alone, thus influencing the ability of this aspect of everyday mobility to contribute to personal development. Analysis of debates around traffic and transport in urban areas demonstrates that concern about congestion is of long standing in British cities, and we examine the ways in which changing everyday mobility impacts upon traffic congestion in urban areas, drawing out implications for contemporary transport policy. We also focus, more briefly, on travel for leisure and tourism, examining continuity and change in leisure travel over the past 60 years.

In each chapter of the book we argue that whilst there have been some obvious and important changes in the experience of everyday mobility over the twentieth century, when the trends are examined more closely there is remarkable stability over the last 60 years at least. Moreover, whilst there have been significant changes in the modes of transport used, there remains considerable individual variability in everyday mobility experiences, and the underlying structures and decision-making process that produce everyday movement have changed little since at least the 1940s. It is thus argued that whilst most of the discourses of mobility (outlined above) focus on change, and especially on the impact of increased mobility, there is a risk of over-stating the extent to which mobility change has occurred. For most people everyday mobility remains short distance, structured around local communities and for some, especially children, it is the discourse of risk that may be having the greatest impact on everyday lives.

Mobility and the Transport Infrastructure

As outlined in Chapter 1 everyday mobility is influenced by many factors, but clearly access to transport is crucial. It is also the factor that has most impact on modal change and the implications of this for urban congestion and pollution. Most fundamentally, transport change has helped to shape the geography of Britain's towns and cities, both through the provision of new routes and technologies and through the mobility choices that travellers have made in their everyday lives. This section briefly outlines some key changes in the transport infrastructure, and in access to transport, in Britain over the twentieth century. The following sections explore these themes in more detail in the context of the four case study towns.

At the end of the nineteenth century most people had very limited choice for their everyday mobility. Most cities were still relatively compact and the majority of everyday journeys were undertaken on foot. Only those with higher and more regular incomes would use public transport for intra-urban journeys: either the horse-drawn omnibus or the tram (Dyos and Aldcroft, 1969; Freeman and Aldcroft, 1988). Although most urban areas in Britain had trams from the late-nineteenth century, it was the early decades of the twentieth century before they became a popular form of mass transport. The development of tram networks is explored in more detail below in the context of specific cities and towns. The bicycle also enjoyed growing popularity in the late-nineteenth century, but initially only as a leisure pursuit for the middle classes. Again, it was the 1920s before mass-produced new bicycles and a large second-hand market in bikes enabled large numbers of working men to adopt the bicycle as a means of travelling to work on a daily basis (Lloyd Jones and Lewis, 2000). For longer, inter-urban, travel in 1900 most people used the train. Although cars were appearing on the roads, and some people continued to travel by horse, the train offered a fast and efficient means of transport that many could afford, with the provision of first, second and third class carriages providing an acceptable social milieu. The British rail network was also more-or-less at its peak by the turn of the century with, by 1912, over 32,000kms of track penetrating almost all corners of Britain (Perkin, 1970; Freeman, 1986). In 1900 the train offered the possibility of travelling to within a few miles of even small places (Figure 2.1).

There have been three really significant periods of change in the provision of public transport in twentieth-century Britain. First, in the 1920s and 1930s most towns gradually introduced motorbuses which initially competed with, and then replaced, trams (and trolley buses) as the main form of urban public transport provided for commuters and others who moved around the city on a regular basis. Second, following the Beeching Report (1963) there was a dramatic reduction in

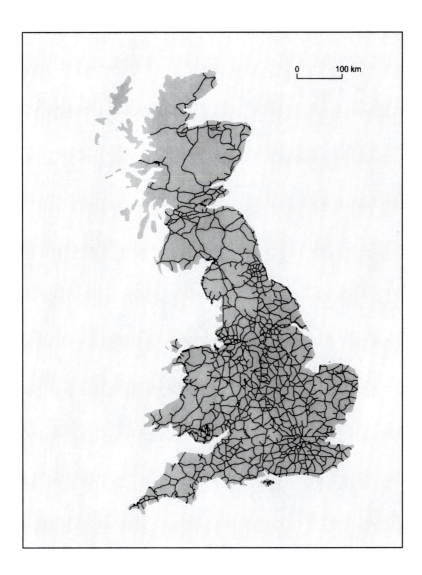

Figure 2.1 The Railway Network in Britain circa 1900

Source: Based on Freeman, (1986), p. 89.

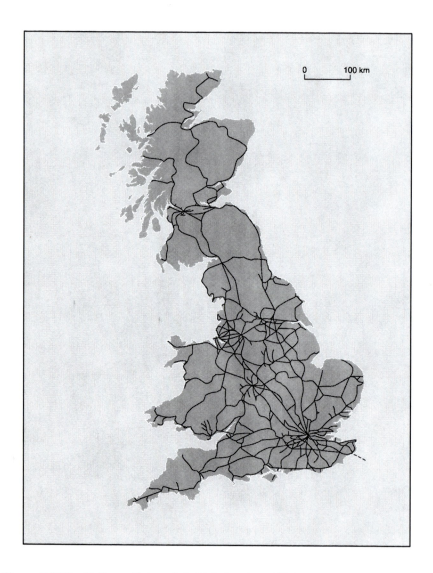

Figure 2.2 The Railway Network in Britain circa 2004

Source: National Rail network website
(http://www.nationalrail.co.uk/tocs_maps/maps/network_rail_maps.htm).

the rail network with the closure of many rural and suburban lines that were considered uneconomic. In the late-twentieth century the rail network has focused on connecting mainly larger settlements, with most smaller and remoter towns losing their rail connection (Figure 2.2). Third, in 1985, deregulation of bus provision had a similar effect on the bus network. Competition between competing bus companies led to the reduction or removal of many uneconomic rural and suburban bus services, with only a minimal (subsidised) service available in many rural areas. The net effect of these latter two changes has, inevitably, been to push more people towards travelling by car. All these trends are reflected in the histories of the case study towns (outlined below).

Car ownership and car use in Britain increased exponentially over the twentieth century. In 1904 there were just 8,465 private cars in use in Britain, but by the eve of the Second World War in 1938 this had risen over 200-fold to in excess of 1.9 million vehicles (Dyos and Aldcroft, 1969). During the second half of the twentieth century, although the rate of increase necessarily slowed, the absolute numbers of private vehicles on the roads rose rapidly with over 24.5 million privately registered cars in Britain in 2002 (Department for Transport web pages, 2004) (Table 2.1). The number of individuals with full car driving licences

Table 2.1 Motor Vehicles Licensed in Britain, 1950-2002 (000s)

Year	Private cars	All vehicles
1950	1,979	3,970
1955	3,109	5,822
1960	4,900	8,512
1965	7,732	11,697
1970	9,971	13,548
1975	12,526	16,511
1980	14,660	19,199
1985	16,454	21,159
1990	19,742	24,673
1995	20,505	25,369
2000	23,196	28,898
2002	24,543	30,557

Source: Department for Transport Web Pages: *Transport Statistics* (accessed 8/10/2004).

similarly increased from some 19.4 million in 1975/6 to 32.1 million in 1998/2000. The most rapid rise was amongst women: in 1975/6 only 29 per cent of females aged over 17 years could drive but by 2003 some 61 per cent of all such women held a car driving licence, compared to 70 per cent of males (Table 2.2) (National Statistics, 2003). The impacts of these changes in car ownership have been felt both in increased traffic congestion and the environmental impacts of new road schemes designed to meet the demand. However, access to a private car is still far from universal and in 2001 27.4 per cent of households in the UK did not have access to a car or van (National Statistics web pages, 2004). Moreover, there are significant geographical variations in car access, with the lowest rates of car ownership mainly in urban areas (Figure 2.3). For many who do not own or have regular access to a car the changes in public transport provision outlined above have had serious consequences.

Table 2.2 Full Driving Licence Holders by Age and Gender, 1975/76 to 2003 (Per cent)

Year	All 17+	17-20	21-29	30-39	40-49	50-59	60-69	70+
All adults								
1975/76	48	28	59	67	60	50	35	15
1985/86	57	33	63	74	71	60	47	27
1992/94	67	48	75	82	79	72	57	33
1998/2000	71	41	74	84	84	78	68	41
2003*	70	28	68	82	84	79	73	45
Males								
1975/76	69	36	78	85	83	75	58	32
1985/86	74	37	73	86	87	81	72	51
1992/94	81	54	83	91	88	88	81	59
1998/2000	82	45	81	90	92	89	84	65
2003*	81	31	74	88	91	90	87	69
Females								
1975/76	29	20	43	48	37	24	15	4
1985/86	41	29	54	62	56	41	24	11
1992/94	54	42	68	73	70	57	37	16
1998/2000	60	37	69	78	77	68	54	22
2003*	61	24	62	77	78	69	59	27

*Provisional figures.
Source: National Statistics, (2003) p. 5.

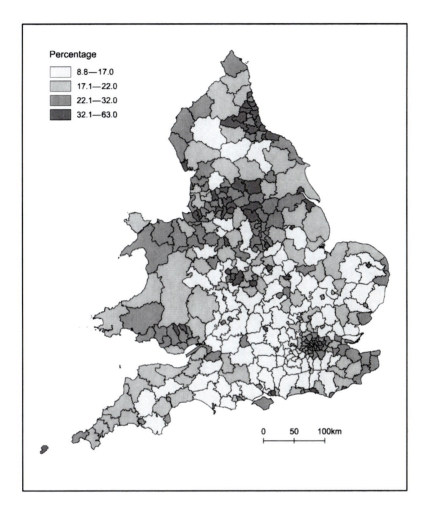

**Figure 2.3 Spatial Variations in Car Ownership in England and Wales, 2001
(Percentage Without Access to a Car)**

Source: Census of England and Wales, (2001).

At the national level there have thus been well-charted changes in transport
provision with consequent impacts on opportunities for personal mobility. Whilst
car ownership has increased, by no means everyone has access to a vehicle, and
public transport has declined markedly. However, although these general trends
affected all of Britain, the changes have been worked out in rather different ways
in particular places. To enable the following analysis to be placed in its local
contexts we now examine some of the key changes in transport provision in the
four case study towns, moving from the smallest (Lancaster and Morecambe) to

the largest (London). In doing so, we also demonstrate the extent to which there was local variability in changes to the national transport infrastructure.

Lancaster and Morecambe

The towns of Lancaster and Morecambe, situated in north Lancashire, form a relatively small urban area in terms of population with the modern Lancaster District (comprising Lancaster, Morecambe, Heysham, Carnforth and surrounding villages) containing 110,540 people in 1951 and 133,914 in 2001. However, although Lancaster, Morecambe and Heysham now effectively form a continuous urban area, this is spatially quite spread out, with Lancaster and Morecambe comprising two distinct towns some 6km apart and divided by the river Lune. This inevitably funnels all traffic over the bridges and restricts travel between the two centres. It can thus be suggested that physical factors may have played a significant role in limiting travel between Lancaster and Morecambe and in focusing most everyday mobility on either one town or the other.

Over the past century Lancaster and Morecambe residents have had a fairly restricted range of options for travelling around the two urban areas, with much movement undertaken either on foot or (more rarely) by bicycle. Morecambe's trams were withdrawn in 1926 (the last operational horse-drawn tram system on the British mainland) and Lancaster's (electric) trams, introduced in 1905, were withdrawn in 1930. Thus from the 1930s onwards, public transport consisted only of motorbuses and the railway lines between Lancaster and Morecambe. Prior to 1974 bus services in the area were provided by three main operators: Morecambe and Heysham Corporation, Lancaster City Transport and Ribble. Following local government reorganisation in 1974 the Morecambe and Lancaster bus fleets were amalgamated. Bus deregulation in 1985 led to the privatisation of the corporation services and the eventual dominance of the system by Stagecoach. Bus use peaked in Lancaster in 1952 when some 14,079,770 passengers per annum were carried by Lancaster City buses, and in Morecambe in 1956 when the corporation buses carried 12,942,987 passengers. By the time the two services were amalgamated in 1974 the annual total of passengers had approximately halved. Nonetheless, the bus service continues to provide an important means of transport both within Lancaster and Morecambe and between the two towns (Shuttleworth, 1976; Knowles, 1983; Constantine and Warde, 2000; White, 2003).

Travel between Lancaster and Morecambe can also be undertaken by train. Today, the only route is from Lancaster Castle station via a loop from the west coast main line through Bare. However, until 1966 a separate line ran from Lancaster's Green Ayre station direct to Morecambe Promenade and on to Heysham. This line was unusual in that it was used for early experimentation with electrification and it provided a fast electric service linking the two towns with an average journey time of just eight minutes between Lancaster Green Ayre and Morecambe Promenade in 1964. From 1957 until 1966 there was also an intermediate station at Scale Hall, serving those people who lived between Lancaster and Morecambe. The line through Green Ayre station, and on up the Lune valley, was closed to passenger traffic in 1966, thus removing a fast and efficient link between the main urban centres of the small conurbation (White, 2003).

The town centres of Lancaster and Morecambe have suffered from road traffic congestion since at least the 1940s, and as early as 1949 there was a plan to introduce a one-way system into Lancaster to relieve congestion in Market Square. Some relief from through traffic came in 1960 with the construction of the Lancaster Bypass as part of the new M6 motorway, and from 1973 a one-way system was introduced in Lancaster with progressive pedestrianisation of the central retail area. However, there has been continuing concern both about traffic congestion in Lancaster and about congestion over the two road bridges that link Lancaster and Morecambe. Since the 1970s there have been repeated calls for a variety of new road schemes including an eastern relief road for Lancaster, and either a western or northern bypass linking the M6 with Morecambe and Heysham. All schemes have met with strong objections on environmental and cost grounds, and despite several public enquiries the road system in Lancaster and Morecambe has not changed significantly over the past 30 years (Constantine and Warde, 2000).

Manchester and Salford

The conurbation of Manchester and Salford, situated in south Lancashire prior to 1974 and now part of the County of Greater Manchester, reached its peak population (989,816) in 1931, and thereafter both cities have lost population through decentralisation within North-west England, and out-migration to the Midlands and southern England. Although administratively separate, Manchester and Salford merge to form a single urban area and, for the most part, they are considered together in this research. The physical extent of the built-up urban area grew rapidly in the late-nineteenth century, and this was recognised by a series of boundary extensions to the City of Manchester, which increased its extent from 5,935 acres in 1890 to 21,645 acres in 1913 (Simon, 1938; Rodgers, 1986; Kidd, 1993). By 1930 the City of Manchester had been further extended to include new corporation housing developments such as Wythenshawe (population 35,000 in 1935 and 100,000 in 1964), and the city stretched some 13km from the city centre to the municipal boundary. The urban structure of Manchester and Salford thus reflected early decentralisation, not only of housing, but also of industry, most notably through the development of the Trafford Park industrial and housing estate from 1896. This massive development, built on a triangle of land between the Manchester Ship Canal and other waterways, employed some 30,000 people in 1923, and 75,000 at its height in 1945 (Clay and Brady, 1929; Simon and Inman, 1935; Russell and Walker, 1979; Farnie, 1980). Thus although Manchester city centre continued to provide jobs in finance and commerce, and some manufacturing industry, by the 1930s much new employment in sectors such as oil, chemicals, electrical engineering and foodstuffs, and an increasing amount of housing, was located on the periphery of the built-up area, with consequent implications for commuting patterns. Some of these issues were recognised by contemporary plans for urban renewal and overspill developments, which moved increasing numbers of people to peripheral housing developments after 1945, although plans for one or more new towns to accommodate Manchester's overspill were repeatedly frustrated by opposition from Cheshire County Council until the 1970s (Hall et al, 1973; Rodgers, 1986; HMSO, 1995).

For the first 30 years of the twentieth century Manchester commuters depended on the municipal tram networks run by the separate corporations of Manchester and Salford. Thus by 1926 Manchester Corporation tramways operated 892 tram cars, 258 miles of track and recorded over 300 million passenger journeys in the year. Reciprocal agreements between Manchester, Salford and other surrounding local authorities meant that co-ordinated tram services could run throughout the whole conurbation and tram lines extended to most of the new industrial and housing estates that were developed prior to 1930 (Manchester Corporation Tramways Department (MCTramD), 1926; Simon, 1938; Gray, 1967; Frangopulo, 1977). At this time motorbuses run by Manchester Corporation complemented, and were secondary to, the tram service; but from 1929 the Corporation pursued a deliberate policy of replacing trams with motorbuses on certain routes. Trams were increasingly blamed for causing urban traffic congestion, buses were seen to be faster and more flexible and could more cheaply provide services to new suburban developments such as Wythenshawe. The Corporation's decision to gradually switch from trams to buses was increasingly driven by competition from private bus companies in the city, particularly the introduction of express services, which led the Corporation to introduce its own express service from Cheadle to Heywood in 1927. In the year 1930-1931 over 39 miles of tram route were converted to motorbus operation. Thus whilst in 1931 84 per cent of passengers on Manchester Corporation's public transport system travelled by tram, by 1941 this had fallen to 23.9 per cent. By 1941 64.6 per cent of passengers were carried on motorbuses and 11.5 per cent on trolley buses which were introduced to the streets of Manchester for the first time in 1938. The last tram of this era ran in the city in January 1949 (in Salford two years earlier in 1947) and motorbuses provided the main public transport system in Manchester and Salford, with a small trolley bus network carrying 10-15 per cent of passengers until 1966 when this system also disappeared. By the late 1930s the Corporation had bought up all bar one of its competitor bus companies but, despite proposals in 1933, an integrated public transport system for the whole conurbation (including Salford and surrounding towns) did not emerge until the formation of the South East Lancashire and North East Cheshire Passenger Transport Authority in 1969 (Bruton, 1927; Clay and Brady, 1929; Manchester Corporation Transport Department (MCTranspD), 1935; Simon and Ingham, 1935; Eyre, 1971; Joyce, 1982).

The Manchester conurbation was also relatively well served by suburban rail routes, with electrified lines to Bury (1916), Altrincham (1931) and Glossop (1954) amongst other destinations. These, too, competed with the municipal tramway system and following electrification of the Altrincham line the tram route to this destination was closed. There were also early plans for an underground link between Manchester's main line stations but, despite serious consideration in the 1920s, 1930s, 1940s and 1970s, they were never developed. From the 1950s the use of private cars for commuting (and other journeys) reduced the number of people travelling by public transport, and passengers carried on Manchester Corporation's transport system fell from a peak of 488 million passenger journeys per year in 1950 to 327 million 15 years later. Increased car use also placed new strains on the city's urban structure from the 1950s. Thus, for much of the period 1930-70, commuters in the Manchester conurbation had access to a reasonably flexible and integrated public transport system, though policy decisions taken by Manchester and Salford Corporations (for instance to switch from trams to motor buses) considerably reduced choice in some areas (Clay and Brady, 1929; MCTramD, 1902-28; MCTranspD, 1929-65; Knowles et al, 1991; Kidd, 1993).

Over the past 30 years or so the motorcar has come to increasingly dominate travel and transport in Manchester. The conurbation is surrounded by a motorway box and has connections to six motorways radiating out in all directions from this ring. Manchester and Salford probably have a larger number of motorway connections than any other city in Britain, with spurs from these routes delivering traffic into the centre of the city. However, despite this expansion of road transport, and the impact of deregulation in 1985, the Manchester conurbation is still served by an extensive bus and coach system with some 52 commercial operators providing services in and around the conurbation, co-ordinated through the Greater Manchester Passenger Transport Executive (GMPTE). The conurbation also continues to be served by an extensive system of suburban and main line railways, with intra-urban transport supplemented from 1992 by the construction of the Metrolink Rapid Transit Tram system. This currently links the city centre with Altrincham, Eccles and Bury. Further extensions are planned in phase three, though the finance for this is not yet assured. Thus, over 40 years after the closure of the first Manchester tram system, a new network has been developed, and it is estimated that it has already led to a 10 per cent reduction of car journeys within the city (GMTPE website, 2004).

Glasgow

A brief history of the development of transport and urban form in Glasgow embraces many of the same themes as that for Manchester but with varied chronology and emphasis. Like Manchester, Glasgow grew rapidly in the late-nineteenth and early-twentieth centuries: the city's population peaked at 1,128,473 in the 1939 mid-year estimate, and Glasgow was reputed to have one of the most densely populated central areas of any city in Europe in 1914. Repeated boundary extensions virtually doubled the city's administrative area between 1912 and the 1930s but, despite this, Glasgow retained a relatively compact urban form in the early-twentieth century giving many Glaswegians the opportunity to walk to work. By the 1930s all Glasgow's traditional industries (iron and steel, shipbuilding, engineering) were in decline and the city was much less successful than Manchester at attracting new investment. The main centres of industrial employment were distributed along Clydeside, creating complex commuting patterns as many workers who continued to live in the city centre travelled towards peripheral dockland industrial areas, whilst others travelled in to commercial and related employment in the city centre. Although employment remained in largely traditional locations, and only the affluent suburbanised early, from the 1920s Glasgow Corporation developed substantial peripheral housing estates. Although some were relatively low density others, such as Blackhill, were of high-rise construction and proved unpopular with tenants. The theme of suburbanisation and inner city reconstruction continued after the Second World War, stimulated by the 1946 Clyde Valley Plan. From the late-1940s Glasgow's urban population was increasingly rehoused on both green field housing estates and the three new towns of Cumbernauld, East Kilbride and Irvine, the adoption of both strategies being a compromise between the different aspirations of the Scottish Development Office (which favoured new towns) and Glasgow Corporation, which preferred overspill estates. By 1970 some 200,000 people had moved to peripheral estates around Glasgow, fundamentally changing patterns of daily commuting in the city (Ministry of Transport, 1955; Slaven, 1975; Checkland, 1981; Gibb, 1983; Wannup, 1986; Pacione, 1995; Glasgow City Council, 1996).

In 1871 Glasgow Corporation promoted one of the first tramways in the country (it built lines but leased operation to a private company until 1894 when the Corporation took full control), and the tramway dominated Glasgow's urban transport system from the 1910s, when lines were extended into commuter suburbs, until the 1960s. Although from the 1920s trams faced competition from private bus companies, and the Corporation introduced motorbuses on some routes from 1924, these did not have the same impact as in Manchester. First, the Corporation reacted to private bus competition by reducing tram fares and investing in new tram cars, regarded as the best in Europe in the 1930s; second they only introduced their own motor buses on routes not served by trams; and, third, in 1930 they introduced the Glasgow Corporation (Monopoly) Act which severely restricted private bus operation in the city. Although by 1938 the Corporation operated some 600 motorbuses, these complemented the tram service, largely linking the city centre to new peripheral housing and industrial estates not served by the tramway system. Thus in 1947 the trams were still carrying four times the number of passengers carried by motorbuses and in 1948 (the time that trams disappeared from the streets of Manchester) the corporation took delivery of 100 new tramcars. However, from the mid-1940s there was increasing debate about the role of trams in the urban transport system, and the corporation embarked on a programme of gradually replacing its tram services with motorbuses and trolley buses. The first trolley buses were introduced in 1949 and, with some 195 vehicles, Glasgow had the largest fleet of trolley buses outside London. However, trams continued to be widely available and popular with the travelling public despite the removal of some routes. In 1953 the Corporation supplemented the tram fleet with the purchase of second-hand tram cars from Liverpool and in 1957 there were still 1,027 trams in Glasgow, carrying over 300 million passengers a year over 256 route miles. However, despite their popularity the trams were the only section of the City Transport department to make a loss from the mid-1950s. As in Manchester trams were also blamed for causing congestion, and the motorbus came to dominate public transport. The last trams ran in Glasgow in 1962 (despite continuing to carry more passengers than any other form of public transport), and trolley buses were withdrawn in 1967. The number of passengers travelling by bus peaked in the early 1960s (following the closure of the tram network), but thereafter passenger numbers dropped dramatically (from 419 million trips per annum 1964-1965 to 264 million 1969-1970) as commuters and other travellers switched to the private car (Glasgow Corporation Transport Committee (GCTC), 1929-1970; Glasgow Herald, 1937-1938; 1956-1957; Bruce, 1945; Fitzpayne, 1948; Corporation of Glasgow, 1969; Simpson, 1971-1972; Strathclyde Passenger Transport, 1974; Longworth, 1994).

Although carrying a relatively small proportion of travellers, Glasgow commuters in the mid-twentieth century also had the possibility of travelling by rail. A small (six and a half mile) circular underground system was opened in 1896, serving the central area. Originally operated on a cable system by the Glasgow District Subway Company, it was sold to the Corporation in 1922 and was electrified in 1935. Never particularly profitable or convenient for most commuters it had just 50 passenger cars in 1954 and conveyed about 5 per cent of passengers using public transport in the city. Some Glasgow suburbs were also relatively well-served by main line trains from the late-nineteenth century and, in the 1940s and 1950s, there were calls to make increasing use of the rail network for commuting journeys. However, trains only ever served a minority of commuters and the service declined substantially from the 1960s with the closure of a number of lines and suburban stations (GCTC, 1929-1970; Inglis, 1951; Ministry of Transport, 1955; Simpson, 1971-1972; Kellett, 1979; Pacione, 1995). Although, as in Manchester, there had been calls for an integrated public transport system from the 1940s, little was achieved until the Trans-Clyde Transport System was set up in the late 1970s, based on proposals developed a decade earlier. However, as elsewhere, by the 1960s Glasgow was experiencing rapid growth in car ownership (from 59 per thousand in 1961 to 85 per thousand in 1965), with associated inevitable problems of congestion and urban pollution. Despite some early calls for improved traffic management, the 1960s and early 1970s saw extensive road improvement schemes in and around the city. During the 40 years from 1930, commuters in Glasgow increasingly, and repeatedly, found their travel options affected by decisions of councillors and others in authority. The Monopoly Act restricted private bus operations, a widely used (though unprofitable) tram system was withdrawn and most planning decisions increasingly favoured the motorcar rather than integrated public transport (Bruce, 1945; Inglis, 1951; Hodgson and Cullen, 1969; Glasgow Corporation, 1967-1975; Greater Glasgow Passenger Transport, 1980; Wannup, 1986; Pacione, 1995).

Like Manchester, although the needs of the motorcar have increasingly dominated transport planning in Glasgow over the past 30 years and the city is well connected to the UK motorway network, there has also been substantial and renewed investment in public transport. The Strathclyde Passenger Transport Authority (SPT), which covers Glasgow and a huge swathe of western Scotland, has responsibility for co-ordinating, integrating and promoting public transport within the region. There has been substantial investment in the modernisation of the underground, the expansion of the suburban rail network and the promotion of bus transport since deregulation. Glasgow has the largest suburban rail network outside London, consisting of some 181 stations and 334 miles of track with, in the past 30 years, dozens of new stations opened and others regenerated (SPT website, 2004). Most Glaswegians thus still have access to a substantial, if changed, public transport system.

London

The transport history of London is relatively well known, and only a brief overview can be given in this chapter (Barker and Robbins, 1963-1974). As the capital city, both the scale of the urban area and the diversity of demands that are placed upon the transport infrastructure complicate transport provision in London. Whereas the conurbations of Manchester and Glasgow have clearly-defined cores, and a mainly radial transport network, London can be viewed much more as a collection of towns with complex cross-city flows in addition to daily movement into and out of the centre (Hoggart and Green, 1991). The population history of London mirrors that of Manchester and Glasgow, with Greater London consisting of 6.6 million people in 1901, rising to 8.7 million in 1939, but thereafter declining slightly (with some fluctuations) to 7.2 million people in the Greater London region in 2001. Although there has been a substantial shift of population to the suburbs, recent redevelopment of inner city areas, especially the London Docklands, has led to an increased population in many of these areas, further complicating transport movements in and around the conurbation. In many ways the basic structure of London changed little over the twentieth century. Since the nineteenth century London's economy has been based on a wide range of manufacturing industry and an increasingly dominant service sector, which by the late-twentieth century accounted for approximately 80 per cent of all jobs in London (Government Office for London, 1996). In physical terms the size and shape of London also changed little during the twentieth century, with green belt legislation restricting suburban expansion after 1945 and leading instead to the development of eight New Towns some 30 miles from London (Jackson, 1973). However, London has seen dramatic changes in the structure of urban government. Until 1965 control was highly dispersed with some 122 separate local authorities having some influence over Greater London by 1923 (Barker and Robbins, 1963-1974), but this changed dramatically in 1965 with the creation of the Greater London Council (GLC) which contained 34 new boroughs plus the city of London. However, this structure was short-lived with the abolition of the GLC in 1986 and all powers devolved to the individual boroughs. Yet further change occurred in 1999 with the creation of a Greater London Authority led by a powerful Mayor and responsibility for a wide range of strategic planning in London, including transport (Young and Garside, 1982; Greater London Authority (GLA) website, 2004).

London has one of the most complex public transport systems in the world, due in part to the scale and complexity of the city, but in part to the piecemeal and fragmented way in which the system developed (Association of London Authorities (ALA), nd). This problem was recognised from an early date when a Royal Commission of 1905 called for a more co-ordinated approach to transport planning in London and a Select Committee of 1919 made similar recommendations (Barker and Robbins, 1963-1974). In 1933 tram, bus and underground services were brought under unified control with the establishment of the London Passenger Transport Board (LPTB), but the legacy of earlier developments continued to be felt for some years (Mumby, 1978). Compared to most other British cities Londoners continue to rely heavily on public transport for daily travel with, in 2003, 34 per cent of all trips undertaken by public transport, 43 per cent by car/motorcycle and 22.6 per cent on foot or by bicycle (Transport for London, 2003). However, as in other cities, journeys by public transport peaked in the mid-twentieth century (1950). Within this, travel by tram was most popular in the 1930s, by trolley bus in 1945 and by motorbus in 1955, but travel on the underground increased throughout the twentieth century and in 2002/3 was at a higher level than in any previous period. Following new investment in buses, and the introduction of congestion charging in London in 2003, travel by bus has also begun to increase again and there are now more passenger journeys by bus than at any time since 1965 (London Passenger Transport Board (LPTB), 1934-1948; British Transport Commission, 1948-1962; London Transport Board, 1963-1969; London Transport Executive, 1970-85; Transport for London, 2003).

London was, and still is, served by complex system of mainline and underground railways with some 250 million passenger journeys undertaken in Greater London on mainline trains in 1903. These lines linked central London employment areas to the expanding suburbs and cheap workmen's fares enabled an increasing proportion of Londoners to commute to work by train (Jackson, 1973; Barker and Robbins, 1963-1974). The unusual importance of mainline trains to travel within London was again emphasised in the 1960s when the Beeching Report (1963) estimated that 86 per cent of all British Rail suburban revenue was generated in the London area, and the development of park-and-ride facilities at suburban stations from this period has continued to ensure that mainline trains provide the principal means of longer-distance commuting into London, accounting for 42.2 per cent of all trips into central London during the morning peak from 0700-1000hrs (Transport for London, 2003). The first electric underground railway in the world was opened in London in 1890 and during the first decade of the twentieth century London's existing underground network was both electrified and expanded with 26.5 miles of new track constructed 1903-1907. By 1920 the underground network was carrying some 690 million passengers per year, though this accounted for only 25.7 per cent of all trips by public transport (excluding mainline trains) and was dwarfed by the numbers travelling by tram and bus (Barker and Robbins, 1963-1974). However, unlike bus and tram use, underground rail journeys have increased for most of the twentieth century and in 2003 the underground accounted for 54.7 per cent of all morning peak journeys to work (including transfers from mainline services) (Transport for London, 2003).

The London County Council (LCC) took control of central London's horse-drawn tram system in 1899, with electrification taking place from 1901, but there was no unified system throughout the Greater London area and two central London boroughs (Kensington and Chelsea) refused to allow trams onto their streets. By 1909 the LCC operated 135 miles of (mainly electrified) tramway and local authorities and private companies in outer London operated a further 110 miles. As in Glasgow and Manchester, by the 1930s trams were facing competition from motorbuses and were increasingly seen as an outmoded form of transport. For instance, the 1931 Royal Commission on Transport recommended that trams should gradually be phased out in London. One way in which the LPTB responded was by converting tram routes to trolley buses, which used the existing infrastructure but were viewed as more modern, comfortable and efficient. In 1937 the LPTB committed itself to converting the whole of its tram network to trolleybuses. Although trams persisted for another 15 years (the last tram of this era ran in London in 1952) passenger numbers declined rapidly and trolleybuses lasted only a further decade although they were still carrying some 475 million passengers a year when the service was withdrawn in 1962 (Barker and Robbins, 1963-1974). However, as in Manchester, trams and light rail systems have recently been re-introduced into London with the Dockland Light Railway opened in 1987 and the Croydon Tramlink in 2000. By 2003 these services carried some 18 million passengers annually and there are plans to extend the tram network to other parts of the city, thus recreating a public transport system that disappeared half a century ago (Transport for London, 2003).

Road traffic congestion was identified as a problem in London from the early-twentieth century. It was attributed largely to the rapid growth in private cars and was blamed for increasing operational difficulties faced by motorbuses. Thus a census of 1937 showed that private cars accounted for 37 per cent of total road traffic flow and pedal cycles 21 per cent, whilst only 14 per cent was generated by public service passenger vehicles (LPTB Annual Report, 1937). The Board identified the problem as due to: 'badly planned streets, the abuse of street accommodation by waiting vehicles, and the ill-considered driving of vehicles' (LPTB Annual Report, 1937, p. 20). Road traffic management schemes were increasingly introduced into London from the 1950s, and the potential pressure that cars placed on London's road system was emphasised by Buchanan (1963) who noted that although less than five per cent of those working in inner London travelled by car, some 70 per cent would choose to travel by car if restraints were removed. Successive reports through the 1970s and 1980s highlighted the inefficiencies of car transport in London but, despite the fact that car ownership rates in London are lower than elsewhere in Britain, and both walking and cycling remain important ways of moving around the city, the problem was not tackled in a comprehensive and effective way until Ken Livingstone, as Mayor of London, introduced congestion charging in February 2003. This has resulted in an 18 per cent drop in cars entering central London and an approximate 30 per cent increase in cycling (GLA website, 2004). As noted above, expansion and modernisation of the bus network has also produced significant increases in bus use and passengers numbers on the London underground are at their highest ever level. Thus although Greater London still suffers from many of the problems of road congestion and excessive car use seen in other cities, especially in the outer districts and around the M25 London orbital motorway, the Greater London Authority has tackled urban traffic congestion more effectively than any other city in Britain.

Conclusion: Mobility and Meaning

This chapter has, first, examined the ways in which everyday mobility is connected to wider society through the identification of six discourses of mobility that relate to the extensive theoretical and empirical literature. Second, we have focused on the ways in which the transport infrastructure has changed over the past century, examining in some detail the changes that have occurred in the four case study towns. This material provides a context for the detailed analysis that follows, and some aspects will be returned to in the final chapter that reviews implications of the research for contemporary transport policy.

However, one aspect of mobility has been given only passing mention in the above analysis. Previous research has tended to focus on the implications of mobility for society, economy and environment, but the meaning of mobility for ordinary people has been largely neglected. This dimension forms an important part of the following historical analysis. Through the use of oral evidence collected from in-depth life histories we examine ways in which the individual experience of everyday mobility has changed over the past 60 years, the strategies employed and constraints encountered in carrying out everyday mobility, and the ways in which daily mobility impacted upon people's lives.

Chapter 3

Reconstructing Mobilities

Introduction: What Do We Need to Know?

There is a paucity of empirical information on everyday mobility and the ways in which it has changed in Britain over the past century. This is one reason why assumptions about mobility change are based on broad-brush interpretations of global change rather than on detailed assessments of what has actually happened. Because everyday mobility is viewed as mundane and commonplace, such movement has been neglected in the compilation of official statistics and reports and in detailed academic studies. Most everyday mobility requires little thought or planning, it is just something that is done on a daily basis and the routine nature of such movement means that it disappears from view. Thus, whereas a family may spend weeks discussing, planning and booking a holiday trip to the Mediterranean; travelling to work, going to the supermarket, or taking children to school are activities that are all completed without a second thought. However, whilst a holiday appears to be an expensive and exciting event, it probably occupies just two weeks and in total will almost certainly cost much less than the real costs of travel for everyday purposes on the other 50 weeks of the year. However, because we do such trips regularly we do not usually think about, plan, or record them systematically.

To study everyday mobility we thus, first, need to gain access to good quality data that record where, when, how and why people travel on a daily basis. Whilst much of this information can be recorded systematically, for instance as a travel diary or daily log of journeys, explanation of why people chose to travel to a particular place or in a specific way, and of the impacts of such travel on the individual, requires the production of detailed individual accounts. It is thus necessary to produce both quantitative data relating to the distance, direction, time and mode of travel and qualitative evidence on the reasons why trips occurred, the ways in which modal choices were made, and on the opportunities and constraints that affected daily travel. Such information should also reflect both the diversity of the population and the varied geography of the country. Thus there needs to be recognition that whilst some travel decisions are taken by family groups (most obviously a family's annual holiday) in most such decisions there will be a dominant voice and that travel demands, opportunities and constraints will be different for men and for women, and will vary between children, adolescents and adults. Moreover, even for adults, the factors affecting travel will vary over the life course. Geography is important because, most obviously, travel demands will vary between urban and rural areas, but even in urban areas variations in urban structure and the transport infrastructure will influence travel behaviour. Thus, ideally, any data on everyday mobility should take into account all the above factors to produce a comprehensive picture of mobility change in the past.

What Data are Available and What Do They Tell Us?

Existing information on mobility change over the past century come from three main sources: official national surveys and reports; one-off surveys and studies of particular places; and mobility accounts provided by individuals. We briefly review each of these and assess the problems and limitations of extant data. It should be noted that much of the information that is available was originally conceived for a purpose other than recording everyday mobility. Useful data on everyday mobility are available as a by-product, or form a small part of the whole, but because the survey or study was not constructed with the sole purpose of measuring everyday mobility, the extent and nature of the data may be less than ideal. This is a familiar problem for historical geographers, especially when dealing with the more distant past when change in society and economy has to be inferred from scanty evidence (Baker, Hamshere and Langton, 1970; Butlin, 1993). However, there is a tendency to assume that for more recent periods good quality data will be readily available. This is certainly not the case for many everyday events, including routine daily mobility.

Official statistics on mobility come from two main sources, the census and the National Travel Survey (NTS). Current information is made readily available on the National Statistics web site (www.statistics.gov.uk), or in annual publications such as *Social Trends* (also available on-line at the above site), but most historical data must be culled from a variety of reports. There has been a decadal census in Great Britain since 1801, with the only gap during the Second World War in 1941. In 1966 there was also a mid-term sample census (Rhind, 1983). However, during the nineteenth century no data were collected on mobility, and the only question on migration related to place of birth (Wrigley, 1972; Lawton, 1978). In 1921 the census asked a question on the journey to work and this was repeated in 1951. From 1961 onwards there have been a small number of questions on commuting including information on transport mode. However, such data have only limited use. Census tabulations record only journey to work movement between local authority areas, thus ignoring the majority of flows that occur within an urban area and they are presented only as broad aggregate statistics. They give a snapshot of longer distance movement, but certainly do not reflect all commuting trips. Moreover, the census does not collect any information on other travel such as the journey to school or to shop, even though in terms of transport planning it can be suggested that such trips have at least as great an impact on traffic flows and urban congestion. They have been used to good effect to examine past national level commuting flows between urban areas (Lawton, 1963; 1968; Warnes, 1972), but tell us nothing of the majority of everyday movement.

The National Travel Survey (NTS) provides much more data for the recent past, and was designed specifically to collect information on daily travel patterns.

The first NTS was carried out in 1965/6, with further ad hoc surveys through the 1970s and early 1980s, and with the collection of continuous survey data since 1988. Some 11 National Travel Surveys are currently available, with the most recent accessible via the National Statistics web site. The first full-scale survey was completed during the 12 months from 20th February 1965 to 18th February 1966. Over 15,000 households were sampled from all areas of Britain and asked to complete a travel diary and provide additional information for a randomly selected week. The survey produced a 71.4 per cent response rate. Subsequent surveys have followed a similar, though not identical, methodology. The main purpose of the survey was to collect information on those aspects of everyday travel that had the most impact on traffic, and especially on transport planning in both rural and urban areas, with considerable emphasis given to car use and access to public transport.

Although providing a large amount of detailed information on most aspects of everyday travel since the 1960s, it is difficult to construct accurate longitudinal data from these surveys. We attempt to provide some analysis in Chapter 4, but limitations inherent in the NTS methodologies must be borne in mind. Most importantly, there have been a number of significant changes in the methods used to collect data and the categories used to present evidence in the NTS reports. These are detailed in the relevant reports, but are often ignored when NTS data are referred to in other studies. In particular, the NTS methodology understates the total amount of short distance mobility undertaken, especially short trips on foot. Thus in 1965 no journeys less than one mile (1.6km) were included, and in subsequent surveys trips of under one mile were only recorded on the last day of the seven-day survey. Walking distances of under 50 yards are excluded from all surveys, as too is children's play in the street or neighbourhood. With the exception of the 1965/6 survey all travel off a public road (for instance walks in parks) is excluded. These factors obviously limit the extent to which the surveys can be used to examine changes in the amount that people walked, or shifts in patterns of outdoor play by children.

Second, the NTS methodology relies on the calculation of aggregate data about annual travel patterns from data collected over a randomly selected week. The sample framework ensures that for different families sample weeks were distributed throughout the year so that seasonal effects were taken into account, but clearly it is possible that the week sampled could have been atypical, either overstating or understating mobility. Third, there have been some changes in the ways in which distances were calculated, thus in 1965/6 respondents were asked to estimate the distance travelled whilst in 1975/6 distances were calculated according to a fixed formula based on respondents' statements of the time taken for a trip. Fourth, the age categories used to record mobility have also changed over time, restricting direct comparison of the travel behaviour of children and adults at different stages of the life course. Fifth, there have been substantial changes to the categorisation of trip purpose, restricting the extent to which long-term comparisons can be made. Sixth, there is only limited information on variations between different geographical regions, or between urban and rural areas, and the geographical definitions used have also changed over time. Finally, the ways in which the data are presented vary from report to report, though the more recent publications do attempt to provide comparable data on key trends since the 1970s.

In addition to the above national surveys, concerns about traffic congestion, the impact of commuting on towns and the emergence of new urban and transport planning policies have led to a large number of one-off studies and surveys that have examined aspects of everyday movement. However, as with the NTS, the main focus of these has been to deal with perceived problems of transport planning, caused particularly by the growth of motor traffic, and such studies have paid little attention to walking or cycling. The town planning movement in Britain emerged from the 1920s with the development of a number of urban and regional plans in the interwar period and, especially, after the Second World War (Cherry, 1988). Thus planning documents such as the Thompson Plan for Merseyside (1944), the City of Manchester Plan (1945) and, especially, Abercrombie's famous plan for London (1944), all focused on transport planning, and the problems produced by large volumes of daily movement as part of an overall approach to restructuring housing, employment and transport in urban areas (Hall et al, 1973). One of the first studies that focused specifically on the journey to work was carried out (mainly in London) by Liepmann (1944), but earlier social enquiries did provide some relevant data for other localities, for instance Caradog Jones's (1934) extensive survey of Merseyside. In the 1950s and 1960s attention shifted even more clearly to the problems of traffic in towns with further research on London (Westergaard, 1957) and, especially, Colin Buchanan's influential report on traffic in towns (1963). Although this paved the way for major road building and urban restructuring to accommodate the car, it also provided considerable information on everyday mobility patterns. Since the 1970s the planning framework has required authorities to produce regular land-use plans in which transport planning has played a major role and, since the 1990s, attention has shifted towards the need for more sustainable transport policies with a raft of government reports (DETR 1998a,b,c; 1999; 2001; DfT, 2004a,b), and critical commentary (Docherty and Shaw, 2003). However, it can be argued that all of these reports are very narrowly focused. They are concerned almost exclusively with the impact of motor traffic in towns and with the provision of public transport. Commuting flows are privileged over other trips, and they pay little attention to walking or cycling, to the myriad of short everyday trips that people make around town, or to children's outdoor play. Moreover, these reports are mainly concerned with reporting aggregate trends: they say little about the decision-making processes that lie behind everyday travel behaviour.

At the other end of the spectrum, rare individual accounts of everyday travel given in diaries, autobiographies and other writing, together with data culled from oral history interviews, can begin to provide the individual insights into daily mobility that national statistics and large-scale surveys necessarily miss. These are almost the only sources available for the detailed examination of everyday mobility prior to the 1920s, and a small number of studies have used life histories and other contemporary records to reconstruct journey to work patterns in the late-nineteenth century (Lawton and Pooley, 1975; Green, 1988; Pooley and Turnbull, 1997). Personal diaries, though rare, can provide particularly good insights into everyday travel patterns as they do record the mundane and allow the reconstruction of daily movement in a way that few other sources allow (Pooley, 2004; Pooley and Pooley, 2004). There are also now large collections of oral history recollections held in archives and libraries and many of these tapes and transcripts include information about everyday travel. However, like official documents, most such sources – diaries, life histories, oral testimonies – have been produced for a purpose other than the collection of information on everyday mobility. They may contain relevant data, but it is a by-product from a source that could have been produced for a whole range of (often unknown) motives. Such limitations must be recognised fully when these sources are utilised.

In order to undertake a detailed study of all aspects of everyday mobility it is thus necessary to collect original data that is specifically focused on the research question in hand. Although such data can never provide the comprehensive coverage of national censuses and surveys, it is the only way in which more detailed questions relating to both the structure of, and motives for, all aspects of everyday mobility can be uncovered. Thus research reported in this book draws mainly on data produced by two separate investigations: one that examined changes in the journey to work over the century since 1890 focusing particularly on the three urban areas of London, Manchester/Salford and Glasgow; and one that studied all aspects of everyday mobility since the 1940s in the Manchester/Salford conurbation and in the urban area of Lancaster and Morecambe situated in north Lancashire. Full details of the methodologies used are outlined below, but here we summarise the overall approach.

In both research studies we adopted a life history approach and combined survey methodologies with the use of in-depth oral history interviews. There are two key beliefs underlying this approach. First, it is argued that any aspect of mobility, be it residential migration or the journey to school, can only be understood within the context of an individual's life history. All too often studies of migration and mobility treat movement as discrete and separate events that are unconnected to each other, and that are divorced form the life course of the individual (Halfacree and Boyle, 1993). We argue that mobility experience is both cumulative over time and embedded in the life history of the individual. Thus any movement has to be placed in context and needs to be recalled within the framework of an individual life history. This approach was pioneered in a previous study of residential migration in Britain since the eighteenth century (Pooley and Turnbull, 1998) and has been adapted for this research. Second, we believe firmly in the importance of combining quantitative and qualitative evidence to produce a holistic view of the mobility process. Both large-scale surveys and in-depth interviews are by themselves limited, but in combination they can produce powerful evidence. Thus a mixed methodology, that first collects some broad survey data that is capable of quantification and, secondly, then uses this information to construct in-depth oral history interviews, allows both the reconstruction of past mobility patterns and the explanation of how and why mobility change has occurred. By definition, all such work is dependent to some degree on the recall of respondents who are providing information on past mobility. In this sense the data are inferior to the NTS surveys that record actual travel patterns through a travel diary, but in the absence of good retrospective evidence there is no other way in which historical data on mobility trends can be collected. Some of the problems associated with these sorts of data are outlined below.

The Journey to Work Since 1890

Data on changes in the journey to work were collected during 1996 as part of a project funded by The Leverhulme Trust. Information was collected, first, from a survey of 1,834 individuals scattered throughout Britain who began work after 1890 and who provided detailed information on their employment life histories, including 12,439 separate journeys to work; and, second, from 90 in-depth semi-structured interviews with respondents living in the case study cities of London, Glasgow and Manchester/Salford. These interviews probed the structure and context of journey to work decisions. Respondents were identified in a number of ways. Our main source (providing 77.4 per cent of respondents) was a network of genealogists and family historians, which we had utilised in a previous project (Pooley and Turnbull, 1998), through which individuals provided information both about themselves and their immediate ancestors; but we also sought respondents by contacting large employers in selected towns and by placing advertisements in the local press. All those expressing interest in the project were sent a detailed data entry form which requested information on a person's employment history, residential history, details of every new journey to work (including mode of transport, time taken, cost and reasons for choosing a particular mode) and personal characteristics. Those completing forms for themselves (rather than immediate ancestors) were asked if they were prepared to participate in a subsequent interview. Most interviews were carried out face-to-face, but for some younger respondents interviews were conducted by 'phone due to the difficulty of arranging a meeting. All interviews were taped, fully transcribed and prepared for analysis in much the same way as explained in more detail for the everyday mobility data (discussed below).

A data collection procedure such as this, which relies on a self-selected sample responding to an open request for information, creates many problems and potential biases. It is not possible to use the aggregate data to relate journey to work characteristics to specific labour markets as, in most cases, the number of responses is too small. For analysis, we have divided respondents into those working in London, other towns over 100,000 population (in 1951) and other places. There is a fairly even split between these three categories. We also failed to get an even response between decades, with less information for those starting work in the 1890s and most for the 1930s and 1940s. The relative lack of data on people who are no longer alive is understandable; slightly more surprising is the low response from people who began work in the 1970s and 1980s. Older people were much more likely to respond and complete our forms than those who began work recently (Table 3.1). The characteristics of all those in our sample who were

Table 3.1 Characteristics of the Journey to Work Data Set

Decade	Sample size*					
	Males		Females		Total	
	No.	%**	No.	%**	No.	%+
1890-1899	77	81.9	17	18.1	94	5.1
1900-1909	101	73.7	36	26.3	137	7.5
1910-1919	108	65.9	56	34.1	164	8.9
1920-1929	94	60.6	61	39.4	155	8.5
1930-1939	166	58.9	116	41.1	282	15.4
1940-1949	193	52.2	177	47.8	370	20.2
1950-1959	100	41.3	142	58.7	242	13.2
1960-1969	57	39.0	89	61.0	146	8.0
1970-1979	63	46.0	74	54.0	137	7.4
1980-1989	51	47.7	56	52.3	107	5.8
Total	1010	55.1	824	44.9	1834	100.0

* Number of males and females in the sample who started work in each decade.

** Percentage of total starting work in that decade.

\+ Percentage of total sample.

Table 3.2 Comparison of Journey to Work Sample and Census Population Characteristics* (Per cent)

Characteristic	1931		1951		1971	
	Census	Sample	Census	Sample	Census	Sample
(a) Gender						
Males	70.3	81.4	69.2	72.8	63.3	65.6
Females	29.7	18.6	30.8	27.2	36.7	34.4
(b) Age						
14-24 years	33.0	24.0	23.2	19.1	21.0	4.6
25-34 years	23.0	27.3	21.8	28.9	19.4	11.4
35-54 years	32.8	45.7	42.7	37.6	41.8	68.8
55-64 years	10.8	3.0	12.3	14.4	17.8	15.2
(c) Marital status						
Single	48.7	36.0	34.3	34.1	23.3	15.6
Married	46.8	61.6	61.2	63.9	66.5	80.3
Widowed	4.5	2.4	4.5	2.0	10.2	4.1
(d) Socio-economic status						
Professional	2.2	17.4	3.1	21.2	3.6	41.0
Intermediate	12.9	13.0	13.7	15.6	17.8	17.0
Skilled	48.9	47.5	52.6	46.2	49.5	34.7
Semi-skilled	18.2	11.6	16.0	9.1	20.9	3.5
Unskilled	17.8	10.5	14.6	7.9	8.2	3.8
Sample size	339		607		665	

* Comparison of the employed sample population alive in 1931, 1951 and 1971 with the employed population in the relevant census of population for England and Wales and Scotland.

in the workforce in 1931, 1951 and 1971 were compared with the relevant census workforce characteristics (Table 3.2). The sample is quite representative of the total population with respect to gender, has some under-representation of the young and single, and contains a substantial bias towards those in higher socio-economic groups.

It is almost inevitable that a self-selected sample will be biased towards those with more education and in higher status occupations. It can be suggested that family historians (our main providers of information) are themselves most likely to come from middle class and professional backgrounds and that white-collar employees are most likely to receive and respond to calls for information disseminated within a company. It can also be suggested that there will be other demographic biases in data provided about the ancestors of family historians. In particular, there will be a bias towards those who married and had children to continue a family line. In addition, all research that collects life history data from individuals will be affected by errors of recall and possible misrepresentation. All the biases and omissions noted above are inevitable in a project such as this and must be taken into account in interpretation. It is not claimed that the data set is totally representative of the population as a whole and the data are not being used for inferential purposes. However, it is argued that there are sufficiently large numbers of responses for most decades for secure conclusions to be drawn. The fact that journey to work distances and transport modes recorded in this project for the 1990s are very similar to those found in recent surveys (National Statistics, 2003) suggests that the biases have not unduly distorted the picture of commuting. In addition, the second stage of the research (in-depth interviews) was used to try to correct some of the biases. Those interviewed all began work in London, Manchester/Salford or Glasgow and in this way we can relate the detailed accounts to specific labour market characteristics, local topography and transport infrastructure. In selecting those to be interviewed we also over-sampled respondents in lower-status occupations to ensure that the second stage sample was more broadly representative of the population as a whole.

Everyday Mobility Since the 1940s in Manchester/Salford and Lancaster/Morecambe

During 2001-2003 data on all aspects of everyday mobility since the 1940s were collected as part of a project funded by the Economic and Social Research Council. Again, a mixed method life history approach was used that combined the collection of quantitative survey data with in-depth life histories. In this study most emphasis was placed on the collection of qualitative evidence and data were collected from a total of 156 individuals (75 in Lancaster/Morecambe and 81 in Manchester/Salford). Some 160 hours of interviews (producing over 3,200 pages of typed transcripts) delivered a rich data source that provides unparalleled insights into everyday mobility over the past 60 years.

Table 3.3 Everyday Mobility Sample Population: Manchester/Salford and Lancaster/Morecambe

Birth year	Age at interview	Sample size				Life-cycle stage	Interview periods
		Manchester		Lancaster			
		Male	Female	Male	Female		
1932-41	60-69	11	14	11	10	Retiring/retired/family left home	Age 10/11 Age 17/18 Age 30s Age 60s
1962-71	30-39	8	8	7	7	Young/teenage family	Age 10/11 Age 17/18 Age 30s
1983-84	17/18	11	9	10	10	End of secondary education/first job	Age 10/11 Age 17/18
1990-91	10/11	9	11	10	10	Last year of primary education	Age 10/11
Total		39	42	38	37		

The aim of the project was to collect detailed information on everyday mobility for people of different ages and at different times from the 1940s to the present. To achieve this we have used an oral history approach in which particular cohorts of individuals were questioned about their mobility experience at particular stages of their life. Four cohorts of respondents were identified: those born 1932-1941, 1962-1971, 1983-1984, and 1990-1991. Information on everyday mobility was collected for up to four time slices (as appropriate) designed to match key life course stages: age 10/11, age 17/18, age 30-39, and age 60-69 (Table 3.3). To standardise for the impact of different urban structures on mobility, it was a requirement that all individuals included in the survey should have lived in the same urban area throughout their lives (or at least at the dates for which data were collected).

During the early stages of the research we undertook a number of pilot surveys and interviews and refined the methodology several times before settling on a standard approach. This was largely because we were experimenting with the balance between the use of a relatively structured questionnaire survey to collect mobility data and semi-structured in-depth interviews to probe meanings and experiences of mobility. Whereas the survey approach allowed a large amount of information to be collected quickly, the interviews took much longer and enabled us to collect detailed data on a smaller number of respondents. However, interviews with older respondents who were reporting mobility for four time slices could take a very long time (in some cases 3-4 hours) so we had to restrict the extent to which such data were collected. In the end we agreed a compromise that combined both survey and interview techniques and allowed the data to be collected reasonably quickly and efficiently.

Respondents were identified by a variety of means. Those born 1990-1991 were contacted through primary schools, chosen to reflect a cross-section of communities and catchment areas. Respondents born 1983-1984 were mainly recruited through schools and FE Colleges together with a small number not currently in education identified through personal contacts. This provided a good cross-section of respondents. Most children were interviewed at school, though in some cases interviews took place in the respondent's home. For those aged 10/11, parental permission was gained before an interview took place and parents could be present at the interview if they wished. A wide range of strategies was used to identify older respondents (born 1962-1971 and 1932-1941). Articles were placed in local newspapers and other media (including the web), information was posted in libraries and other public places, leaflets were distributed via a selection of large employers and flyers were posted through letter boxes in a selection of residential areas. In addition personal contacts were used to identify suitable respondents and a snowballing technique was employed where one respondent could suggest others who would fit our strict criteria with respect to age and residential history. All methods yielded some respondents. All adults who expressed an interest in the project were sent further information and a survey form. Not all completed this, but those who did were then asked to fix a date for a follow-up interview. There was a small drop-out rate at this stage, but most respondents who completed a questionnaire also agreed to be interviewed.

Most interviews with adults took place in the respondent's home, though some were carried out in a workplace or at Lancaster University. In Lancaster/Morecambe all interviews were carried out face-to-face, and all interviews with children aged 10/11 and 17/18 were also face-to-face, but in Manchester/Salford it was decided to use telephone interviews for most adults. This was because we found it increasingly difficult to schedule interviews, and contact by 'phone was the only viable means of collecting the data within the time available. Having used some telephone interviews for younger respondents in the journey-to-work study we had extensive experience of carrying out and recording such material. Although telephone interviews inevitably lose some of the immediacy of face-to-face encounters, they lasted approximately the same length of time as face-to-face interviews with adults in Lancaster. We have carefully compared evidence from the telephone interviews in Manchester and the face-to-face interviews in Lancaster, and can find no systematic or significant differences in the quality of information provided.

Two main methods of data collection were used. For children all data were collected through a single interview that both recorded factual data about everyday mobility and explored the reasons and motivations behind these trips. On average, interviews lasted 45 minutes with those aged 10/11 and 90 minutes for those aged 17/18. All interviews were taped and transcribed and from these transcripts both quantitative and qualitative data were extracted for further analysis. In the case of adult respondents a two-stage approach was adopted. This was because pilot interviews showed that with three or four time slices of data to collect, the collation of all data in a single interview was too time consuming. All respondents were first sent a detailed questionnaire on which they recorded factual information about their mobility aged 10, 17, 35 and 65 (as appropriate). From this information an interview schedule was designed that probed an individual's mobility experience and collected qualitative explanatory data as efficiently as possible. For those in their 30s these focused interviews lasted around 45 minutes, whilst those in their 60s were interviewed for approximately one hour. All interviews were again taped and fully transcribed. This combined approach provided good quality quantitative and qualitative data relatively quickly.

Two members of the research team (Jean Turnbull and Mags Adams) were responsible for all interviews and at the start of the project several joint interviews were conducted to ensure that all data were comparable. Throughout the research regular team meetings ensured that this comparability continued. At the start of the research we undertook an ethical review of the research methodology and gained clearance from the Criminal Records Bureau to work with children. All interviews with children were carried out with permission from both the school through which the child was recruited and the child's parent. A full risk assessment was also carried out for the two members of the research team undertaking interviews.

Transcribing the interviews and extracting the quantitative data from the children's interviews and adults' questionnaires were time-consuming tasks (when aggregated over a 12 month period we have information on almost one million individual trips). Geraldine Byrne undertook all transcription and Cait Griffiths completed all coding and data entry of the quantitative material into an Access database. There were several stages to the data manipulation phase of the project. For adults the survey form was checked and used as a framework from which the in-depth interview was constructed. Data on the form were then coded and entered into an Access database. Following the interview the tapes were transcribed and read carefully. A system of hierarchical coding of key themes arising from the interviews was identified and the transcripts were entered into the text analysis programme Atlas ti, and coded appropriately. For children all data were gained from the structured interview and thus quantitative data were extracted and coded from a careful reading of the transcript before being entered into the Access database. Once again the full transcript was entered into Atlas ti and coded appropriately. Further analysis required the use of SPSS and Excel for manipulation of quantitative data and the use of ArcView for spatial analysis and representation. For the textual data the coding system worked well and allowed relevant segments of interviews to be recalled. However, we deliberately coded large segments of text to ensure that quotes were set within a context and also used quite high-level codes to retrieve data. For all queries in Atlas there was thus a further manual stage of carefully reading and reviewing the relevant segments of text to establish meaning and context prior to interpretation.

Problems of Data Analysis and Interpretation

All data present problems of analysis and interpretation. Two key issues are relevant to both the journey to work data and the information on all forms of everyday mobility: the ability of respondents to recall and provide accurate information about their mobility and the representativeness of the samples. All information provided in surveys and interviews depends to some extent on the respondents' ability to remember and there is a large literature that deals with the role of memory in oral history (Perks, 1992; Fields, 1989; Thomson et al, 1994). In general, it is usually suggested that people are more likely to remember unusual or traumatic events than they are the mundane and that recall for the recent past will be better than for events that took place a long time before the date of interview. However, many other factors can also affect and influence the ability of respondents to remember information. Memories of well-known events may have been affected by later information gained from books or television programmes, the frequency with which an event occurred will influence how it is remembered, as too will the degree of subsequent association with a place or context. All these factors potentially affect the data analysed in this study.

In this research we were asking respondents to recall mundane events that mostly occurred regularly and frequently: the journey to work and to school, trips to shops, visits to relatives and friends and simply going out to play as a child. Although such events are mundane and, in one sense easily forgotten, they also occurred regularly and the memory is unlikely to have been unduly affected by outside influences. In both projects data were collected by taking respondents through their life history and by encouraging them to recall what they did on a daily basis in a chronological order. In doing this we found that the quality of recall that elderly respondents had of their play as a child or their journey to work as a young man or woman was extremely good. In the everyday mobility project, their memory of place was also enhanced by the fact that they had lived in the same area for most, if not all, of their life. Undoubtedly our respondents did not have total recall and some journeys may have been missed. But all respondents engaged closely with the interview and were able to provide a full and detailed account of their daily activities.

One specific and unusual problem does occur with the data on everyday mobility: we are using oral evidence to recall change over time. Most oral history studies focus on a single event or set of experiences and all the respondents will be subject to the same memory bias. This is not true with our data. Thus, whereas a ten year old should have good recall of (for instance) their current journey to school, a 65 year old may have a very sketchy memory of the journey to school they undertook when they were ten. In examining change over time we are thus trying to compare two (or more) sets of data that have different (and unknown) memory biases. This problem is unavoidable, and there are no other ways of generating similar data, but this issue needs to be borne in mind when interpreting the results. In general, we believe that by adopting a life history approach and getting older respondents to talk about their everyday mobility in the context of other aspects of their life at the time, the quality of data collected is good for those journeys on which we have information. It seems likely that data on trips that were made regularly (such as the journey to school) were relatively easily remembered by 65 year olds; however other journeys that were undertaken irregularly may have been omitted or distorted by older respondents, whereas when talking about current mobility respondents would recall these trips. We thus believe that the problem of partial recall relates principally to the extent to which some trips were omitted by older respondents, rather than to the quality of data on those trips that were recalled.

In most cases interviews themselves did not present problems and the nature of the subject matter was not sufficiently sensitive or personal to create tensions between the interviewer and the interviewee. However, interviews with children aged 10/11 did present especial problems. There are two key issues. First, where such interviews were carried out with the child alone (with the permission of the parent and school) then we found the ability of the child to explain why a particular journey was undertaken highly variable. Clearly it was often a parental decision about which the child had limited knowledge. Thus some (though by no means all) interviews were rather short and lacking detail. Second, where the interview was carried out in the presence of a parent, although the parent was able to provide prompts to the child and give more explanatory information, the quality of data on what the child actually did and where they went was often less good. It was clear that the child was inhibited by their parent's presence and, not surprisingly, when they were alone 10 year olds were prepared to say things that they would not reveal to their parents. There is also the possibility that, when alone, some children would brag or exaggerate certain aspects of their mobility. We tried to check this by triangulating information throughout the interview and identifying any inconsistencies in the information revealed. One solution would have been to interview both parents and children separately, but this proved too time-consuming. One further, and related, problem pertains to the journey to work data set. Here, data for those that entered the labour force in the early-twentieth century came not from the individuals themselves, but from their descendents drawing on detailed knowledge of their close relatives. However, this will not provide the same quality of data as a direct testimony and, once again, it is not possible to precisely compare like with like.

In one sense representativeness is not an issue in this study: the intention was not to produce a statistically valid sample of a total population, but rather to focus in depth on the qualitative life histories of a relatively small number of respondents. It is the quality of individual testimonies that is important rather than the validity of the sample. However, we do use some of the data collected to examine broad mobility trends and it is important to assess the extent to which there may be bias in the data that will affect these results. Bias in the journey to work survey data is outlined above and in Table 3.2. As stated previously, to some extent this was corrected for when selecting the 90 respondents who were interviewed as we over-sampled those categories that were under-represented in the survey data. The everyday mobility data are more balanced in terms of occupations and socio-economic group, partly because the requirement that respondents had lived in the same area all their life excluded many with better education and higher-status employment, although the small numbers involved preclude meaningful comparisons with census data. However, we did have real difficulty recruiting respondents in their 30s (Table 3.3). This was because we found most people aged 30-39 were simply too busy to both complete a survey and undertake an in-depth interview. We had far more refusals in this age category than in any other group. It should also be emphasised that although in the context of a qualitative study the total sample size is large, when broken down into sub categories the number of respondents in each group can be quite small. Thus one or two respondents with what appeared to be unusual mobility can distort the overall picture. This occurred with one cohort in Lancaster and will be noted where relevant in the analysis.

Conclusions: Space, Time and Mobility

A focus on individual action spaces and space-time geographies is not new. In the 1960s Wolpert (1965) highlighted the concept of action space in the context of residential migration and Hagerstrand (1975) developed the notion of time geography in which he and others plotted space-time prisms of individual movement, stressing the constraints that influenced everyday mobility behaviour. However, such studies were set mainly within the framework of quantitative behavioural geography and they made little attempt to explore the factors underlying mobility decisions or the meanings associated with everyday mobility. Although various strands of cultural studies have focused on the meanings associated with everyday life, especially in the context of the production and consumption of material cultures (see Chapter 2), individual everyday mobility has been relatively neglected in recent years. This is almost certainly due to the paucity of easily available data, and the difficulty of collecting original data on mobility change over time.

As outlined above, published data sources are geared towards the needs of transport planning and tend to ignore the role of non-vehicular everyday movement. Moreover, the National Travel Survey deliberately excludes a number of important types of mobility, including walks off public roads and children's play. There has thus been a need to construct new data sets. The surveys and interviews analysed and interpreted in the remainder of this book are certainly not without their problems, some of which are outlined above. However, they do provide original new evidence on the ways in which all forms of everyday mobility have changed over the last century. By focusing on a restricted number of places (four case study towns) and controlling for variations in urban form, and by examining change over a relatively long time period, it is possible to construct a clearer picture of how all aspects of mobility have altered during the past century. Wherever possible these data are compared to, and supplemented by, information drawn from other sources. In combination these sources are used to qualify, and in some cases challenge, some popular assumptions about mobility change over the twentieth century.

Chapter 4

Changes in Everyday Mobility:
An Overview

Introduction

This chapter provides a starting point for more detailed later analysis by examining long-run trends in everyday travel behaviour. Although as outlined in Chapter 2 national-level data on long-term trends in everyday mobility are limited, there is some information on the journey to work from the 1920s and much more data on daily mobility and travel from the 1960s. First, these national-level data sets are reviewed and main trends identified. More detailed analysis of journeys for specific purposes is mostly left for later chapters. Second, we focus on the headline results from our study of everyday mobility in two towns from the 1940s to the present. We compare these data with National Travel Survey information and explain differences between the data sets. This aggregate analysis provides a context for the more detailed examinations of mobility for different reasons that follow in later chapters.

It should be stressed that much of the analysis presented in this chapter can provide only an aggregate view of changing patterns of everyday mobility. One of the themes that will be explored in later chapters is the degree to which there was a high degree of individual variability in mobility patterns in Britain, and the extent to which, for any individual, mobility behaviour may vary greatly from day to day or week to week. These individual variations are illustrated by focusing especially on qualitative evidence from in-depth interviews that highlight the personal factors that influence mobility. One example is given here, but in general data presented in this chapter, whilst representing broad trends of change in mobility over time, cannot reflect accurately the individual mobility experiences of particular people. There will always be many exceptions to the broad trends identified in aggregate statistics.

Everyday Mobility in the First Half of the Twentieth Century

There is very little direct evidence pertaining to daily mobility in the first half of the twentieth century. The British censuses of 1921 and 1951 collected both residence and workplace information and tabulated commuting journeys between local authorities (Warnes, 1972) and a small number of studies have focused on the journey to work in particular localities (Hewitt, 1928; Liepmann, 1944;

Westergaard, 1957). Most research focused on the problems of congestion caused by commuting (especially in London) and contributed to the development of urban planning after the Second World War (Barlow Report, 1940; Sneed, 1961; Buchannan, 1963). Apart from these sources, information on daily travel in the first half of the twentieth century has to come from anecdotal sources including diaries, accounts and oral histories.

Lawton (1963) and Warnes (1972) have both explicitly analysed changes in the journey to work in England between 1921 and 1951. Lawton (1963) focused on simple movement in and out of local authority areas, and showed that between the two censuses the total amount of movement increased substantially, and commuting between local authority areas spread from being focused mainly around large cities in 1921 to most parts of the country by 1951 (Figures 4.1 and 4.2). Thus in towns such as Coventry, Croydon, Leicester, Nottingham, Plymouth and Portsmouth daily in-movement for work more than doubled between 1921 and 1951, and the City of London was the only urban area studied that experienced a decline in daily in-movement of commuters (Table 4.1). Warnes (1972) extended this analysis and attempted to calculate changes in the mean distance travelled for the journey to work between 1921 and 1951. Although a somewhat crude analysis, based only on distance between the centroids of local authority areas, this showed a clear trend of increasing commuting distances within the study area of North West England. Thus the mean journey to work distance in North West England increased from 2.35km to 3.01km between 1921 and 1951 with longer commuting distances and the greatest increases in the more rural local authorities.

Table 4.1   Changes in Daily In-movement for Work to Selected Towns, 1921-1951

Town	Daily in-movement		% change
	1921	**1951**	
City of London	424,875	335,682	-21.0
Birmingham	51,703	97,736	+89.0
Bradford	19,234	24,255	+26.1
Bristol	14,906	23,124	+55.1
Cardiff	13,662	23,773	+74.0
Coventry	14,256	33,277	+133.4
Croyden	7,088	24,284	+242.6
Hull	9,244	15,764	+41.4
Leeds	19,637	33,502	+70.6
Leicester	10,566	28,453	+169.3
Liverpool	60,787	87,996	+24.2
Manchester	117,194	137,485	+17.3
Newcastle	40,888	64,805	+58.5
Nottingham	19,572	43,136	+120.4
Plymouth	5,349	11,843	+121.5
Portsmouth	4,355	13,182	+202.8
Sheffield	16,456	26,309	+59.9
Stoke	17,411	27,870	+60.0

Source: Lawton, (1963) pp. 66-67.

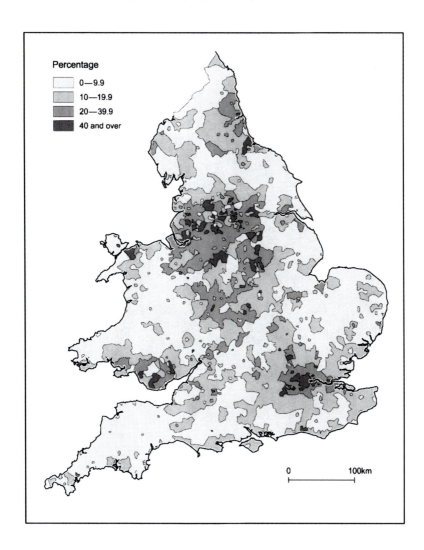

Figure 4.1 Total Daily Movement for Work, 1921 (Percentage of Total Resident Population)

Source: Lawton (1963), p. 63.

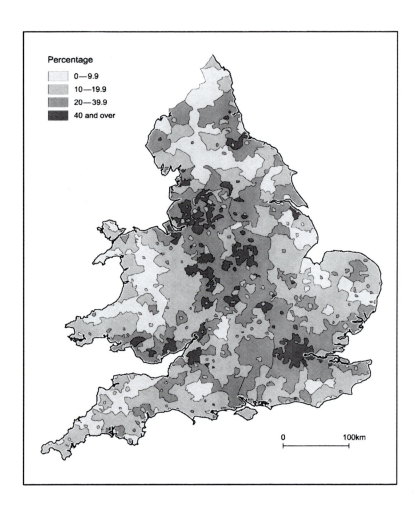

Figure 4.2 Total Daily Movement for Work, 1951 (Percentage of Total Resident Population)

Source: Lawton, (1963), p. 63.

Such aggregate analysis can only indicate broad trends, and the data available relate only to one dimension of everyday travel: the journey to work. An alternative perspective on everyday mobility in the first half of the twentieth century may be provided through analysis of diaries, accounts and oral evidence. An unusually detailed unpublished diary that recorded the daily movements of a young woman in London between 1938 and (in detail) 1942 provides some insights. This material has been analysed more fully elsewhere (Pooley, 1999; 2004). Here we focus on selected extracts from her diary to examine the way in which daily mobility around the city was structured during her first year of residence in London.

R arrived in London as an 18 year old in January 1938 with a job as a typist in the Inland Revenue and accommodation arranged at a girls' hostel in Earl's Court. Most of her everyday movement around the city was undertaken either on foot or on the underground and, initially, she rarely used the buses because she found them harder to negotiate. For her first journey to work she relied on another girl in the hostel to show her the way, writing in her diary 'I met D. and we went and got our tickets 3/-. We walked through a little green place and up to Somerset House. D. took me to the new wing' (31st January 1938). However by the following day she had established her own routine of a tube journey from Earl's Court to Charing Cross and then a short walk to her office. In total the trip took around 45 minutes and she described it in detail in her diary:

> After that [breakfast] I went to the station. From there to Charing Cross. I walked through a little park, through Somerset House, across the road, through Bush House, up Aldwych to Kingsway and so to Holborn. Turnstile House is a modern building. I think I can do the things better now. At lunchtime I went to the Milk Bar where I had steak and kidney pie and chips 4d. Then I went for a walk and found myself in Lincoln Inns Fields where the solicitors are. I walked round them and saw some men who fed the pigeons and sparrows (1st February 1938).

The following day she followed exactly the same routine, but the day after gradually became more adventurous, visiting the British Museum in her lunch break and after work met a girl from the hostel and visited Big Ben, the Houses of Parliament and Westminster Abbey. During her first two weeks in London R's routine varied little. She almost always took the same route to work, mostly went to the same Milk Bar for lunch, and then walked round Lincolns Inn Fields and adjacent streets, or visited the British Museum. Some evenings she attended secretarial classes at Bush House after work. She quickly established a restricted action space around her work environment, in which she felt comfortable and which seemed to meet her needs, but she rarely strayed from familiar territory (partly restricted by the length of her lunch break). Similarly, she quickly established a regular routine of activity around her hostel in Earl's Court and in both localities had an action space with which she was familiar and through which she travelled on a regular basis either on foot or by underground train.

During her first few weeks in London R made a deliberate attempt to explore at weekends at least the main tourist areas of London. She usually travelled with friends from the hostel and often described the journeys in detail:

> We went down Constitution Hill (which is not a hill) to Hyde Park Corner. We went down and looked at the 'Duke of Kents' home 3 Belgravia Square. It is not an extra nice house. There was a policeman outside it. After this D and I went down Piccadilly to Piccadilly Circus. On the way I saw fine shops and hotels. I saw Eros in the middle of the Circus. I saw the Mall, the Wellington Memorial and the Duke of York's Monument. We passed

through Trafalger Square on our way to Charing Cross station (19th February 1938).

A few weeks later in May 1938 R became more adventurous and travelled alone by tram to parts of the city that she had not visited before. This was a deviation both from her usual territory and her normal modes of transport and indicated that she was becoming increasingly familiar with London and its urban transport system. Again she described the trip in some detail, including comments on the areas through which she passed:

> I then decided to do some exploring. I bought a 1/- tram ticket and went off to Hampstead Heath. I arrived at South End Road Gate. There was a Punch and Judy show ... I had a good walk about the Heath. It is very nice but there are far too many people about it. The weather was somewhat cool. I ended up by coming out at the tram terminus at Highgate. I took a trip from there right past the East India Dock. The route there is most interesting and you do see some queer looking people. There is one place I noticed which was very Jewish. It was all not at all like what I thought the East End was. It is very nice indeed in parts ... The roadways are all railed in in the East-end and there are only openings for crossings (8th May 1938).

Although she rapidly gained confidence in travelling around the city, and her everyday mobility became routine and unexceptional, she did also sometimes make mistakes, especially during her first few months in the city. Thus in February 1938 she described in her usual detail an occasion when she and her friends got muddled in the tube, despite travelling parts of that route on a daily basis:

> We decided to take a 1[d] ride from Holborn to Charing Cross. We went down two escalators, down it seemed into the depths of the earth. We went to platform 4. We got on a train. We had to change at Leicester Square. We got off alright and went up a couple of escalators. At the top we went to the Baker line. We went down a long escalator. We got on the wrong train. It took us to Warren Road, the opposite direction to Charing Cross. We got off at Warren Road, we tried to get off at Goodge Street but the doors shut before we could get out. We got safely in a train that took us straight to Charing Cross. We got to P just in time for tea at 5 (27th February 1938).

Evidence from this one diary adds another dimension to the picture of everyday mobility painted by census evidence. R's daily journey to work of approximately six kilometres by tube and foot, taking some 45 minutes, was longer than most people experienced in provincial towns, but was not atypical for London (Warnes, 1972; Westergaard, 1957). Aside from this, most of her everyday travel was relatively short and was confined to localities that she knew well and through which she moved with ease. Longer trips were mostly undertaken for pleasure and to explore the city, either alone or with friends. Where possible R walked around London, but for longer trips she travelled by tube and more occasionally (but increasingly as she lived in London longer) by tram and bus. These everyday movements thus formed an essential part of R's life. They enabled her to carry out

both essential and leisure activities, they connected her to both a local comm
and a wider network of friends and they helped to construct her identity
Londoner (Pooley, 1999). At no time in her diary did she ever express any
significant concerns about travelling around the city, either alone or with friends,
and risk did not seem to be a concept that troubled her. This was reinforced by oral
evidence from an interview with R conducted in 1996:

> I was quite safe. It never crossed my mind for a minute that I was not safe.
> The only time I thought I was unsafe was once on the Strand when a man
> was trying to pick me up. He bought me an ice cream, he was being, you
> know, very friendly. I was a bit nervous then (Interview, 1996).

Everyday Mobility in the Second Half of the Twentieth Century:
Evidence from the National Travel Survey

As outlined in Chapter 3, although a National Travel Survey (NTS) has been
conducted periodically since 1965 the data they produce have not always been
directly comparable and some categories of travel (especially some short trips on
foot) have often been omitted. Thus the construction of long-run data from NTS
reports can only be done with difficulty and there may be some categories where
data are not directly comparable. However, it is possible to construct a broad
picture of everyday travel trends in Britain since the mid-twentieth century. This
section reviews selected evidence from NTS data, where possible constructing and
interpreting trends over time. More detailed analysis of trips for specific purposes
is left for later chapters. Questions on travel to work have also been included in
British censuses over the past 50 years. However, these data only allow the
analysis of movement between local authority areas and, for the most part, NTS
data provide much deeper insights into changes in the structure of all types of
mobility.

The trend of increased everyday mobility demonstrated by the journey to work
data for the first half of the twentieth century is continued if aggregate (non-
walking) travel patterns are analysed. The total distance travelled by British
residents by road and rail within Great Britain more than trebled between 1952 and
2002, rising from around 220 billion passenger kilometres to 746 billion passenger
kilometres. By comparison the British population only increased from 50.2 to 58.8
million people 1951-2001. Unsurprisingly most of this increase was in travel by
car, with movement by car, van and taxi increasing from 58 to 634 billion
passenger kilometres 1952-2002. In contrast travel by train increased only slightly
and use of buses and coaches almost halved (Figure 4.3). There has thus been a
substantial real increase in total movement and not just a switch from one travel
mode to another (National Statistics, 2004, p. 180). When related to individual
mobility the mean distance travelled per person per year by all modes of transport
(including some walking trips) has increased from 5,882km in 1965 to 10,965km
in 2001, and the mean distance travelled per person per trip has increased from 5.0

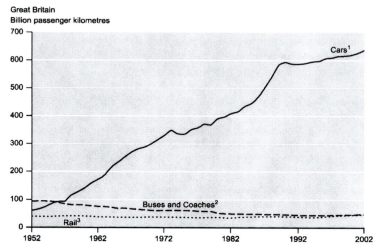

Great Britain
Billion passenger kilometres

1 Road transport data from 1993 are calculated on a new basis and are not directly comparable
with earlier years.
2 Includes vans and taxis.
3 Financial years. National rail, urban metros and modern trams.

**Figure 4.3   Changes in Distance Travelled by Mode (Passenger Transport),
1952-2002**

Source: Social Trends, (2004), p. 180.

to 10.8km over the same period (Table 4.2). Provisional figures for 2003 show a
slight drop from the 2002 high of 11,068km to 10,994km per person per year,
suggesting that levels of mobility may be stabilising at approximately double the
level of 1965 (Department of Transport, 1979; National Statistics, 2003). Thus the
main change in overall mobility has been an increase in trip length, especially by
car, rather than an increase in the number of individual trips undertaken. Indeed,
the mean number of trips per person per year has remained quite stable at around
one thousand since the 1970s. Likewise, there has been almost no change since
1972 in the average trip time of around 20 minutes (National Statistics, 2003).

   All people in Britain have not experienced these changes in everyday travel
equally, and there are significant variations both by age and gender (Table 4.3).
Comparison of data for 1965 and 1999/2001 shows that whereas in 1965 total
everyday mobility was greatest amongst young adults aged 21-29 years, by
1999/2001 those aged 40-49 travelled the greatest distances per annum. This may
reflect two trends. First, a mobile generation in the 1960s and 1970s may have
continued to exhibit high levels of mobility as they aged; and, secondly, changed
life-cycle constraints have meant that those currently in their 40s have both more
affluence and fewer mobility constraints than in the past. The fact that increases in

Table 4.2 Changes in Personal Travel 1965 to 1999/2001*

	1965	1975/76	1985/86	1992/94	1999/2001
Mean distance travelled per person per year (km)	5882	7627	8555	10360	10965
Mean distance travelled per person per trip (km)	5.0	8.2	8.4	9.8	10.8
% of trips undertaken for:					
Work and work related reasons	39.3	30.0	20.5	18.7	18.7
Education	7.0	7.3	7.5	6.4	6.6
Shopping	12.7	16.6	20.5	21.4	21.0
Entertainment	4.8	3.8	4.0	3.8	3.7
Social activities (visiting friends)	14.3	16.8	18.7	17.8	17.6
Sport	1.6	2.6	1.9	2.1	2.5
Other personal business	7.2	8.9	9.5	10.2	10.3
% of trips undertaken by:					
Walking		34.8	34.2	29.1	25.8
Walking (excluding trips of under 1.6km)	12.1	13.0	-	-	8.1
Bicycle	7.6	3.2	2.4	1.7	1.6
Car or van (driver or passenger)	40.1	45.8	50.5	58.7	62.6
Bus (public and private)	32.9	11.6	8.3	6.6	5.8
Train (surface and underground)	7.4	1.6	1.8	1.6	2.0

*Data for 1965 and 1975/76 are not always directly comparable with later figures. The main differences are as follows:
All data for 1965 exclude trips less than 1.6km (1 mile). Walking trips of less than 50 yards are excluded from all surveys, as are children's play and all off-road travel. For 1965 data on mode of transport relates to journey stage (i.e. several modes can be recorded for a single trip): later data relate only to the main mode used.
Sources: Department of Transport, 1979; Department for Transport, 2001.

A Mobile Century?

Table 4.3 Total Everyday Mobility by Age and Gender, 1965 and 1999/2001

| | Total km per person per year | |
	Male	Female
1965		
All children age 3-15	3,280	
16-20	9,446	7,363
21-29	11,739	5,823
30-64	9,455	4,886*
65+	3,012	2,544*
1999/2001		
<17	6,396	6,372
17-20	9,905	9,369
21-29	16,494	11,973
30-39	17,976	11,664
40-49	18,983	12,019
50-59	16,623	11,043
60-69	11,865	8,697
70+	7,054	4,566

*Females age 30-59 and 60+

Data for 1965 exclude travel of less than 1.6km (1 mile).

Sources: Department of Transport, 1979; Department for Transport, 2001.

overall mobility have slowed in the 1990s (and there may now possibly be some reduction) suggests that the impact of a particularly mobile generation may have been significant. In both 1965 and 1999/2001 the lowest levels of mobility were amongst children and the elderly.

Unfortunately, data do not allow a detailed assessment of change over time by age group, as the age divisions for 1965 are very broad. However, it is clear that everyday mobility has changed much more for some than for others. Thus, amongst adolescents and young adults aged 16/17-20 the mean total distance travelled per year has scarcely changed over the past 40 years, whereas for those aged 20-29 distances have increased by 40 per cent for males and have more than doubled for females. However, the greatest increases in total mobility have been experienced by the elderly with, on average, those aged over 70 in 1999/2001 travelling more than double the annual distance that the over-65s travelled in 1965. This clearly reflects a combination of increased longevity into an active retirement and increased affluence as the retired population are able to use their leisure time more fully.

There are consistent gender differences in the total mobility of people in Britain with males travelling more than females in all age groups and each time period. However, the extent of the differentials does vary with age, and the differences between male and female mobility have decreased over time. Gender differences are least amongst children with almost no difference between male and female mobility amongst those under 17 today. Not surprisingly, the gap widens during the family-rearing stage of the life cycle and narrows again slightly in old age. Whereas in 1965 men aged 21-64 travelled more than twice the distance that women covered in their everyday mobility, by 1999/2001 the differential had been reduced to around 30 per cent. Thus although, the total distance travelled per year has increased relatively more quickly for females than for males, adult women still appear to experience more mobility constraints, or choose to travel less, than their male counterparts.

There have also been significant changes in the reasons for everyday mobility and in the mode of transport used (Table 4.2). Although data are computed for 1965 to 2001, it should be stressed that the information for 1965 is not directly comparable with later figures due to changes in the categories used and the ways in which statistics were compiled. In general, over the past 40 years, there has been an increase in the proportion of trips undertaken for leisure and pleasure, and a decrease in the proportion of trips undertaken for work. Thus travel for work and work-related reasons decrease from some 39 per cent of all journeys in 1965 to 18 per cent in 1999/2001. At the same time, travel for shopping, entertainment, social activities and sport all increased their share of total travel distance. These trends again reflect a combination of increased affluence and leisure time and indicate that the mobility increase has been focused mainly on what might be considered non-essential travel activities that reflect changing life styles and aspirations.

Changes in the modes of transport used are also predictable, but when examined in terms of the proportion of trips undertaken by different modes, as opposed to the total distance travelled (see Figure 4.3) the changes are rather less dramatic (Table 4.2). The greatest reduction has been in bus use, with walking trips falling from 34.8 per cent of all journeys in 1975/76 to 25.8 per cent in 1999/2001, and car trips increasing from 45.8 per cent to 62.6 per cent of all journeys over the same period. It must be remembered that the NTS data exclude all walking trips of less than 50yds, data for 1965 exclude walking trips of under one mile, and all surveys exclude children's play and all off-road travel. Thus many activities in which walking is important are excluded from the surveys, but despite this travel on foot still accounts for over one quarter of all everyday mobility in the early twenty-first century. It is estimated that the total distance walked per person per year has dropped by about 25 per cent from 410km in 1975/6 to 309km in 2003, though the NTS admits that short walks were under-recorded in 2002 and 2003 compared to earlier years, and there has been no recorded change in the distance walked since the 1998/2000 data were collected.

Although the car now dominates everyday travel, there is some evidence that the rate of increase is slowing. This is emphasised by data on full driving licence holders (Table 2.2). Whilst the proportion of all adults holding a driving licence increased rapidly from 48 per cent in 1975/76 to 71 per cent in 1998/2000, thereafter the figure has stabilised and provisional data for 2003 show a slight fall to 70 per cent. This is most marked amongst young adults. The percentage of adults aged 17-20 with a full licence peaked in 1992/4 at 48 per cent and in 2003 stood at only 28 per cent. At the very least adolescents appear to be delaying learning to drive thus reducing the total amount of travel undertaken by car. As with other aspects of mobility there are persistent differences between males and females – in 1975/6 69 per cent of adult males had a driving licence compared to only 29 per cent of females – but that differential has reduced considerably in the past decade (National Statistics, 2003).

The National Travel Survey thus provides a reasonably clear picture of changes in some aspects of everyday mobility at a national level. The key trends can be summarised as an approximate doubling of the total distance travelled and the mean trip length over the past 40 years, but very little change in the total number of trips undertaken. There are consistent gender differences, with males more mobile than females, but with a narrowing difference between the mobility of men and women. The greatest mobility change has been experienced by those aged over 65. Increased car use accounts for most of the increase in total distance travelled, with a substantial reduction in both walking and bus use, however travel on foot still accounts for some 25 per cent of all trips covered by the NTS data. Although there are no directly comparable data for the first half of the twentieth century, census travel to work information and qualitative evidence cited above suggest that these trends have been apparent for much of the twentieth century.

Everyday Mobility in Manchester/Salford and Lancaster/Morecambe: An Overview

As outlined in Chapter Three analysis of all everyday mobility presented in this volume is largely based on data collected from in-depth life histories conducted in the two northern conurbations of Manchester/Salford and Lancaster/Morecambe (for brevity the two conurbations are often referred to in the text as Manchester and Lancaster). These data are now used to provide an overview of mobility change in two specific localities and to create a framework for the following chapters that focus on specific aspects of mobility. Attention is focused especially on the mobility of children aged 10/11 and adolescents aged 17/18, as these are the two age groups for which we have the longest time span of data. It should be emphasised that data drawn from our survey will give a rather different perspective on everyday mobility than that of the National Travel Survey. There are four main points of contrast. First, we used in-depth interviews to probe all everyday mobility including short walks and children's play, thus covering important categories of travel not included in the NTS. Second, our sample is drawn from two urban areas and limited evidence in the NTS shows that in towns there are both higher rates of walking and shorter mean journey distances than in rural areas or in the country as a whole. For instance, the 1985/6 NTS demonstrated that people in rural areas walked half the distance of those in urban areas (DoT, 1988). Third, our sample focuses on two specific age groups whereas NTS data only provide information for children in broad age categories. It is likely that childhood mobility may vary substantially within these age groups. Fourth, it is possible that the different methodologies used to collect data may produce rather different results.

Compared to NTS data for the entire population there has been much less change in the amount of mobility undertaken by children and adolescents in Manchester and Lancaster over the past 60 years (Table 4.4). For children aged

Table 4.4 Distance and Time Travelled for Everyday Mobility (Averages for all Trips Over 12 Month Period)

Cohort born:	Mean distance per person per year (km)		Mean trip distance (km)		Mean trip time (min)	
	Manchester	Lancaster	Manchester	Lancaster	Manchester	Lancaster
Age 10/11						
1990-91	4,494	6,054	1.5	1.8	8.6	10.7
1983-84	3,606	6,109	1.5	2.4	9.8	14.6
1962-71	4,545	5,217	1.7	2.1	10.8	12.6
1932-41	3,526	3,477	1.3	1.2	12.8	13.2
All	3,986	5,176	1.5	1.8	10.8	12.6
Sample size	222,530	212,948	222,530	212,948	247,546	212,366
Age 17/18						
1983-84	5,563	6,658	2.8	2.6	16.0	13.8
1962-71	7,316	13,837	3.8	6.0*	20.7	21.6
1932-41	8,602	6,054	4.2	2.6	25.1	21.1
All	7,279	8,255	3.7	3.4	21.1	18.5
Sample size	121,232	133,202	121,232	133,202	145,770	139,342
Age 30s						
1962-71	11,532	12,224	6.4	5.6	22.3	18.8
1932-41	7,375	6,215	4.5	3.5	27.3	16.1
All	8,997	8,619	5.3	4.5	25.1	17.3
Sample size	70,138	67,744	70,138	67,744	90,850	71,198
Age 60s						
1932-41	10,025	7,318	6.1	5.8	22.7	21.7
Sample size	40,812	26,428	40,812	28,428	46,750	28,202

Data relate to all journeys recorded aggregated over a 12-month period. Totals for distance and time vary because it was not possible to calculate distances for all recorded journeys. *Distances for this group are affected by a small number of respondents undertaking some very long journeys.

Source: Everyday mobility sample, Manchester/Salford and Lancaster/Morecambe, 2001-2003.

10/11 in Manchester the total mean distance travelled per annum has fluctuated between 3,500 and 4,500 kilometres per year since the 1940s, and for adolescents aged 17/18 the annual distance travelled has fallen substantially from some 8,602km per year in the 1950s to 5,563km per year at the time of the survey. In the smaller towns of Lancaster and Morecambe there has been a more sustained increase in distance travelled by children aged 10/11 from 3,477 per year to 6,054km per year, but little change in the distance travelled by adolescents. The data for 17/18 year olds in Lancaster and Morecambe born 1962-1971 is slightly aberrant due to some respondents having unusually long journeys to school. However, this does emphasise the individual variability that occurs within everyday travel behaviour. Likewise the mean trip distance has changed relatively little since the 1940s, but the mean trip time has decreased in both settlements as more people have gained access to faster modes of transport. These data suggest that young children and adolescents in urban areas have not necessarily shared in or contributed to the national increase in total everyday travel recorded in the National Travel Surveys. It also suggests that for those aged 17/18 today, there may be constraints that restrict mobility compared to the 1950s. This theme is explored in more detail in later chapters.

Travel characteristics can be examined from a number of different perspectives, each of which gives a slightly different take on travel behaviour. In particular we can look at variations in the proportion of trips undertaken by (for instance) different modes; changes in the distances travelled by each mode; and differences in the time spent travelling by each mode. In this analysis we use these three approaches to examine variations in the travel behaviour of children and adolescents.

With regard to travel mode the case study data reflect the broad trends of the NTS data, with predictable declines in bus use and walking and an increase in car use, but there are also more subtle variations that need to be highlighted (Tables 4.5, 4.6, 4.7). In particular, the data suggest that walking continues to be rather more significant for children and adolescents in urban areas than is sometimes assumed. In both study areas walking accounted for around 89 per cent of all trips by children aged 10/11 in the 1940s, it accounted for 60 per cent of distance travelled in Lancaster and Morecambe and 45 per cent in the Manchester conurbation (where buses were much more widely used), and it occupied some 70 per cent of all travel time by children aged 10/11 in both urban areas. At the time of the survey in 2001-3 children aged 10/11 still undertook some 61-65 per cent of their everyday trips on foot, though walking accounted for only 15-18 per cent of distance travelled but occupied around 49 per cent of total travel time. Thus although the extent of walking has reduced from the 1940s to the present, it still accounts for the majority (over 60 per cent) of all trips by children aged 10/11, and for approximately half of travel time. Most everyday mobility around an urban area is over short distances, and the mean distance travelled on foot was predictably short at each time period. However, there has been a decline in the average walking trip distance for children aged 10/11 of one third to one half, from around 0.8km to 0.5km in Lancaster, and from 0.6km to 0.3km in Manchester.

Table 4.5 Mode of Transport used for all Journeys (Per cent of all Trips)

Cohort born:	Car		Walk		Bus		Cycle		Other*	
	M	L	M	L	M	L	M	L	M	L
Age 10/11										
1990-91	28.5	26.4	64.7	61.4	1.5	1.6	3.7	7.1	1.6	3.5
1983-84	26.5	27.3	64.7	61.3	1.5	2.7	5.2	4.2	2.2	4.5
1962-71	8.3	13.3	84.7	76.8	3.7	3.9	3.2	5.0	0.2	1.0
1932-41	0.3	0.3	88.0	89.1	9.6	8.2	1.4	1.7	0.7	0.6
All	14.0	17.4	77.1	71.5	4.8	4.1	3.0	4.6	1.0	2.6
N (000s)	34.8	36.9	190.8	151.7	12.0	8.6	7.6	9.7	2.5	5.4
Age 17/18										
1983-84	15.7	18.9	48.2	67.8	33.6	8.4	0.0	2.1	2.5	2.8
1962-71	7.4	43.7	48.8	39.8	30.6	7.2	3.9	4.5	9.3	4.8
1932-41	4.7	0.5	48.7	56.7	35.3	28.4	10.8	13.2	0.6	1.2
All	8.4	18.4	48.6	56.7	33.6	15.5	6.0	6.8	3.5	2.7
N (000s)	12.2	25.5	70.8	78.9	48.9	21.5	8.8	9.5	5.1	3.7
Age 30s										
1962-71	44.3	67.4	28.0	25.7	12.9	3.9	7.8	2.2	7.0	0.8
1932-41	31.8	46.5	33.8	40.5	20.1	9.1	1.2	0.0	13.1	3.9
All	37.4	56.0	31.2	33.8	16.9	6.7	4.1	1.0	10.4	2.5
N (000s)	33.9	39.9	28.3	24.1	15.4	4.8	3.7	0.7	9.5	1.8
Age 60s										
1932-41	58.3	74.6	29.4	21.1	10.0	1.5	1.8	1.1	0.5	1.8
N (000s)	27.2	21.0	13.7	6.0	4.7	0.4	0.9	0.3	0.2	0.5

Data relate to all journeys recorded aggregated over a 12-month period. *Includes travel by train, taxi and motor cycle. N = sample size.

Source: Everyday mobility sample, Manchester/Salford (M) and Lancaster/Morecambe (L), 2001-2003.

Table 4.6 Mode of Transport used for all Journeys (Per cent of Total Distance)

Cohort born:	Car		Walk		Bus		Cycle		Other*	
	M	L	M	L	M	L	M	L	M	L
Age 10/11										
1990-91	75.3	64.8	14.8	18.3	5.4	9.1	3.5	3.9	0.9	3.8
1983-84	56.9	67.1	20.7	16.5	9.6	8.3	1.4	4.0	11.4	4.1
1962-71	58.9	51.4	26.1	24.2	10.0	6.8	3.6	12.7	1.3	5.0
1932-41	10.7	5.2	45.1	60.3	37.3	28.7	0.6	2.4	6.2	3.3
Age 17/18										
1983-84	24.3	39.0	14.6	28.8	57.3	16.1	0.0	4.3	2.8	11.8
1962-71	17.9	77.0	10.9	4.9	40.7	10.4	2.6	3.7	27.9	4.0
1932-41	10.0	3.5	9.6	23.6	51.9	44.9	22.4	16.3	6.1	10.6
Age 30s										
1962-71	70.8	89.2	2.5	3.5	14.7	2.3	6.1	1.3	5.9	3.7
1932-41	49.8	77.7	5.6	11.5	22.1	7.8	1.8	0.0	20.5	3.0
Age 60s										
1932-41	83.3	87.3	2.4	3.9	12.6	5.5	0.7	0.0	1.0	0.6

Data relate to all journeys recorded aggregated over a 12-month period. See Table 4.5 for sample size. *Includes travel by train, taxi and motor cycle.

Source: Everyday mobility sample, Manchester/Salford (M) and Lancaster/Morecambe (L), 2001-2003.

Table 4.7 Mode of Transport used for all Journeys (Per cent of Total Travel Time)

Cohort born:	Car		Walk		Bus		Cycle		Other*	
	M	L	M	L	M	L	M	L	M	L
Age 10/11										
1990-91	39.1	35.9	49.1	48.7	5.9	5.7	4.9	7.2	1.0	2.5
1983-84	40.6	31.6	46.4	44.1	6.4	7.1	4.5	10.0	2.2	7.1
1962-71	18.1	24.3	68.0	52.2	8.8	6.8	4.5	14.9	0.6	1.8
1932-41	1.3	1.2	70.3	71.4	23.0	16.8	3.9	9.2	1.5	1.4
Age 17/18										
1983-84	14.7	24.7	32.0	52.1	50.7	15.1	0.0	3.1	2.6	5.0
1962-71	5.8	48.9	30.4	19.1	40.6	8.9	7.8	20.0	15.4	3.1
1932-41	5.3	0.8	21.9	33.1	46.6	33.9	24.1	28.1	2.2	4.0
Age 30s										
1962-71	40.0	74.0	27.2	17.3	14.1	4.3	9.4	1.8	9.8	2.6
1932-41	36.8	55.5	18.6	30.0	23.8	9.3	4.3	0.0	16.5	5.3
Age 60s										
1932-41	63.6	65.4	13.5	15.6	15.3	2.7	6.2	11.8	1.3	4.6

Data relate to all journeys recorded aggregated over a 12-month period. See Table 4.5 for sample size. *Includes travel by train, taxi and motor cycle.

Source: Everyday mobility sample, Manchester/Salford (M) and Lancaster/Morecambe (L), 2001-2003.

For adolescents aged 17/18 walking has tended to be less important than for younger children as teenagers have made much greater use of public transport, especially buses in Manchester, but there has also been much less decline in travel on foot by adolescents than by younger children. In Manchester and Salford walking has consistently accounted for about 48 per cent of all trips by adolescents aged 17/18 since the 1950s, approximately 10 per cent of all distance travelled and 20-30 per cent of the time spent travelling. In Lancaster and Morecambe walking was even more important, due probably to shorter distances in a small town and a less well-developed public transport system, and the proportion of trips undertaken on foot has actually risen since the 1950s from 56 per cent to almost 68 per cent today (but with a drop for those born 1962-1971, due mainly to the inclusion in this cohort of small number of respondents with unusual travel patterns). Distance and time data for Lancaster and Morecambe reflect these trends with little change from the 1950s to the present, but with a dip in walking for the middle cohort. Mean distances travelled on foot have also hardly changed, remaining at around one kilometre in Lancaster/Morecambe and 0.9km in Manchester/Salford. Bus travel in the Manchester conurbation has consistently accounted for around one third of all trips, but in Lancaster this has always been both lower and more variable. In Manchester buses also consistently account for 40-50 per cent of both travel time and distance and the mean trip distance by bus was around five kilometres at each time period. Thus everyday mobility for adolescents aged 17/18 shows considerable stability over the past 50 years, with both walking and bus use continuing to be important.

There have also been changes in the companions that children travel with (Table 4.8). In general, the proportion of journeys undertaken without an adult present have decreased, with children apparently given less freedom to move around the city independently. This theme is explored in more detail in Chapter 7. However, the data also show that even today over half of all trips by children aged 10/11 are undertaken without an adult present, rising to over 80 per cent of journeys by adolescents aged 17/18. Again, it can be suggested that the degree of change that has occurred over the past 60 years is rather less than is popularly assumed. Not surprisingly, there are large variations in the mode of transport used when children and adolescents travel with different companions (Table 4.9). Travel on foot is overwhelming undertaken alone or with others of approximately the same age, whilst travel by car (obviously for those aged 10/11) for both groups and by bus for those aged 10/11 is mainly with adults. However, these differentials have changed relatively little over time. Thus, examining the data in Table 4.9 from a different perspective, for children aged 10/11 in Lancaster in the 1940s just 22.8 per cent of walking trips were with an adult whereas the figure for those aged 10/11 at the time of interview was 23.7 per cent. The figure for adolescents aged 17/18 in Manchester in the 1950s was 11.0 per cent and today just 9.2 per cent. There has been a little more change in travel by bus for those aged 10/11 with the proportion of accompanied trips increasing from 45.0 per cent in Lancaster in the

Table 4.8 Companions on all Journeys (Per cent of all Trips)

Cohort born	Alone		Other Children		Adults /Mixed	
	M	L	M	L	M	L
Age 10/11						
1990-91	19.6	18.3	35.4	37.8	45.0	44.0
1983-84	14.4	11.6	34.0	39.0	51.6	49.4
1962-71	19.0	12.5	41.2	39.0	39.7	48.6
1932-41	23.7	25.3	40.8	48.3	35.5	26.4
All	19.9	17.5	38.2	41.1	41.9	41.4
Sample size	49,312	37,164	94,596	87,302	103,638	87,920
Age 17/18						
1983-84	34.0	31.3	47.3	49.3	18.7	19.4
1962-71	39.4	38.5	37.6	32.2	23.0	29.3
1932-41	46.2	47.7	39.0	39.0	14.8	13.3
All	41.1	39.2	40.9	41.2	18.1	19.7
Sample size	59,856	54,566	59,576	57,392	26,338	27,384
Age 30s						
1962-71	37.3	44.2	20.5	17.6	42.2	38.2
1932-41	37.4	35.7	13.3	23.0	49.3	41.3
All	37.4	39.6	16.5	20.6	46.1	39.9
Sample size	33,956	28,166	15,000	14,639	41,894	28,396
Age 60s						
1932-41	50.2	36.2	1.5	4.7	48.3	59.0
Sample size	23,490	10,212	690	1,338	22,570	16,652

Data relate to all journeys recorded aggregated over a 12-month period.
Source: Everyday mobility sample, Manchester/Salford (M) and Lancaster/Morecambe (L), 2001-2003.

Table 4.9 Companions by Mode of Travel on all Journeys (Per cent)

Cohort born	Alone				With other children**				With adults/mixed			
	Car	Walk	Bus	Cycle	Car	Walk	Bus	Cycle	Car	Walk	Bus	Cycle
Manchester and Salford												
Age 10/11												
1990-91	0.0	96.8	0.0	0.0	2.6	87.4	2.7	6.9	61.3	32.9	4.0	1.4
1983-84	0.0	99.7	0.3	0.0	4.0	83.1	0.7	12.1	48.7	42.8	5.8	2.0
1962-71	0.0	95.0	0.7	4.3	0.4	92.8	1.1	5.6	20.4	71.4	7.9	0.1
1932-41	0.0	92.2	7.0	0.4	0.1	90.7	7.5	1.7	0.9	82.8	13.9	1.7
Age 17/18												
1983-84	0.7	60.8	33.9	0.0	9.3	48.7	41.2	0.0	59.2	23.8	15.4	0.0
1962-71	2.8	45.3	39.1	4.8	6.6	49.3	32.5	0.8	16.7	53.6	12.8	7.5
1932-41	0.0	40.4	42.2	17.4	0.5	63.2	29.8	5.5	30.3	36.3	28.4	4.0
Age 30s												
1962-71	34.4	17.4	22.4	17.5	68.8	23.3	8.1	0.0	41.3	39.6	7.4	1.0
1932-41	15.1	36.1	25.3	2.7	24.7	56.9	16.9	0.0	46.3	25.7	18.3	0.4
Age 60s												
1932-41	34.7	47.1	14.5	3.6	91.3	8.7	0.0	0.0	81.8	11.7	5.8	0.0

Companions and mode of travel*

Table 4.9 (Continued)

Cohort born	Alone				With other children**				With adults/mixed			
	Car	Walk	Bus	Cycle	Car	Walk	Bus	Cycle	Car	Walk	Bus	Cycle
Lancaster and Morecambe												
Age 10/11												
1990-91	0.0	83.2	0.0	16.7	7.8	84.9	2.1	5.2	52.2	33.0	6.2	4.9
1983-84	0.0	86.8	0.0	0.0	7.9	80.8	2.0	4.1	49.0	40.0	8.8	2.1
1962-71	0.0	88.7	2.3	9.0	0.9	93.2	0.0	5.2	22.6	60.7	8.7	3.7
1932-41	0.0	89.3	10.0	0.7	0.0	93.0	3.1	2.8	1.3	81.2	16.3	0.8
Age 17/18												
1983-84	2.4	83.6	4.5	3.6	12.6	74.8	10.9	0.5	61.7	24.6	8.9	3.9
1962-71	32.4	44.4	7.1	11.3	25.7	57.1	7.6	0.6	77.1	15.6	7.3	0.0
1932-41	0.0	44.6	31.7	23.7	0.5	69.9	24.2	2.6	2.1	62.1	28.6	7.1
Age 30s												
1962-71	61.6	27.1	6.3	4.8	81.4	12.2	6.1	0.1	67.7	30.2	0.1	0.0
1932-41	33.2	43.3	14.9	0.0	28.5	60.3	11.2	0.0	68.0	27.1	3.0	0.0
Age 60s												
1932-41	68.6	26.5	1.1	2.9	90.4	7.5	0.0	0.0	76.9	18.9	2.2	0.0

*In each category data show the percentage of those travelling with particular companions who use each transport mode. 'Other' category is excluded. **Includes siblings/friends under 18 who can drive. Data relate to all journeys recorded aggregated over a 12 month period.

Source: Everyday mobility sample, Manchester/Salford and Lancaster/Morecambe, 2001-2003.

Table 4.10 All Everyday Mobility by Journey Purpose (Per cent)

Cohort born	Work	Educ	Shop	Pers	Eat	Social	Ent	Sport	Hols	Other
	Journey purpose*									
Manchester and Salford										
Age 10/11										
1990-91	0.0	13.0	15.2	8.9	4.9	45.5	4.7	5.8	0.5	1.5
1983-84	0.0	16.7	15.8	11.6	2.6	39.3	3.9	7.4	0.1	2.6
1962-71	0.0	15.0	7.5	8.3	1.2	57.9	3.1	5.3	1.3	0.3
1932-41	0.0	13.7	8.9	11.4	2.5	49.0	6.2	7.1	1.0	0.3
Age 17/18										
1983-84	9.7	18.4	17.7	12.0	6.3	14.6	8.7	10.4	0.8	1.3
1963-71	14.6	6.4	9.6	20.0	17.6	18.5	7.6	3.3	0.7	1.7
1932-41	20.8	3.7	8.4	12.4	8.9	17.3	13.6	10.2	3.3	2.4
Age 30s										
1963-71	16.1	0.0	9.7	10.5	8.6	28.2	4.0	10.8	1.6	10.5
1932-41	18.3	0.0	16.7	10.4	11.8	19.5	10.5	5.3	1.4	6.2
Age 60s										
1932-41	3.5	0.0	26.7	14.0	11.6	20.2	8.0	8.9	1.3	5.8
Lancaster and Morecambe										
Age 10/11										
1990-91	0.0	12.2	18.1	7.4	3.3	42.3	5.9	8.6	0.4	1.8
1983-84	0.0	15.8	14.0	8.7	2.5	36.9	6.0	14.5	0.5	1.1
1962-71	0.0	16.0	11.8	9.0	2.7	44.8	5.7	6.5	2.7	0.8
1932-41	0.0	15.7	7.9	13.1	2.6	39.8	11.1	7.0	1.3	1.5
Age 17/18										
1983-84	9.3	16.2	13.9	14.9	10.1	16.3	6.8	8.8	0.1	3.8
1963-71	17.8	9.3	5.2	18.0	12.9	14.2	9.9	7.2	3.8	1.8
1932-41	23.9	2.3	5.7	15.4	8.6	10.7	17.7	12.5	2.7	0.5
Age 30s										
1962-71	16.6	0.0	27.5	8.8	7.9	18.5	6.6	2.9	1.9	9.3
1932-41	20.4	0.5	18.3	8.1	8.2	19.9	5.8	2.5	5.3	11.0
Age 60s										
1932-41	6.8	0.0	18.9	14.0	13.8	11.8	10.7	9.6	5.6	8.7

* Fuller definitions of journey purpose are as follows: 'Work' and 'Educ' include both full and part-time work and education; 'Shop' refers to shopping including children accompanying a parent who is shopping; 'Pers' refers to all personal business; 'Eat' refers to all trips principally for eating or drinking; 'Social' refers to all social activities not otherwise classified; 'Ent' refers to all trips principally for paid entertainment; 'Sport' includes both watching and participating in sporting activities; 'Hols' includes both day trips and holidays away from home; 'Other' refers to all other travel including escorting. Data relate to all journeys recorded aggregated over a 12-month period.

Source: Everyday mobility sample, Manchester/Salford and Lancaster/Morecambe, 2001-2003.

1940s (51.2 per cent in Manchester) to 77.8 per cent today (65.5 per cent in Manchester). Thus whilst children are still allowed to walk short distances without an adult, longer journeys by bus are more likely to be accompanied than in the past.

Changes in the frequency of trips for different purposes are also quite predictable, and support National Travel Survey data outlined above (Table 4.10). For children aged 10/11 at all time periods some 40-50 per cent of all trips were undertaken for social activities, followed in importance by travel to school. Trips to participate in sporting activities are also important, but the only category that has increased markedly in the late-twentieth century is travel for shopping. For those aged 17/18 trips were more evenly divided between a number of different purposes including personal business, shopping, social activities eating out and, today, education. In the past, for this age group, travel for education was, of course, largely replaced by travel for work. A similar overall pattern is reflected if the data are analysed in terms of distance covered rather than trip frequency. There are, however, variations in the mean distances and times travelled for different journey purposes (Tables 4.11, 4.12). Whilst most distances and times travelled for everyday mobility around town are short, rather longer distances and journey times were recorded for travel to work, to watch or participate in sport (especially for adolescents), for escorting duties and, obviously, for holidays and day trips. Thus for children aged 10/11 in Lancaster the mean distance travelled to school in the 1940s was 1km and is just 0.8km today, whereas travel to watch sport increased from a mean of 6.5km in the 1940s to 12.3km today. Other categories (including shopping, personal business and eating out) have also increased in proportional terms, but remain relatively short. Thus mean trip distances for personal business for children aged 10/11 in Lancaster have increased from 1.2km in the 1940s to 2.5km at the time of interview. Thus whilst travel distances have doubled most trips still occur over a short distance and within walking distance for most people. There are also predicable variations in the mode of transport used for different trips. These are summarised in Table 4.13. Within the broad trend of increasing car use and decreasing travel by public transport and on foot outlined above, walking continues to be particularly important for trips for social activities, for shopping and for education, whereas travel to work has become much more car-dependent. Also, not surprisingly, children are much more likely than adults to walk for their social and shopping activities. Travel for many of these activities is explored in more detail in later chapters.

Everyday mobility over the past 60 years appears to have varied relatively little by gender and most of the variations that do occur are predictable and quite consistent over time (Tables 4.14 and 4.15). With the exception of Lancaster 17/18 year olds born in the 1960s (where the sample is distorted by a small number of males with very long journeys to school), there is almost no difference in the mean distances or times travelled by males and females aged 10/11 and 17/18 at any time period. There are larger differences between adult males and females (especially those in their 30s) relating mainly to the impact of life-cycle stage and childcare responsibilities. These are dealt with in Chapter 8. Overall, females are a little less

Table 4.11 Mean Distance Travelled (km) by Journey Purpose

Cohort born	Work	Educ	Shop	Pers	Eat	Social	Ent	Sp P	Sp W	Hol	Day	Esc
Manchester and Salford												
Age 10/11												
1990-91	0.0	1.4	0.9	1.6	3.0	1.1	1.0	1.1	5.4	99.4	20.3	1.6
1983-84	0.0	0.9	1.0	1.1	2.0	1.7	2.2	1.7	5.3	162.4	30.0	0.0
1962-71	0.0	0.6	1.4	0.9	2.2	1.2	1.5	2.9	2.2	136.1	36.2	66.6
1932-41	0.0	1.3	1.3	1.2	0.8	0.8	1.0	2.2	1.9	91.2	17.5	30.1
Age 17/18												
1983-84	2.7	4.0	2.4	1.4	1.7	3.6	4.3	2.2	0.0	297.9	49.2	0.3
1963-71	4.8	4.7	3.6	2.1	3.8	2.0	3.8	4.8	5.6	111.0	44.8	11.8
1932-41	4.1	6.5	3.2	3.1	1.2	2.4	2.1	8.9	5.7	101.4	26.4	48.2
Age 30												
1963-71	12.1	0.0	4.5	2.1	5.3	4.5	2.9	9.4	2.6	115.8	26.7	3.4
1932-41	4.5	0.0	3.3	1.7	2.0	4.7	3.2	4.1	4.1	134.9	58.5	2.1
Age 60s												
1932-41	7.8	0.0	3.1	2.2	9.8	8.0	4.6	3.1	4.2	110.0	63.9	8.0
Lancaster and Morecambe												
Age 10/11												
1990-91	0.0	0.8	1.9	2.5	2.3	1.4	2.2	2.0	12.3	242.9	7.2	2.4
1983-84	0.0	1.5	1.3	2.1	1.6	1.8	1.4	5.5	22.1	150.3	11.1	0.0
1962-71	0.0	0.8	1.2	1.5	1.2	1.4	2.0	5.5	5.6	150.2	13.9	0.0
1932-41	0.0	1.0	0.5	1.2	0.5	1.2	1.2	1.0	6.5	55.8	9.7	0.0
Age 17/18												
1983-84	2.0	2.1	2.2	0.9	1.5	4.6	2.9	4.8	0.0	147.5	60.6	0.0
1963-71	6.2	6.0	1.6	4.8	1.9	4.5	2.3	13.7	4.9	88.3	28.7	22.0
1932-41	2.4	1.6	2.0	1.5	1.8	2.8	1.7	2.1	3.7	109.9	19.3	0.0
Age 30s												
1962-71	9.3	0.0	4.9	6.3	1.8	3.0	2.0	5.5	11.1	185.0	33.7	2.7
1932-41	3.8	12.4	1.3	4.4	1.4	3.1	5.5	8.1	1.8	215.6	10.4	2.0
Age 60s												
1932-41	3.4	0.0	3.0	1.8	6.9	9.7	4.8	8.7	0.0	253.0	15.8	3.5

* Fuller definitions of journey purpose are as follows: 'Work' and 'Educ' include both full and part-time work and education; 'Shop' refers to shopping including children accompanying a parent who is shopping; 'Pers' refers to all personal business; 'Eat' refers to all trips principally for eating or drinking; 'Social' refers to all social activities not otherwise classified; 'Ent' refers to all trips principally for paid entertainment; 'Sp P' refers to participating in sporting activities; 'Sp W' refers to watching sporting activities; 'Hol' refers to holidays away from home; 'Day' refers to day trips from home; 'Esc' refers to escorting. Data relate to all journeys recorded aggregated over a 12-month period.
Source: Everyday mobility sample, Manchester/Salford and Lancaster/Morecambe, 2001-2003.

Table 4.12 Mean Time Travelled (min) by Journey Purpose

Cohort born	Work	Educ	Shop	Pers	Eat	Social	Ent	Sp P	Sp W	Hol	Day	Esc
Manchester and Salford												
Age 10/11												
1990-91	0.0	10.6	9.4	8.3	9.4	6.4	10.8	10.5	16.5	166.2	24.7	10.0
1983-84	0.0	10.2	9.7	7.8	10.8	7.9	11.0	12.1	19.4	286.2	80.0	0.0
1962-71	0.0	13.9	14.1	11.5	8.7	7.4	12.2	17.5	17.0	200.5	54.5	70.0
1932-41	0.0	16.3	13.0	13.8	9.4	9.1	14.5	22.8	16.3	171.4	51.8	112.5
Age 17/18												
1983-84	12.6	27.1	14.9	8.8	7.8	13.2	19.3	17.4	0.0	228.8	47.5	5.5
1963-71	25.0	34.3	19.6	12.0	17.3	17.3	22.9	45.3	34.9	173.3	63.5	31.2
1932-41	32.9	31.1	17.4	18.4	13.3	15.2	19.1	53.2	31.9	258.3	117.2	29.0
Age 30s												
1963-71	32.5	0.0	20.6	15.2	22.2	22.4	20.7	21.6	13.0	147.3	45.3	14.5
1932-41	38.2	0.0	19.2	10.9	24.5	19.2	17.8	75.3	61.8	159.9	99.6	21.2
Age 60s												
1932-41	54.0	0.0	17.0	15.0	20.7	18.3	18.3	34.4	20.3	205.1	91.6	21.3
Lancaster and Morecambe												
Age 10/11												
1990-91	0.0	8.7	12.2	13.3	12.5	8.7	12.6	13.8	31.7	349.1	14.0	6.4
1983-84	0.0	15.1	11.4	13.2	12.7	9.4	12.2	30.6	25.4	238.0	20.1	0.0
1962-71	0.0	10.4	10.6	11.7	12.3	8.1	11.0	35.0	16.6	168.0	52.8	0.0
1932-41	0.0	15.3	9.2	12.4	6.0	10.0	15.8	26.4	33.8	132.0	38.2	0.0
Age 17/18												
1983-84	16.1	15.5	12.3	8.9	12.4	12.7	16.3	18.0	0.0	214.5	84.2	20.8
1963-71	22.3	19.8	11.1	16.7	10.4	12.9	10.1	75.0	14.6	225.0	43.9	64.2
1932-41	19.9	20.5	19.9	10.4	14.1	19.4	16.3	34.3	13.7	360.0	108.7	0.0
Age 30s												
1962-71	26.3	0.0	16.4	12.6	10.7	14.3	11.7	22.5	32.3	256.8	86.3	17.0
1932-41	15.8	67.5	11.1	13.6	10.0	13.0	16.2	48.1	12.5	277.5	43.1	13.2
Age 60s												
1932-41	17.8	0.0	13.4	13.0	18.4	20.6	16.6	49.2	45.0	621.2	32.2	12.3

* Fuller definitions of journey purpose are as follows: 'Work' and 'Educ' include both full and part-time work and education; 'Shop' refers to shopping including children accompanying a parent who is shopping; 'Pers' refers to all personal business; 'Eat' refers to all trips principally for eating or drinking; 'Social' refers to all social activities not otherwise classified; 'Ent' refers to all trips principally for paid entertainment; 'Sp P' refers to participating in sporting activities; 'Sp W' refers to watching sporting activities; 'Hol' refers to holidays away from home; 'Day' refers to day trips from home; 'Esc' refers to escorting. Data relate to all journeys recorded aggregated over a 12-month period.

Source: Everyday mobility sample, Manchester/Salford and Lancaster/Morecambe, 2001-2003.

Table 4.13 Main Mode of Travel by Selected Journey Purpose (Per cent)

Cohort born	Manchester			Lancaster			Manchester			Lancaster		
	Car	Walk	Bus	Car	Walk	Bus	Car	Walk	Bus	Car	Walk	Bus
	Shopping						Social/Entertainment					
Age 10/11												
1990-91	32.6	54.0	5.7	30.7	61.2	0.8	22.7	70.6	2.7	21.1	64.2	4.8
1983-84	19.9	68.9	1.3	39.3	57.8	1.4	25.9	63.8	4.5	25.1	61.4	5.9
1962-71	21.5	56.2	7.1	25.2	72.1	2.6	6.3	88.4	2.8	11.6	77.1	4.4
1932-41	0.0	81.2	18.7	0.0	95.8	4.2	0.2	91.3	6.9	0.4	91.4	5.1
Age 17/18												
1983-84	8.9	41.9	46.3	29.5	66.7	3.4	15.0	57.2	26.1	17.4	73.9	3.1
1962-71	6.4	50.3	41.1	30.2	61.0	8.6	8.8	56.1	23.3	41.5	46.3	3.0
1932-41	1.3	46.7	48.3	0.0	67.9	27.4	5.9	63.0	23.4	0.7	66.6	24.1
Age 30s												
1962-71	25.6	56.7	15.2	66.2	23.6	9.2	42.8	29.1	11.7	59.1	38.0	0.7
1932-41	42.7	30.1	20.9	24.8	56.4	18.7	27.2	40.1	18.5	47.9	44.2	5.8
Age 60s												
1932-41	67.3	23.1	9.4	68.6	29.4	2.0	51.3	36.8	8.7	70.0	23.9	2.2
	Education						Work					
Age 10/11												
1990-91	47.5	52.5	0.0	47.7	47.4	0.0	-	-	-	-	-	-
1983-84	35.0	65.0	0.0	24.7	65.4	4.9	-	-	-	-	-	-
1962-71	6.3	87.5	6.3	7.1	85.7	7.1	-	-	-	-	-	-
1932-41	0.0	76.0	20.0	0.0	81.8	18.2	-	-	-	-	-	-
Age 17/18												
1983-84	22.2	27.8	50.0	16.7	47.6	33.3	21.2	44.4	26.5	17.8	62.7	9.5
1962-71	0.0	0.0	85.0	35.3	14.7	50.0	1.9	31.1	45.2	49.9	33.3	0.0
1932-41	0.0	21.1	78.9	0.0	36.4	27.3	0.0	4.2	67.5	0.0	31.8	40.3
Age 30s												
1962-71	-	-	-	-	-	-	47.9	10.4	23.6	82.5	2.0	7.7
1932-41	-	-	-	-	-	-	24.3	17.3	36.0	47.1	25.4	13.7
Age 60s												
1932-41	-	-	-	-	-	-	65.0	0.0	35.0	100.0	0.0	0.0

Table should be read as follows: For children in Manchester/Salford aged 10/11, born 1990-91, 32.6 per cent of shopping trips are by car and 54.0 per cent are on foot. Manchester refers to Manchester and Salford; Lancaster refers to Lancaster and Morecambe. Totals do not sum to 100 per cent due to omission of some transport modes. Data relate to all journeys recorded aggregated over a 12-month period.
Source: Everyday mobility sample, Manchester/Salford and Lancaster/Morecambe, 2001-2003.

likely than males to travel alone: girls possibly because they are given less independence (see Chapter 7) and women because of childcare responsibilities. In Lancaster, in particular, females are also more likely than males to walk or use public transport, but none of these variations is large and there are

Table 4.14 Distance, Time and Mode of Travel by Gender

Cohort born	Mean dist (km) M	F	Mean time (min) M	F	% of all trips undertaken by: Car M	F	Walk M	F	Cycle M	F	Bus M	F
Manchester and Salford													
Age 10/11													
1990-91	1.5	1.4	8.4	8.7	26.3	31.0	67.5	61.6	4.2	3.1	0.8	2.2
1983-84	1.4	1.7	9.4	10.3	22.4	32.0	70.9	56.5	3.4	7.5	2.1	0.7
1962-71	1.9	1.5	10.8	10.9	6.2	11.0	83.7	86.0	5.7	0.0	4.2	2.9
1932-41	1.1	1.4	13.8	11.9	0.0	0.6	86.9	89.3	2.9	0.1	10.0	9.4
Age 17/18													
1983-84	2.9	2.7	16.9	14.5	10.5	25.0	49.7	45.4	0.0	0.0	36.6	23.8
1963-71	4.8	2.9	22.6	18.7	4.4	10.4	47.7	49.8	7.9	0.0	23.8	37.1
1932-41	4.2	4.2	23.6	26.9	2.6	6.9	56.4	39.6	16.1	4.9	24.0	47.9
Age 30s													
1963-71	8.5	4.9	24.4	20.5	34.4	52.5	16.4	37.5	15.6	1.3	19.1	7.8
1932-41	4.8	4.2	33.6	20.6	14.2	50.7	36.0	31.3	1.9	0.4	23.2	16.8
Age 60s													
1932-41	4.8	7.4	22.7	25.3	38.1	79.0	41.9	16.5	3.6	0.0	15.9	4.0
Lancaster and Morecambe													
Age 10/11													
1990-91	1.8	1.8	9.8	11.7	25.0	27.9	57.8	65.3	10.2	3.7	2.4	0.8
1983-84	2.3	2.5	11.1	17.5	33.3	22.2	53.3	68.2	5.7	2.9	2.9	2.6
1962-71	2.3	1.8	13.7	11.4	15.2	11.0	72.3	82.2	9.2	0.0	2.6	5.6
1932-41	1.2	1.3	13.8	12.7	0.4	0.2	89.1	89.1	3.5	0.3	6.9	9.3
Age 17/18													
1983-84	2.6	2.5	13.6	14.0	18.4	19.3	65.4	70.0	4.5	0.0	8.3	8.5
1963-71	9.5	3.1	32.0	12.6	47.1	40.8	32.3	46.2	9.4	0.3	5.8	8.3
1932-41	2.6	2.6	19.3	22.8	0.8	0.2	54.1	59.2	18.4	8.4	25.0	31.6
Age 30s													
1962-71	9.4	2.7	23.4	14.9	66.3	68.4	25.9	25.5	4.7	0.0	2.4	5.1
1932-41	5.2	2.6	16.3	16.1	65.3	34.7	22.8	51.6	0.0	0.0	3.9	12.3
Age 60s													
1932-41	5.0	6.5	22.4	21.1	73.5	75.5	23.7	18.8	2.2	0.0	0.0	2.8

Data relate to all journeys recorded aggregated over a 12-month period.
Source: Everyday mobility sample, Manchester/Salford and Lancaster/Morecambe, 2001-2003.

only small differences between Lancaster/Morecambe and Manchester/Salford. We do not present any analysis by socio-economic group, as even with rudimentary categories the number of respondents in each group is too small for reliable analysis. However, it should be stressed that the data were collected to ensure a range of social and occupational groups amongst both adult respondents and the parents of children and the individual variations that occur do not appear to be related to socio-economic position.

Table 4.15 Companions and Travel Purpose by Gender

Cohort born	Companions						Selected journey purpose*							
	Alone		Children		Adults		Work/Ed		Shopping		Social		Sport	
	M	F	M	F	M	F	M	F	M	F	M	F	M	F
Manchester and Salford														
Age 10/11														
1990-91	22.5	16.3	37.9	32.9	39.6	51.1	11.0	15.2	7.9	23.5	51.8	38.3	7.3	4.0
1983-84	22.9	3.0	34.7	33.2	42.5	63.8	15.9	17.7	13.9	18.5	40.9	37.2	10.1	3.7
1962-71	24.9	11.6	35.6	48.3	39.4	40.0	14.6	15.5	8.5	6.6	58.7	57.2	8.3	2.1
1932-41	13.9	31.6	47.5	35.3	38.5	33.3	14.2	13.3	6.0	11.3	45.8	51.6	14.1	1.4
Age 17/18														
1983-84	31.3	38.8	52.1	38.8	16.6	22.4	24.7	34.1	18.9	15.6	10.5	21.9	13.4	5.2
1963-71	47.1	31.9	34.8	40.3	18.1	27.8	18.7	24.2	6.5	12.4	21.4	16.0	5.2	1.8
1932-41	43.2	49.5	42.0	35.7	14.8	14.8	22.6	26.4	4.6	12.0	16.5	18.2	13.5	5.0
Age 30s														
1963-71	55.9	22.1	8.7	30.1	35.4	47.8	21.6	12.2	7.6	11.2	16.9	36.4	13.9	8.5
1932-41	49.7	24.2	2.8	24.7	47.5	51.1	17.3	19.3	12.7	20.6	18.0	20.9	10.0	0.6
Age 60s														
1932-41	56.3	44.1	0.0	3.0	43.7	52.9	4.9	2.3	28.4	25.2	20.3	20.2	13.7	4.4

Table 4.15 (Continued)

Cohort born	Companions						Selected journey purpose*							
	Alone		Children		Adults		Work/Ed		Shopping		Social		Sport	
	M	F	M	F	M	F	M	F	M	F	M	F	M	F
Lancaster and Morecambe														
Age 10/11														
1990-91	24.6	11.4	41.6	33.6	33.8	54.9	12.2	12.3	15.3	21.1	44.0	40.5	12.2	4.9
1983-84	14.3	9.3	41.6	36.7	44.1	54.0	17.8	14.3	11.4	16.2	38.6	35.4	16.3	13.1
1962-71	16.2	8.1	46.5	30.1	37.3	61.8	15.0	17.1	6.8	17.6	45.9	43.5	10.0	2.7
1932-41	29.6	21.6	55.8	42.1	14.6	36.2	18.5	13.2	5.4	10.1	40.8	38.8	12.2	2.5
Age 17/18														
1983-84	31.3	38.8	52.1	38.8	16.6	22.4	23.9	26.7	9.0	18.3	16.4	16.3	11.3	6.6
1963-71	47.1	31.9	34.8	40.3	18.1	27.8	30.1	24.7	1.0	8.7	8.0	19.3	12.0	3.1
1932-41	43.2	49.5	42.0	35.7	14.8	14.8	30.3	22.3	2.2	9.0	8.9	12.4	16.6	8.6
Age 30s														
1962-71	56.5	33.9	2.9	29.9	40.6	36.1	22.7	12.9	16.2	34.3	19.8	17.7	4.2	2.1
1932-41	47.3	28.4	3.9	34.9	48.8	36.6	36.3	11.9	5.4	25.9	17.6	21.2	3.7	1.7
Age 60s														
1932-41	29.9	41.6	4.5	5.0	65.6	53.1	5.1	8.1	15.2	21.9	13.3	10.7	14.4	5.7

Data relate to all journeys recorded aggregated over a 12-month period.

*Work/Ed refers to work and education combined (as appropriate for each age group); Social excludes social travel to eat/drink or for specific entertainment; Sport includes both watching and participating in sport.

Source: Everyday mobility sample, Manchester/Salford and Lancaster/Morecambe, 2001-2003.

Table 4.16 The Changing Relationship Between Home and Workplace as Expressed Through the Journey to Work, 1890–1998 (Per cent)

			Time period			
	1890-1919	1920-39	1940-59	1960-79	1980-98	All
Change of home but no change of workplace	18.2	31.6	3.2	3.2	5.1	4.4
Change of workplace but no change of home	20.8	23.7	30.0	37.4	43.8	33.1
Change of home and workplace	59.1	41.9	41.8	33.9	23.7	37.5
Change of journey mode or route, but no change of home or workplace	1.9	2.8	5.0	5.5	7.4	5.0
Sample size	913	1,778	3,822	3,780	2,146	12,439

Source: Details of 12,439 journeys to work taken from 1,834 individual life histories. Statistics relate to all modes of transport and are calculated for the decade in which a particular journey to work started.

The Changing Relationship Between Mobility and Migration

Whilst there is an extensive literature on residential migration in both the past and the present (White and Woods, 1980; Champion and Fielding, 1992; Pooley and Turnbull, 1998; Whyte, 2000), academic research has paid much less attention to everyday mobility. However, it can be suggested that over the twentieth century a much closer relationship between migration and mobility has developed, with many people gaining the ability to exchange some aspects of mobility for residential migration. This theme has been explored elsewhere (Pooley and Turnbull, 1999; Green, Hogarth and Shackleton, 1999; Pooley, 2003) and is picked up in Chapter 6 in the context of the journey to work. However, some general issues are introduced here.

In particular, it can be suggested that the ability to commute over longer distances, without significantly increasing travel times, has given people the opportunity to adjust their mobility behaviour by substituting commuting for residential migration. Green, Hogarth and Shackleton (1999) identify this as a recent trend, but life history data discussed in this volume suggest that the same processes have been operating for much of the twentieth century. Thus, according to our data, in the period 1890-1919, 59.1 per cent of people who moved home also changed their workplace; but in the period 1980-1998 only 23.7 per cent of respondents who moved home also changed where they worked (Table 4.16). Conversely, whereas in the period 1890-1919 only 20.8 per cent of people changed their workplace without moving home, in the 1980s and 1990s 43.8 per cent changed their job but remained in the same house.

It can thus be suggested that the twentieth century has seen the interaction of two rather contradictory mobility trends. On the one hand, people have progressively moved home more frequently and over longer distances. On the other hand, the ability to commute over increasing distances in approximately the same time has allowed people to either change their job without moving home, or to move house without changing their work. This leads to relatively less residential mobility for employment reasons, but more for housing, environmental and life-style reasons. This is borne out by migration life history data where, in the period 1880-1919, 38.8 per cent of moves were for work reasons, 16.0 per cent for housing reasons and 2.9 per cent for family reasons; but in the period 1920-1994 only 26.3 per cent of moves were for work reasons, with 23.6 per cent for housing reasons and 5.7 per cent for family reasons (Pooley and Turnbull, 1998). Whereas in the early-twentieth century, when most people walked or cycled to work, a 30 minute journey restricted them to living within a few kilometres of their workplace, in the late-twentieth century these restrictions have been significantly reduced. These changes have acted both to increase the potential for residential mobility (people can move freely and improve their housing status within an acceptable commuting radius of their work), and to reduce it (people can more easily change employment without moving home). The modest increase in mobility (especially the journey to work) indicated by the life history data is thus a compromise arising from these competing trends. Moreover, it can be suggested that the most important factor in this balance is the interaction between the length of time that people are prepared to spend commuting, the speed of available transport and the strength of ties to a particular neighbourhood. Changes in the journey to work over the twentieth century are explored in more detail in Chapter 6.

Conclusions

This chapter has examined long-run trends in everyday mobility in Britain, using the limited evidence that exists in secondary sources such as the census and the National Travel Survey and new data on everyday mobility collected from selected sample towns. Inevitably, such data present a picture that is generalised and which ignores variations between individual people and places. Some of these subtleties will be drawn out in later chapters in relation to specific aspects of mobility. However, certain key trends are clear. On the one hand, the data demonstrate some expected and widely recognised increases in everyday mobility, especially in the distances over which some journeys are undertaken and in the use of the car. On the other hand, however, the data also demonstrate a perhaps surprising degree of stability in mobility patterns over the last century. Most everyday travel remains short distance and, especially for children, travel on foot continues to be important. There has also been relatively little change in the structure of children's mobility in relation to either the extent to which children were accompanied by adults, or the reasons why mobility occurred. This overview thus suggests that whilst some changes are obvious and important, these are underpinned by considerable stability in the pattern and process of everyday mobility. We argue that this at least questions some of the assumptions about mobility change built into the main theoretical discourses concerning mobility. More detailed evidence to support these assertions is examined in relation to specific aspects of mobility in the following chapters.

Chapter 5

Travelling to School

Introduction: The Changing Significance of School Travel

It can be suggested that the journey to school may have changed more over the twentieth century than most other forms of everyday mobility. In addition to the changes in transport technology, economy and society that have affected all forms of mobility, and all age groups, there are a series of further factors that have fundamentally restructured the relationship of children and their families to schooling. First, the twentieth century has seen successive changes in the school leaving age and in the proportion of children attending school and college for post-compulsory education. Thus in England and Wales in 1900 compulsory state-funded education was under the control of elected school boards, with a school leaving age of 12. For most children this was the extent of their formal education. The 1902 Education Act transferred control of state education to county boroughs and county councils, establishing the primacy of local authority educational provision, and the 1918 act raised the school leaving age to 14. Following the widespread educational reforms of 1944, which established general primary and selective secondary education, the school leaving age was raised to 15, and it was increased again in 1971 to the age of 16 (Lawson and Silver, 1973; Royle, 1997; Doyle, 2000). In addition the last 50 years have seen a massive increase in the proportion of children over 15 staying at school after the compulsory school leaving age. Thus in 1951 19 per cent of children aged 16 and 9.8 per cent of children aged 17 were in education, whereas in 2001 77.6 per cent of children aged 16 and 17 were attending school or college. Although the provision of compulsory schooling did not have an immediate effect on all children and areas, for instance in 1904 the London School Board noted an attendance rate of 88 per cent (compared to 66 per cent in 1870 at the beginning of compulsory schooling), and in rural areas (especially at harvest time) school attendance continued to fluctuate, in general by the early-twentieth century most children under the age of 12 were attending school regularly (Gilbert and Southall, 2000). Gradually, during the twentieth century, going to school also became a normal rather than an exceptional, experience for most teenagers and the journey to school became a major, but routine, part of their life.

If an increase in the proportion of children aged over 12 attending school has been the main change affecting the journey to school over the twentieth century, there have also been many other trends that have had an influence. In the first half of the twentieth century school choice was limited for anyone staying in post-compulsory education and, thus, the journey to school was determined by distance from the small number of grammar schools that provided education after the compulsory school leaving age. From the 1960s an increasing proportion of, mostly comprehensive, schools offered post-compulsory education and thus it was much more likely that a 16 year old could find an appropriate school or college close to home. For at least some adolescents in post-compulsory education it can thus be suggested that the journey to school will have got shorter over time. Conversely greater parental choice in the selection of an appropriate school has had the opposite effect for many younger children. It can be suggested that in the first half of the century most children under the school leaving age would have attended their local school. The main alternatives occurred where parents could afford to send their child to a private school, or where school choice was determined by religion, especially for some Catholic families. Parents may have expressed some preferences, but for the most part schools were strongly catchmented. Over the last three decades this has changed significantly with the introduction of greater parental choice in education, and with some children travelling long distances to what parents perceive as a more suitable school. Over the same period there have also been changes, both nationally and locally, in policies regarding the provision of free school transport. This may also have influenced school choice (Johnson, 1990; Stead, 1998; Parsons, Chalkley and Jones, 2000).

The journey to school has also had an increasing influence on other aspects of travel, society and urban structure. For many parents residential location is affected by the need to be in the catchment area for a suitable school, and the 'school run' has become a major source of traffic congestion in many towns, with traffic jams reducing or even disappearing during school holidays. It can be suggested that the increased traffic generated by school trips can be related to a number of factors. In part, it simply reflects greater affluence and car ownership, but it also signifies the increasingly complex and busy lives of children and their parents as people cram a greater number of activities into a day. The journey to or from school becomes a multi-purpose trip combined with the journey to work or shop for a parent or a trip to an after-school activity for a child (Joshi and Maclean, 1995; Pettitt et al, 1995; Valentine and McKendrick, 1997; O'Brien et al, 2000). It can also be suggested that changes in the nature of the school run reflect broader perceptions of the risks to which children are exposed in urban areas, either from strangers or, paradoxically, from traffic (DiGuiseppi et al, 1998; Dixey, 1998; DETR, 2000; Sjolie, 2002). One effect of this is to push more children into cars. Such trends also have broader implications, particularly with respect to children's health. It has been suggested that as fewer children walk to school, so too there has been a general decrease in the amount of exercise that children (and adults) take, leading to increased obesity and related illness (Prentice and Jebb, 1995). In some areas there have been attempts to counter this with imaginative schemes to encourage more children to walk to school (Black, Collins and Snell, 2001; Kearns, Collins and Neuwelt, 2003).

It is thus possible to suggest a number of key trends that are likely to have influenced the journey to school over the past century. First, schooling has become more ubiquitous for more and older children, second school choice has widened for most children and adolescents and, third, the school run has become increasingly implicated in urban traffic generation. This chapter combines the limited existing evidence with analysis of the journey to school for children aged 10/11 and 17/18 in Manchester/Salford and Lancaster/Morecambe to test some of the assumptions outlined above.

The Journey to School Since 1900: Key Issues and Trends

There are relatively few detailed studies of school attendance and the journey to school in the first half of the twentieth century. Local historical studies of schooling that have been undertaken have usually used surviving nineteenth- and early-twentieth-century school logbooks to identify pupils and trace their place of residence (Marsden, 1977; 1979). Additional information may be drawn from autobiographies and life histories that look back on life in the first half of the century, but few give much information on the journey to school (Roberts, 1971; Forrester, 1974). Although some early-twentieth century social surveys investigated education, they were usually concerned with school attendance and the links between educational attainment and deprivation. They provide few details on the distances that children travelled to school (Caradog Jones, 1934).

At the national level, National Travel Survey data enable broad trends in the journey to school to be established for the past 30 years. There are no comparable data over a longer time period. NTS data show that the mean distance travelled to school has increased by about 700m over the past 30 years for primary school children and by about 800m for children of secondary school age. However, overall, the journey to school remains short at about 2.3km for children under 11 and 4.7km for children aged 11-16. Whilst the proportion of children walking to school has declined, and car use has increased, NTS data also show that at each survey date (including the most recent) walking was the single most important means of travel to school for both primary and secondary school children. Overall, bus use has remained quite stable, with travel by bus the second most important means of travel for children aged 11-16, but over the past 15 years there has been a marked fall in the proportion of children under 11 travelling to school alone (Table 5.1). For older children this figure has not changed. These data thus suggest that whilst there is evidence of some change, a short journey to school on foot continues to be the most common experience for most children.

NTS data provide only limited evidence on geographical variations, but there are considerable and predictable differences in travel to school distances between urban and rural areas. Thus in 1975/76 the mean journey to school in rural areas was more than double that in towns of over 25,000 population (Department of Transport, 1979). Such urban-rural differentials in the journey to school have increased with the closure of rural schools, greater parental choice and, especially continuing counterurbanisation (Champion, 1989; Cross, 1990). Thus, in 1998/2000, the mean journey to school in Britain was 2.5km in metropolitan areas and 8.1km in rural areas. However, the time spent travelling to school is similar in most areas (the main exception being London boroughs where journey to school

Table 5.1 Changes in the Journey to School, 1975-2001

	Age 5-10			Age 11-16		
	1975/6	1985/6	1999/2001	1975/6	1985/6	1999/2001
Mean distance (km)	1.6	1.8	2.3	3.9	3.7	4.7
% walking	73.5	67.0	54.0	53.0	52.0	43.0
% travelling by car	15.0	22.0	39.0	7.0	10.0	19.0
% travelling by bus	9.5	9.0	6.0	31.5	29.0	32.0
% cycling	1.5	1.0	1.0	7.0	6.0	2.0
% travelling alone	*	0.21	0.10	*	0.46	0.46

*Data not available.
Sources: Department of Transport, 1979; Department for Transport, 2001.

times are much longer than average), and for children age 5-10 rural journey to school times are rather shorter than those in urban areas due mainly to the greater use of cars in the countryside (Department for Transport, 2001; National Statistics, 2002).

A study by Hillman, Adams and Whitelegg (1990) examined changes in children's mobility in five locations (the London borough of Islington, suburban Nottingham, Stevenage, Winchester and rural Oxfordshire) between 1971 and 1990. They found similar trends to those shown by NTS data, but focused attention particularly on the role of increased traffic and the restrictions that parents consequently placed on children's independent mobility. The key changes that they observed between the two survey dates were a reduction in the proportion of younger children allowed to cross roads, use buses, cycle on public roads and travel to places other than school alone; an increase in travel to school by car and a decrease in walking; an increase in the extent to which younger children were accompanied on journeys; and a reduction in the number and range of independent activities undertaken by junior school children. However, it can be suggested that by concentrating on change the authors underplay the extent to which many children do still travel independently and on foot. Thus, even in their 1990 survey, 63 per cent of all junior school children walked to school (compared to just over 80 per cent in 1971), and only 33 per cent were taken to school by car. Although travel to school by car increased more than three-fold 1971-1990, walking remained overwhelmingly the single most important way in which children travelled to their junior school. The limited data that exist thus suggest a slightly contradictory picture. Whilst much rhetoric is focused on the increased numbers of children who are taken to school by car, and on the impacts that this has on both urban traffic congestion and children's health, actual evidence suggests that change may not be quite so dramatic, and that many children still travel a short distance to school on foot. Data from Manchester/Salford and Lancaster/Morecambe will now be used to examine the extent to which such change has occurred in two urban areas since the 1940s.

Travel to School Since the 1940s for Children Aged 10/11

Children aged 10/11 have not been affected significantly by the broader structural changes in the educational system outlined above. Throughout the twentieth century, almost all children this age attended school, and most parents will have sought to send a child age 10/11 to the nearest appropriate school. Evidence from the two case study towns suggest even less change in the distances over which children aged 10/11 travel to school than is shown in the NTS data. In both Manchester and Lancaster distances have varied quite randomly around one km, but with some evidence of a reduction in the mean time that children take to travel to school. Almost all school journeys for this age group are short, with the majority under 1500m and taking less than 20 minutes at all time periods. There are no significant differences between boys and girls (Table 5.2). Differences from the NTS data are easily explained. As outlined above there are considerable variations

Table 5.2   Changes Since the 1940s in the Distance Travelled and the Time Spent Travelling on the Journey to School at Age 10/11, Manchester and Lancaster

Birth cohort/ distance/time	Manchester and Salford			Lancaster and Morecambe		
	All	Male	Female	All	Male	Female
Born 1932-41						
Mean distance (km)	1.3	1.3	1.2	1.0	1.0	1.0
Mean time (min)	16	17	16	15	15	16
Born 1962-71						
Mean distance (km)	0.6	0.6	0.6	0.8	0.5	1.2
Mean time (min)	14	14	13	10	9	12
Born 1983-84						
Mean distance (km)	0.9	0.9	0.9	1.5	1.2	1.8
Mean time (min)	10	11	9	15	11	19
Born 1990-91						
Mean distance (km)	1.4	1.8	1.1	0.8	1.0	0.5
Mean time (min)	10	11	10	9	9	8
All						
Mean distance (km)	1.1	1.2	1.0	1.0	1.0	1.1
Mean time (min)	13	13	12	13	11	14
Sample size*	83	39	44	79	42	37

*Sample size is slightly larger than the number of respondents because some children had two different journeys to school depending on which parent they were living with at the time. Data are not aggregated over 12 month period.
Source: Everyday mobility sample, 2001-3.

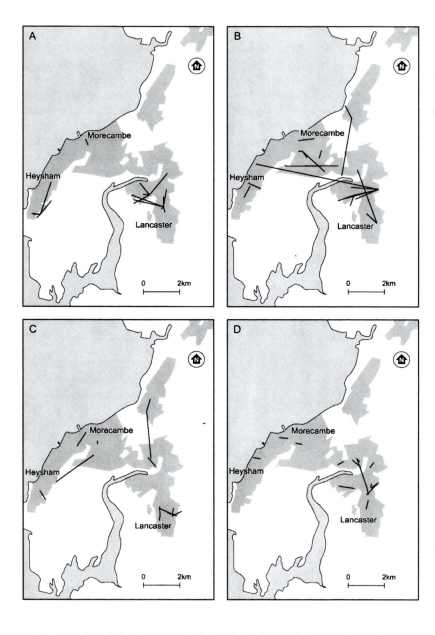

Figure 5.1 Examples of the Journey to School Aged 10/11, Lancaster and Morecambe (A) Cohort born 1990-91, (B) Cohort born 1983-84, (C) Cohort born 1962-71, (D) Cohort born 1932-41

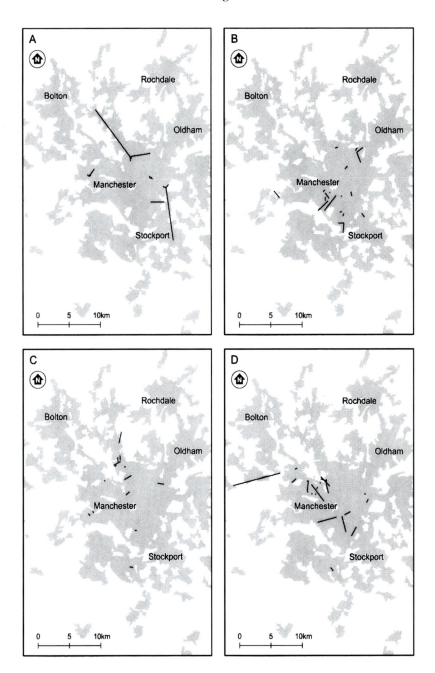

Figure 5.2 Examples of the Journey to School Aged 10/11, Manchester and Salford (A) Cohort born 1990-91, (B) Cohort born 1983-84, (C) Cohort born 1962-71, (D) Cohort born 1932-41

in travel to school distances between children in rural and urban areas, and whereas the NTS data relate to the whole country and broad age categories, our data are drawn from two towns and specific age categories. However, for many urban children change in the distance travelled to school over the past 60 years appears to be relatively small. This is emphasised if individual journeys to school are plotted over time: in both Manchester and Lancaster spatial patterns are similar and relatively constrained, with most children travelling to school within their own communities (Figures 5.1 and 5.2).

Exploration of the reasons why parents chose to send their children to a specific school may begin to explain this surprising degree of stability in the length of the journey to school. It can be suggested that although most parents would wish to minimise the time and cost involved in daily travel to school for their children, the factors outlined above – greater parental choice, together with greater affluence and car ownership – may have led to a lengthening of school trips for many children. However, examination of qualitative evidence relating to the factors that determined which school parents used for their children suggests a high degree of stability over time. In both the 1940s and today most parents chose a local primary school for their child unless other factors intervened. In both time periods such factors included the preference for a school of a particular religious persuasion, choice of a school with a particularly good reputation, or a primary school that fed into a secondary school that was perceived to be good. Some children had a relatively long journey to school due to the fact that they moved home but did not change school because their parents did not want to disrupt their education. In a few cases the choice of school was affected by ease of access.

Examples of all of these reasons relating both to the 1940s and the present day are given in Box 5.1. Thus in 1945 Mary's parents chose the nearest available school that did not entail crossing a main road, in 1947, Olive's parents sent her to the school that gave access to their preferred secondary education, Bob's parents chose a school some distance from home because of its good reputation and for Elizabeth her school was chosen because of her family's religion. Very similar concerns emerge in relation the children who were aged 10/11 at the time of the interview in 2001-2003. Ben stayed at the same school after his parents moved house, Alex moved schools because he was being bullied and Rory's parents selected the school they considered best. Much the same themes also emerge for other time periods, thus Julia (age 10 in 1978) was sent to the nearest Catholic school and in 1993 Ashley's school was selected because of its reputation. However, these accounts of children attending a school some way from home are the exceptions: the vast majority of respondents in all time periods stated that at the age of 10/11 they attended the school closest to their home.

There has been more change in the modes of transport used for the journey to school, but again the decline in walking and increase in car use is not as great as some commentators would suggest. For children aged 10/11 in the 1940s approximately 80 per cent of trips to school were on foot, with most of the remainder undertaken by bus. By the time of the interviews in 2001-2003 this figure had dropped to approximately 50 per cent, with the other half of all school

Box 5.1 **Reasons for Choosing a Particular School, Aged 10/11,**
Manchester and Lancaster

… it was the nearest school when we were born that they didn't have to cross roads If you went to B School you'd a busy road to cross but at C it was straight down (R3, Mary, age 10/11 born 1935, Lancaster).

My parents didn't like B School for some reason, teachers there, so I went down to D Road and I stopped there from being in the infants right through (R113, Bob, age 10/11, born 1940, Lancaster).

Well it was a religious school. So you know the local school was out of/there wasn't, there wasn't a school for our religion there, so it was a case of travelling (R323, Harry, age 10/11, born 1942, Manchester).

Well it was the nearest at the time you know and you usually went to the nearest school, yea (R351, Les, age 10/11, born 1937, Salford).

I, I think my mother wanted me to go to M when I was 11 and I think she thought it would help if you went to the prep for a year first (R357, Olive, age 10/11, born 1937, Salford).

Because we were Catholics, but we couldn't get in the Catholic School because it was overcrowded. And I went to that particular school because there was no other (R339, Elizabeth, age 10/11, born 1940, Manchester).

It's the nearest Roman Catholic school yes (R10, Julia, age 10/11, born 1968, Morecambe).

As far as I'm aware it was because it was a nice school with a nice headmaster (R49, Ashley, age 10/11, born 1983, Lancaster).

No no, there was one quite close, where my brother went, but I went there for I think it was about a week and I didn't like it at all. I was very young, but I remember not liking it at all. And so my mum and dad moved me to a different school, cause my cousins went to a different school (R219 Nazira, age 10/11, born, 1986, Manchester).

It's because when I moved I was in Year Four and my mum said there's no need in changing school because/I know some people that go to the school, but I didn't really want to go to a different school, I don't like making new friends, I just want to stay with the same friends (R206, Ben, age 10/11, Stockport, born 1992).

I've really only come in, just come into this school from Year Four. The last four weeks of Year Four I come to this school, cause in my other school I was being bullied (R207, Alex, age 10/11, born 1991, Manchester).

Because, because my mum want us to finish our school in here because this is the school that she, that she thought would be best for us (R211, Rory, age 10/11, born 1992, Manchester).

Source: Everyday mobility sample.

journeys undertaken by car. There were few differences between the two towns and the decline in walking occurred most rapidly in the 1990s, but even at the time of interview walking remained the single most important method of travelling to school. There were again few differences between boys and girls but in Manchester for children born since the early 1980s there is some evidence that girls were less likely than boys to walk to school and more likely to travel by car. However in Lancaster this trend is reversed (Table 5.3). There is no obvious explanation for these different gender patterns, and they could be a random product of a small sample. However, the fact that the differences between Manchester and Lancaster are consistent across several time periods suggests that this may be a real difference. Possibly in the smaller urban area of Lancaster and Morecambe girls

Table 5.3   Changes Since the 1940s in the Mode of Transport used for the Journey to School at Age 10/11, Manchester and Lancaster (Per cent)

Birth cohort/ mode	Manchester and Salford			Lancaster and Morecambe		
	All	Male	Female	All	Male	Female
Born 1932-41						
Walk	76.0	72.7	78.6	81.8	83.3	80.0
Cycle	4.0	9.1	0.0	0.0	0.0	0.0
Bus	20.0	18.2	21.4	18.2	16.7	20.0
Car	0.0	0.0	0.0	0.0	0.0	0.0
Born 1962-71						
Walk	87.5	87.5	87.5	85.5	85.5	85.5
Cycle	0.0	0.0	0.0	0.0	0.0	0.0
Bus	6.3	12.5	0.0	7.1	0.0	14.3
Car	6.3	0.0	12.5	7.1	14.3	0.0
Born 1983-84						
Walk	65.0	72.7	55.6	66.7	54.5	80.0
Cycle	0.0	0.0	0.0	0.0	0.0	0.0
Bus	0.0	0.0	0.0	4.8	0.0	10.0
Car	35.0	27.3	44.4	28.6	45.5	10.0
Born 1990-91						
Walk	50.0	66.7	38.5	45.0	33.3	60.0
Cycle	0.0	0.0	0.0	4.5	8.3	0.0
Bus	0.0	0.0	0.0	0.0	0.0	0.0
Car	50.0	33.3	61.5	50.0	58.3	40.0
All						
Walk	68.7	74.4	63.6	68.4	61.9	75.7
Cycle	1.2	2.6	0.0	1.3	2.4	0.0
Bus	7.2	7.7	6.8	7.6	4.8	10.8
Car	22.9	15.4	29.5	22.0	31.0	13.5
Sample size*	83	39	44	79	42	37

*Sample size is slightly larger than the number of respondents because some children had two different journeys to school depending on which parent they were living with at the time. Data are not aggregated over a 12 month period.
Source: Everyday mobility sample, 2001-2003.

were given more freedom to walk, and were more willing to walk, than girls in the larger conurbation of Manchester and Salford. It should also be noted that the information recorded in the tables relates to the normal mode of transport. Qualitative evidence showed quite clearly that the mode of transport used for the journey to school actually varied quite a lot for many children, depending on factors such as the weather and other activities that were being undertaken. Thus someone who said they normally walked to school could travel by car on a wet day or when they had to carry (for instance) their saxophone to school; but equally someone who said they normally travelled by car may walk when the weather was fine. This individual variability in daily patterns is missed in large-scale surveys such as the NTS.

Examples of this variability are given in Box 5.2, together with examples of the variety of reasons that respondents gave for choosing a particular means of travelling to school. What is most striking is the consistency of responses across all the four time periods studied. Thus in the 1940s Tony and Bob varied their journeys between walking and the bus depending on the weather; and at the time of interview Dan and Chelsea switched between walking to school and being taken by car depending on the weather and season. Over a period of 60 years, the car has replaced the bus but the reasons for choosing whether or not to walk have remained the same. Some children in each time period found walking fun and travelled to school on foot out of personal preference. Sarah, Daniel and Elizabeth all seemed to enjoy the journey to school, especially walking, though they were also able to use other forms of independent transport: Daniel his bike and Elizabeth her roller skates! Increasing car use over the past few decades is mainly linked to convenience. Those children, such as Alex, who had an especially long journey to school are taken by car, and for others such as Peta and Chloe car use is a reflection of availability and the need to fit in with other journeys. Thus although, as the quantitative data show, car use has increased, this has mainly been at the expense of bus travel and for many children walking remains a common and often enjoyable means of travel to school. Moreover, the underlying reasons why children and their parents choose a particular form of transport have changed little over time.

Changes in the propensity of children aged 10/11 to travel to school alone in Manchester and Lancaster also match NTS data. Overall, whereas approximately 40 per cent of children aged 10/11 travelled alone in the 1940s at the time of the interview it was just 9 per cent. The proportion travelling with other children has also declined, but the percentage accompanied by adults has increased substantially. Thus in Manchester in the 1940s 28 per cent of children aged 10/11 were accompanied by an adult on their journey to school, by 2001-2003 this had risen to over 68 per cent. Gender differences are mostly small, but since the 1980s there is some evidence that girls were less likely to travel alone though possibly more likely than boys to travel with other groups of children. However, in general, constraints that influenced where and how a child of 10/11 went to school seemed to operate equally on both boys and girls (Table 5.4). The increase in adult accompaniment is obviously in part an inevitable consequence of greater car use,

Box 5.2   Reasons for Using Particular Transport Modes for the Journey to School Aged 10/11, Manchester and Lancaster

It was my choice ... If it was chucking it down they'd say catch the bus and maybe you would on the odd occasion. But the bus wasn't a great deal of advantage cause to get from Skerton to C you needed two buses to start off with (R52, Tony, age 10/11, born 1939, Lancaster).

Yea there was a girl lived opposite. She went to D Seniors, which is now C School. They moved out. So we used to go down together on, on the bus. Or if it was a nice day we walked it down (R113, Bob, age 10/11, born 1940, Lancaster).

Oh yea. Yea there was no/it wasn't, it wasn't on a bus route really. It was on a bus/but you couldn't get to/you'd need two buses and it was, it's only about a mile away, so [I walked] (R 325, Derek, age 10/11, born 1937, Salford).

We all walked there. Or roller skated there ... Oh I roller skated there a lot (R339, Elizabeth, age 10/11, born 1940, Manchester).

Um we sort of went through periods of using the bus to go to school maybe for a few months and then we'd go back to walking. And the bus was very cheap then. And it stopped at the end of the road, so it was quite easy. But I don't know, maybe bad weather or something, but that would be all, it would be about it (R60, Craig, age 10/11, born 1962, Morecambe).

Because it was only five minutes walk away. It was on the same side of the main road to where the house was as well so we didn't have to cross the main road (R13, Paul, age 10/11, born, 1968, Lancaster).

My mum didn't work, she didn't go out to work then, so she tended to sort of ferry us around everywhere. It would have been, if we were walking it would have been a 20, 25 minute walk I should think. So I think it was just, just timing and, and ease really taking the car (R389, Peta, age 10/11, born 1971, Manchester).

Walked most of the time. Sometimes I think, when I was 10 I think we were allowed to go on our bikes (R4, Daniel, age 10/11, born 1971, Lancaster).

Because the times my parents were leaving ... were awkward and Mum knew it was safe and we enjoyed just walking with our friends. Just enjoyment I think (R6, Sarah, age 10/11, born 1983, Lancaster).

Well when it was winter and Christmas we used to go in the car so we used the car. And when it was summer like this we'd walk or we'd cycle, so (R16, Dan, age 10/11, born 1983, Morecambe).

I walk to school on like nice days but if it's raining I go with my mum in the car (R29, Chelsea, age 10/11, born 1990, Morecambe).

Because it's too far to walk, cause it's seven miles away ... we just go, go by car (R207, Alex, age 10/11, born 1991, Manchester).

My uncle drops me off so, cause my mum's busy in the morning (R210, Chloe, age 10/11, born 1992, Manchester).

Source: Everyday mobility sample.

Table 5.4 Changes Since the 1940s in the Companions Travelled with on the Journey to School Aged 10/11, Manchester and Lancaster (Per cent)

Birth cohort/ companions	Manchester and Salford			Lancaster and Morecambe		
	All	Male	Female	All	Male	Female
Born 1932-41						
Alone	36.0	36.4	35.7	40.9	41.7	40.0
Other children	36.0	27.3	42.9	40.9	50.0	30.0
Adult	28.0	36.4	21.4	18.2	8.3	30.0
Born 1962-71						
Alone	12.5	12.5	12.5	14.3	14.3	14.3
Other children	43.8	37.5	50.0	28.6	42.9	14.3
Adult	43.8	50.0	37.5	57.1	28.6	71.4
Born 1983-84						
Alone	25.0	45.5	0.0	9.5	18.2	0.0
Other children	30.0	27.3	33.3	42.9	36.4	50.0
Adult	45.0	27.3	66.7	47.6	45.5	50.0
Born 1990-91						
Alone	9.1	11.1	7.7	9.1	16.7	0.0
Other children	22.7	33.3	15.4	36.4	25.0	50.0
Adult	68.2	55.6	76.9	54.5	58.3	50.0
All						
Alone	21.7	28.2	15.9	19.0	23.8	13.5
Other children	32.5	30.8	34.1	38.0	38.1	37.8
Adult	45.8	41.0	50.0	43.0	38.1	48.6
Sample size*	83	39	44	79	42	37

*Sample size is slightly larger than the number of respondents because some children had two different journeys to school depending on which parent they were living with at the time. Data are not aggregated over a 12 month period.
Source: Everyday mobility sample, 2001-2003.

but it can be suggested that other factors may also be important. These can be explored using the qualitative data where, once again, the variability of individual experience comes through as an important variable.

Three themes recur regularly in many of the testimonies and for each time period (Box 5.3). First, the amount of traffic and the proximity of busy main roads determined whether or not a young child was accompanied. As noted above, in the 1940s Mary's parents chose her primary school not because it was nearest but because it could be reached without crossing a main road. Coincidentally, this was a Catholic school, and although Mary did not come from a Catholic family this school choice influenced her religious beliefs throughout her life (see also case study in Chapter 9). Also in the 1940s, Hilda was seen across the road by her brother who was two years older, and rather later in the 1980s the main reason Jane

**Box 5.3   Factors Affecting Whether or Not the Journey to School of
Children Aged 10/11 was Accompanied, Manchester and
Lancaster**

*Nobody bothered you. You could walk home at night in the, in the dark and nobody'd
bother you ...* (R 113, Bob, age 10/11 born 1940, Lancaster).

*Ten, well our Harry'd be 12. I think he used to stand at the corner of the road you
know to see us across, 'cause there's just one main road and then the school was only
five minutes away* (R328, Hilda, age 10/11, born 1940, Manchester).

*I used to walk half way/my friend lived half way up to school, I used to call at her
house and then we went on together* (R367, Beatrice, age 10/11, born 1937,
Manchester).

*Um we lived near the school, it was literally just over the hill and across one main
road. And I always walked to school either with my sister or her friend, but we always
walked cause they went to the S Senior School when I was at the Junior School so they
dropped me off on their way to school and picked me up afterwards* (R5, Nicola, age
10/11, born 1963, Lancaster).

*Might have gone on my own quite a lot then. Might have been with a school friend It
varies. Sometimes mum might have come with us/with me. It would have been me then.
But most times I think I went on my own at 10. Yea most of the time* (R4, Daniel, age
10/11, born 1971, Lancaster).

*We walked, it was just round the corner from our road ... And usually my mum would
take us ... cause John was in two years below so I don't, I can't recall us ever walking
to school on our own ... we had the main road to cross but it was a lollipop lady there
so it wasn't too bad* (R21, Jane, age 10/11, born 1971, Lancaster).

*Yes, because if I was, if I was up early enough I'd walk to school with my sister, who
went to the high school nearby. Or my dad would give me a lift* (R230, Sunil, age
10/11, born 1984, Manchester).

*Well it was in the mornings I walked by myself and on the way back home I'd walk
back with a friend that lived quite near my house and we'd walk back together each
day* (R7 Claire, age 10/11, born 1983, Lancaster).

*I walk with a friend or I will just go the easy way home through ginnels ... If it's
raining dead hard I'll get a lift off J's dad or K's mum* (R214, Nathan, age 10/11, born
1992, Salford).

Yes she (Mum) walks us to the top of the street, then we walk the rest of the way down
(R147, Kylie, age 10/11, born 1992, Manchester).

*On Tuesday I go across to the G School. Across the road. On Wednesday I go home
with a Child Minder. On Thursday my dad picks me up. On a Friday my mum picks me
up* (R1, Katie, age 10/11, born 1989, Lancaster).

*Normally I walk with my sister cause she started this year and my mum. Sometimes I
walk by myself if they're a bit late* (R45, Marty, age 10/11, born 1990, Lancaster).

Source: Everyday mobility sample.

and her younger brother were accompanied by a parent was because of the need to cross a busy road. Second, many accounts of the journey to school stress that this was a sociable occasion, and that trips were deliberately structured to meet friends. In part this was a response to parental concerns, with an assumed safety in numbers or from an older sibling (in the case of Nicola), but for the most part these seemed to be decisions taken by children themselves. Walking with friends was an enjoyable part of the day. This comes through particularly clearly in some accounts of the journey home from school when time was not so pressing and the journey became playtime. For Ruth, Tim and Louise one gets the impression that the journey from school was not a chore, but rather an important part of their life with meaning and purpose.

> Well just we, just we wouldn't rush, we would you know play games or something, a ball game or stand and chat or you know and/I mean we didn't have money to go to sweet shops or anything like that. But we, but we would, we would wander home. We would maybe go onto the promenade before we went home, that sort of thing (R8, Ruth, aged 10/11, born 1936, Morecambe).

> Yea yea safe. I mean there was two particular routes I'd take and I'd invariably meet other lads, other people, other friends going to school anyway, so it was more of an amble as well, there's no, there's no sense of urgency, if you can understand that (R373, Tim, aged 10/11, born 1963, Manchester).

> It was always nice really cause we just all used to walk and talk. And we were all like/we'd pick our other cousins up on the way because they all sort of lived nearby (R358, Louise aged 10/11, born 1963, Salford).

Two factors do appear to have changed quite considerably over time. First, the complexity of travel for many families, thus affecting the extent to which children were accompanied and the variety of ways in which this was achieved; and, second, perceptions of the risks that children face when travelling alone. The two are, of course, closely intertwined in that it is because children are now less likely to be allowed to travel alone that the need for complex parental journeys arises. Katie's school journeys are very complex because she does different activities during the week and is met variably by her mother, her father and a childminder. Although living only about a kilometre from her school she is not allowed to travel home alone (Box 5.3). Many children aged 10/11 at the interview noted that the school run was part of a parent's journey to work, and where these were in very different locations this could cause problems. Noah's account was typical:

> Cause me mum/in the mornings me mum has to drive down here, you know down B, and drop me off at me mates and then she has to drive back up to C to the café (R201, Noah, aged 10/11, born 1992, Manchester).

The extent to which children's mobility has become constrained by parental fears of unspecified danger is explored more fully in Chapter 7 when we consider children's outdoor play and a range of other leisure activities. In some respects children today may be given more freedom on the journey to school than they are for other activities, because travel to school follows a regular and well-known route and thus parents know exactly where a child will be. In contrast, other activities (such as outdoor play) can take a child anywhere and, as will be shown in Chapter 7, knowing where a child is has been a persistent factor structuring the degree of freedom given to young children. Nonetheless, compared to the 1940s, and even the 1980s, children aged 10/11 interviewed in 2001-2003 appeared to be much more constrained by the fear of unspecified dangers. The testimony of Georgia is typical, and such parental concerns could severely affect the journey to school:

> She's [Mum] afraid like because I don't even know our road very well, that I'll get lost somewhere and I won't know my way back. And she's scared that I might go onto somewhere like the main road and someone can snatch me (R216, Georgia aged 10/11, born 1991, Salford).

In fact Georgia normally travels to and from school by car with her father and the main reason she gives is that they live a little too far to walk. However, it is clear that she would not be allowed to do this journey alone and the time that it would take a parent to walk with Georgia is likely to be as important a factor as the absolute distance. After school Georgia does sometimes walk (with her sister) a short distance either to a friend's house or to her father's place of work if it is not convenient for her to be met at the school gate, but she does not travel all the way home alone:

> Well actually our house is a little/it's too far to walk. Well if you walk it'll probably take us longer than it will to get in the car, about half an hour or something like that ... But in the car it takes like ten minutes ... But when we go sometimes, only like a few times, I go and meet him somewhere by walking with my sister, but somewhere close. Yea but most of the times it's in the car (R216, Georgia, aged 10/11, born 1991, Salford).

Travel to School or College Since the 1940s for Adolescents Aged 17/18

In contrast to younger children, the proportion of adolescents aged 17/18 attending school or college has increased dramatically over the past 60 years. This is reflected in the data sets for Lancaster/Morecambe and Manchester/Salford with just 24 per cent of the respondents born 1932-1941 attending school or college at the age of 17/18. The small number of respondents in this category thus restricts the quantitative analysis that can be undertaken, and it must be interpreted with caution, but the qualitative data again provide rich accounts of the experience of the journey to school and the factors that structured travel decisions. Data from the two case study towns confirm the hypothesis (outlined above) that journey to school distances for pupils aged 17/18 will have decreased since the 1940s due to the expansion of post-compulsory education and the greater choice of schools and colleges available to students (Table 5.5). This is particularly marked in

Manchester and Salford where both the distance and time travelled have decreased substantially. In Lancaster the time travelled for education has reduced but the distance has changed less, possibly because of the much smaller size of the urban area. It should be noted that the mean distance travelled to school for the cohort born 1962-1971 in Lancaster and Morecambe is unusually large because it contained a small number of respondents who undertook very long daily journeys to school. This again stresses the individual variability that occurs within everyday travel, but also serves as a reminder that with relatively small samples the mean can be easily distorted by extreme values. Compared to children aged 10/11 adolescents aged 17/18 travel much further for education (on average about four times as far). Plots of individual journeys for education aged 17/18 demonstrate the extent to which some respondents travelled quite widely across their urban area to get to school or college, however others remained within their local community (Figures 5.3 and 5.4).

Table 5.5   Changes Since the 1950s in the Distance Travelled and the Time Spent Travelling on the Journey to School or College at Age 17/18, Manchester and Lancaster

Birth cohort/ distance/time	Manchester and Salford			Lancaster and Morecambe		
	All	**Male**	**Female**	**All**	**Male**	**Female**
Born 1932-41						
Mean distance (km)	7.1	8.9	3.3	2.5	2.5	0.0
Mean time (min)	36	43	23	29	29	0
Born 1962-71						
Mean distance (km)	6.0	3.8	8.2	7.9	18.3	2.7
Mean time (min)	37	23	5	25	50	14
Born 1983-84						
Mean distance (km)	4.1	4.4	3.7	2.0	2.2	1.8
Mean time (min)	28	29	27	15	17	13
All						
Mean distance (km)	5.0	5.3	4.6	3.5	4.9	2.1
Mean time (min)	31	31	31	19	26	13
Sample size	32	18	14	38	19	19

Data are not aggregated over a 12 month period.
Source: Everyday mobility sample, 2001-2003.

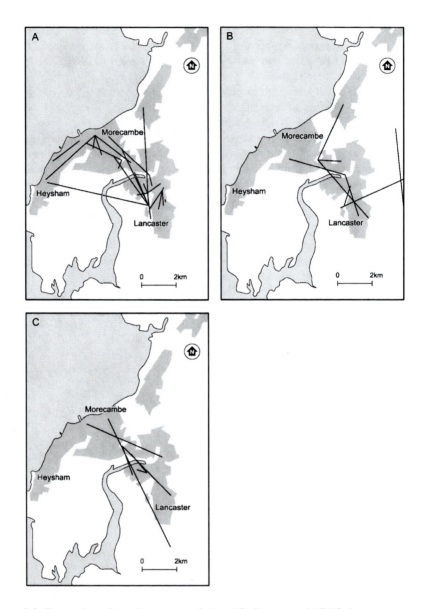

**Figure 5.3 Examples of the Journey to School/College Aged 17/18, Lancaster
and Morecambe (A) Cohort born 1983-84, (B) Cohort born
1962-71, (C) Cohort born 1932-41**

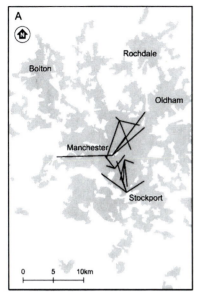

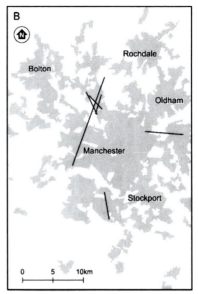

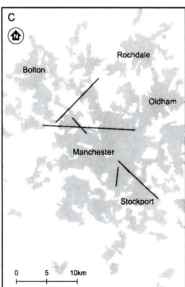

Figure 5.4 Examples of the Journey to School/College Aged 17/18, Manchester and Salford (A) Cohort born 1983-84, (B) Cohort born 1962-71, (C) Cohort born 1932-41

In Lancaster and Morecambe in the 1940s those staying on at school to the age of 17 or 18 had little choice. There was one (mixed) grammar school in Morecambe and two single sex grammar schools in Lancaster. Choice of school was thus not an option, and the distance that pupils travelled depended entirely on where they lived. In the larger urban area of Manchester there was a little more choice and, as with younger children, the choice of school was determined by a mixture of factors including convenience, religion and reputation. A long journey to school could also be created following a parental move as most families were reluctant to disrupt their child's education at that stage. Thus Harry travelled from Stockport back to the (Catholic) college he attended in Manchester. The journey was usually undertaken by bus, but in the summer he sometimes cycled and pocketed the bus fare:

> Um hum. Same school that I'd been going to since 11, but we'd moved
> further away. It's the first time we bought a house/he'd bought a house ...
> In the summer I biked it a lot yea. Cause what happened was you could
> claim your bus fares back from the local council. So I had a, quite a bit of
> free enterprise and claimed. You didn't have to produce the bus tickets
> either, you just had to produce a chitty from the school saying there was so
> many days of term and they paid you at one stage in the game. So of course
> all the cycling to school on fine days and pocketing the bus fare (R323,
> Harry, aged 18, Stockport. Born 1942).

Other accounts stress the extent to which continuing in education in the 1940s depended on a mixture of good fortune and access to sufficient income: thus Barbara was only able to go to college because her aunt and uncle paid. Compared to adolescents today, those aged 17/18 in the 1940s had much less choice about whether they stayed on at school or which school or college they attended (Box 5.4). However, even more recently secondary school children do not necessarily have real choice. Thus for Paul the existence of a combination of selective and church schools in Lancaster, together with his parents' dislike of the alternatives, meant that he ended up travelling some 20km each way for his daily journey to school. For other children the selection of secondary school depended largely on a combination of convenience, the courses available, and the school's reputation: factors that have been consistent over time (Box 5.4).

It is to be expected that adolescents in post-compulsory education will have had much more freedom than their younger brothers and sisters to choose how they travel and whom they travel with. At age 17/18 most adolescents would be treated as young adults, able to take responsibility for their journey to school or college (and for other travel around the urban area). It might thus be expected that there would be rather less change in the modes of transport used to travel to school than for children aged 10/11. Even today, relatively few school pupils aged 17/18 have regular access to a car and many are not able to drive. According to the NTS 1999-2001 just 36 per cent of people aged 17-20 have a full driving licence. This figure has actually fallen from a peak of 48 per cent in 1992-1994 (DfE, 2001). The NTS commentary ascribes this fall to the introduction of the

Box 5.4 Reasons for Attending a Particular School Aged 17/18, Lancaster and Manchester

But I was/you see the trouble was/I don't know whether it was because I went to college, but I wanted to better myself, because I only ever went to S Council School, and I didn't pass my exams for the, for the secondary school because I was told that if I passed anyway I wouldn't be able to go because mum couldn't afford the uniform. So if I'd have passed I wouldn't have been able to go. So I just didn't try for it. And then you see when I was 14 uncle/auntie and her boss decided they'd like to send me to college, and that was why really I was very lucky, because otherwise I would have probably ended up in a factory doing sewing like everybody else did (R369, Barbara, age 17/18, born 1936, Salford).

It was the only one. We all had to go to that college. It was just the course that we all did (R372, Sonia, age 17/18, born 1968, Manchester).

Yea. I failed my Eleven Plus and therefore I didn't get into the Y School. At the time the rules I think/they may be very similar/to get into R where you, you had to have your, almost your card stamped by the vicar to say that you'd been to school/you'd been to church every Sunday since before you were born. We didn't at that time. And so I actually got a place at G, which no longer exists as a school. And we went for an opening evening and myself and my mother and father went, went to the open, open evening. Somebody else who was at the open evening was Mr and Mrs F ... and their son. And my mum and and, and, it was F knew each other and they took one look at G and said our sons are not going here. So we actually both ended up going out to B. Well actually with another one of my friends who'd been at S School with us. So sort of three of us went out there. So that's the reason I went out to B. So it was, it was very much ... [the] Education system and we gave up on it. And it, it ended up actually that one of my brothers went to R and my other brother went to Y so we all went to three different schools. But so that's why, that's why I ended up out at B, and I was there for six, seven idyllic years (R13, Paul, age 17/18, born 1968, Lancaster).

The reason really was cause all my friends from secondary school went there and that/the reason for that is cause I actually/again cause I lived in Manchester, the secondary school I went to was in T purely because I was/the school I was supposed to have gone to was an all boys school up until the year I was due to go and then they were introducing girls to the school which/I can't remember at the time whether it was my decision or my parents, but they didn't think it was a good, a great idea to start going to the school with the first/with it only being the first year of being mixed. And it wasn't a very good school, didn't have a very good reputation (R389, Peta, age 17/18, Manchester, born 1971).

I came here cause I, I know it's got a good reputation for high achieving, you know a high achieve place, so I just came here for/cause it, it, it is a good college, it's a, it's a good college (R236, Greg, age 17/18, born 1985, Manchester).

Source: Everyday mobility sample.

driving theory test in 1996, but it can be suggested that other factors are also involved. More adolescents continue to higher education where access to a car is often less necessary; whilst in education they accumulate debt that reduces their ability to take driving lessons or run a car; and pressures of the post-16 exam system may reduce the amount of free time that teenagers have to learn to drive. There is further evidence of this trend from the two most recent NTS as total car use by people aged 17-20 declined from 52 per cent of all trips in 1995/97 to 48 per cent in 1999/2001. Moreover, whereas in the earlier survey car driving (28 per cent) was more important than travel as a car passenger (24 per cent), by 1999/2001 the situation had reversed (25 per cent passengers and 23 per cent drivers) in the 17-20 age group (DETR, 1998; DfE, 2001).

Table 5.6   Changes Since the 1950s in the Mode of Transport used for the Journey to School or College at Age 17/18, Manchester and Lancaster (Per cent)

Birth cohort/ mode	Manchester and Salford			Lancaster and Morecambe		
	All	Male	Female	All	Male	Female
Born 1932-41						
Walk	16.7	25.0	0.0	20.0	20.0	0.0
Cycle	0.0	0.0	0.0	40.0	40.0	0.0
Bus	83.3	75.0	100.0	40.0	40.0	0.0
Car	0.0	0.0	0.0	0.0	0.0	0.0
Born 1962-71						
Walk	0.0	0.0	0.0	20.0	33.3	14.2
Cycle	16.7	33.3	0.0	0.0	0.0	0.0
Bus	83.3	66.7	100.0	50.0	66.7	42.9
Car	0.0	0.0	0.0	30.0	0.0	42.9
Born 1983-84						
Walk	25.0	36.4	11.1	47.8	54.5	41.7
Cycle	0.0	0.0	0.0	0.0	0.0	0.0
Bus	50.0	63.6	33.3	30.4	36.4	25.0
Car	25.0	0.0	55.6	21.8	9.1	33.3
All						
Walk	18.8	27.8	7.1	36.8	42.1	31.6
Cycle	3.1	5.6	0.0	5.3	10.5	0.0
Bus	62.5	66.7	57.1	36.8	42.1	31.6
Car	15.6	0.0	35.7	21.1	5.3	36.8
Sample size	32	18	14	38	19	19

Data are not aggregated over a 12 month period.
Source: Everyday mobility sample, 2001-2003.

For adolescents aged 17/18, usually (though not always) with a longer journey to school or college than primary school children, the bus was and still is a much more important means of transport to school, especially in Manchester/Salford where, as we have seen, average journeys to school are rather longer than in Lancaster. For the first two cohorts (born 1932-1941 and 1962-1971) the bus was the single most important means of transport in both towns, accounting for over 80 per cent of trips in Manchester/Salford and 40-50 per cent in Lancaster and Morecambe. For those aged 17/18 at the time of interview in 2001-3 bus travel was still the single most important mode of transport in Manchester, though it now accounts for only 50 per cent of all recorded school trips. In Lancaster/Morecambe approximately one third of journeys were by bus with almost half on foot. Again, this may reflect the smaller urban area of Lancaster and Morecambe with more children living close to their school or college. For the earlier cohorts those who did not travel by bus either cycled or walked to school, and even for those aged 17/18 at the time of the interview, only 20-25 per cent said that they normally travelled to school by car (Table 5.6). There were relatively few variations by gender with males slightly more likely to travel by bus or to cycle (though only a small minority ever cycled) in each time period, and females more likely to travel by car today. Thus although bus use has declined and car use increased, the extent of this change has been small, and adolescents aged 17/18 remain some of the most frequent users of public transport, either in the form of special school buses or routine public service bus routes.

Qualitative evidence relating to the reasons why respondents chose to use a particular form of transport to travel to school age 17/18 again stress the variability both of individual circumstances and the extent to which travel mode could vary from day to day depending on weather and other factors (Box 5.5). Thus in the 1950s Arnold varied between walking, cycling and (most usually) travelling by bus depending on how he felt in the morning, and today although Sandra also usually travels by bus (which she dislikes), she sometimes gets a lift from a friend's parent. Many respondents had few alternatives and had to use whatever transport was available. Both Victor in the 1950s and Sonia in the 1980s worked part time and attended college one or two days a week. They had quite long journeys to the colleges in Greater Manchester that offered an appropriate course, and both felt that they had little alternative but to travel by bus, even though at times this could be quite a long and difficult journey across the city. Nicola, attending college in Lancaster in the early 1980s, and Stuart, at school in Lancaster at the time of interview, both walked because they lived close by and there was no point in using any other means of transport. As Stuart added:

> Driving would be silly. A waste of petrol and it would take longer. Cycling would also just be a waste of time, you know getting the bike out (R2, Stuart, aged 17/18, born 1983, Lancaster).

Many respondents, such as Saeeda, stressed that they enjoyed walking to and from school or college, especially in the summer and when the weather was fine, and Nicola explained the way in which in summer she and a friend would dawdle home from college via the lanes, rather than taking the direct route. As for many children aged 10/11 the journey to and from school or college could become a sociable occasion that was enjoyable as well as functional.

Box 5.5 Reasons for Choosing a Particular Form of Transport to School Aged 17/18, Lancaster and Manchester

And so similarly going to school I, I, you know sometimes I may have used the bus and sometimes I may have walked to M School. I had/or, or I had periods of using a bike, sometimes walking, sometimes using a bus ... It's how I felt when I got up in the morning ... Oh the bike probably by '53, '54, I, I don't perhaps think I ever used a bike then much (R331, Arnold, age 17/18, born 1936, Manchester).

Um work was not/only about/well it would be about the same distance away I would think. It never entered my head to go to, to college on my bike. College was in Bolton. And the firm, the works was in Salford. But I could have/it was a lot further away to the college than, than to the/to where I worked (R370, Victor, age 17/18, 1938, Manchester).

Yea, so when I was 17 I only had to go one day a week, so there was some, a couple of people at work, that I worked with, lived not too far away, so sometimes I used to get a lift from them. And other times I just used to get the bus again, so ... Well you see when I went to college when I was 16 it was in Horwich which was like an extra bus journey from Bolton. So it was probably/it would be two buses, one bus into Manchester and then a bus out again. You couldn't, you couldn't really get a bus direct to Bolton from, from Urmston (R372, Sonia, age 17/18, born 1968, Manchester).

Coming back there were four school buses that were laid on that used to stop in the lay-by at the front of the school ... And so it was a case of walking out of the school straight onto the bus, that would be at the school gate, and be dropped off on the other side of the main road and half a mile from home (R10, Julia, age 17/18, born 1968, Morecambe).

Because we had no transport and it was nearby so I walked ... Never looked into it [buses] but they didn't seem [convenient] at the time not. Just assumed we'd walk which we did ... It took us about 15 minutes maybe, casually, dawdling ... Usually dawdling coming back. Yea and about four o'clock, you'd take your time ... The weather, well used to irritate but it never bothered but sometimes we would go, if it was nice you can go down the lanes (R5, Nicola, age 17/18, born 1963, Lancaster).

Because I can't get transport. Well I, I can't get a lift or I wouldn't, I wouldn't want to ask anyone for a lift, so I prefer the bus anyway (R236, Greg, age 18, born 1985, Manchester).

Just I like walking it now, cause like my best friend we just live near each other now you know, and so like we go together, go together (R226, Saeeda, age 18, born 1985, Manchester).

I get to school by bus ... Every weekday. Apart from I get picked up sometimes by my friend and her mum but that's probably about once every two weeks as they drive past, if they see me at the bus stop then they pick me up, but I don't often see them. So it's a bus every day really. I hate it. I hate getting the bus I really do. I have to get up earlier in case the bus is early. It only takes about 15 minutes, 20 minutes to get to school on the bus (R38, Sandra, age 17/18, born 1984, Morecambe).

I always walk. It's about two minutes ... Um it's just the easiest, the easiest way to get there basically (R2, Stuart, age 17/18, born 1983, Lancaster).

Source: Everyday mobility sample.

Even those teenagers that did usually get a lift to school sometimes came home by a different means (usually by bus), and for many the school run became a complex trip for a parent or other relative dropping several children at different locations across town. The reasons why the car was used rather than the bus usually related to a combination of preference, convenience, laziness and distance from a bus stop. Nazira's long account of her journey to a sixth form college in Manchester at the time of the interview is typical of the complex car journeys made by a minority of respondents and their relatives:

> In the mornings I come by car, somebody, somebody will drop me off. And on the way back I can either get the bus or be picked up, whichever. At the beginning of the year it was my brother, but now it's my mum ... Because at the beginning my brother hadn't started university so he had the time. But now he's at university, that's at the same time I start, so it's very hard for him. So my mum drops me off, and then drops my little brother off ... To where my mum drops me off it takes about, about 20 minutes probably by car, and then she, she drops me off. And then I, it takes about a five, maybe 10 minute walk for me to come myself. She drops me/she doesn't actually come onto the Kingsway, she drops me off before that so she can avoid that traffic and/cause she has to go the other way, the opposite way, because of going to Chorlton, so you know. She, and she has to get him there on time as well ... Cause I'm too lazy to take the bus in the morning/no the bus that/the buses/I don't like taking the bus when the bus is very very bad packed and in the morning it's, well the queues to the bus stop are really long. ... cause the bus takes quite a bit of time it'd mean I have to get up early. And I'd, I'd have to/I'd still have to be dropped off to the bus stop, because the bus stop's like, like about 20 minutes away ... Yea 15/it takes about 20 minutes to walk to the bus stop, to that bus stop ... But the bus stop that comes to here it's about 20 minutes from my house, so I have to/I'd have to walk for 20 minutes then get the bus for another 20 minutes (R219, Nazira, aged 17/18, born 1986, Manchester).

Adolescents aged 17/18 are obviously much less constrained in their companions than younger children. For the majority that travel to school by bus, or on foot or by bike, their travel is independent and it can be suggested that the likelihood of them being accompanied by an adult will not have changed substantially since the 1940s. Obviously, those, such as Nazira (above) who are regularly given a lift to college are accompanied by an adult who can drive but, as noted above, this accounts for no more than one quarter of all school trips for this age group. The data from Manchester/Salford and Lancaster/Morecambe bear out these trends (Table 5.7). For the cohort born 1932-1941 the overwhelming majority of the (small) number of respondents who attended school or college travelled alone and none was accompanied by an adult. Many of these respondents attended college part time, combining a course with part-time work. They had already entered the adult world and were essentially fully independent, though usually still living at home (see Chapter 8). For those born 1962-1971 and 1983-1984, approximately 80 per cent of respondents either travelled to school or college alone

Table 5.7   Changes Since the 1950s in the Companions Travelled with on the Journey to School or College Age 17/18, Manchester and Lancaster (Per cent)

Birth cohort/	Manchester and Salford			Lancaster and Morecambe		
companions	All	Male	Female	All	Male	Female
Born 1932-41						
Alone	83.3	100.0	50.0	100.0	100.0	0.0
Other adolescents	16.7	0.0	50.0	0.0	0.0	0.0
Adult	0.0	0.0	0.0	0.0	0.0	0.0
Born 1962-71						
Alone	50.0	66.7	33.3	40.0	66.7	28.6
Other adolescents	33.3	0.0	66.7	40.0	0.0	57.1
Adult	16.7	33.3	0.0	20.0	33.3	14.2
Born 1983-84						
Alone	35.0	45.5	22.2	30.4	27.3	33.3
Other adolescents	50.0	54.5	44.4	43.5	45.4	41.7
Adult	15.0	0.0	33.3	26.1	27.3	25.0
All						
Alone	46.9	61.1	28.6	42.1	52.7	31.6
Other adolescents	40.6	33.3	50.0	36.8	26.3	47.4
Adult	12.5	5.6	21.4	21.1	21.1	21.1
Sample size	32	18	14	38	19	19

Data are not aggregated over a 12 month period.
Source: Everyday mobility sample, 2001-2003.

or with friends. Although dependence on a parent was greater than in the past it is also clear that the majority of respondents in this age group were responsible for arranging their own mobility, and for travelling independently to and from their place of education or training. Often whether or not an adolescent travelled alone or in a group was a matter of chance. There would usually be other children they knew on the bus to school, and sometimes they would meet up with friends walking the same way, but for many these were not regular arrangements. Stuart summed up such attitudes:

> ... just if I saw/if I was with somebody who was going the same way as me/then I would, but I wouldn't arrange to meet someone to walk home with ... Cause it's not worth it (R2, Stuart, age 17/18, born 1983, Lancaster).

As with children aged 10/11 adolescents expressed few fears about travelling to and from school. Such trips usually take place during daylight hours when there are plenty of other people around and the journey is over familiar territory. Similarly, there is little evidence that parents either today or in the past expressed any significant concerns about potential dangers on the way to and from school. In general, the journey to school is perceived as an unproblematic and safe trip for children aged 17/18. However, that is not to say that adolescents of this age (and their parents) do not have concerns about other aspects of their mobility. These, and how they have changed over time, will be explored in Chapter 7 in the context of leisure travel.

Conclusions

We began this chapter by suggesting that, in theory at least, the journey to school should have changed substantially over the past 60 years, especially for older children who are now much more likely to be in education at the age of 17 or 18. It was also suggested that as a common and almost ubiquitous trip for children and adolescents, the journeys for education would have been substantially affected by changes in the factors that structure mobility, including new transport technologies, rising real incomes, increased consumer choice and concerns about safety when travelling. In fact, however, the data suggest that change has been much less than might be expected. At all time periods studied most children had a short journey to school or college and for older children travel for education has decreased over time. This is largely because the factors determining which school a child goes to have altered little over time. The case study data collected from Manchester/Salford and Lancaster/Morecambe confirm NTS data that show that despite a predictable rise in car use, walking continues to be the single most important means of travelling to school for younger children, with the bus continuing to be significant for those aged 17/18. However, our qualitative data stress one element that large-scale surveys cannot show: that is the variability that exists in the nature of the journey to school, both between individuals and for one person depending on weather, whim and many other factors. Certainly the experience of education has changed substantially for those aged 17/18. In the 1950s barely a quarter of such children were in any form of education and many of these were combining part-time study with work. At the time of the interviews almost all respondents were in some form of education. However, again, the nature of the journey, the modes of transport, the degree of independence and the factors structuring travel decisions have changed little over the past 50 years. Children of all ages emphasised that although there are some aspects of the journey to school that they dislike – crowded buses and having to get up early in particular – for many travelling to (and especially from) school was a sociable activity that afforded time for play and gossip with friends. For many the journey home from school was not a walk but a 'dawdle': it was an everyday experience that added meaning to their lives.

It may appear that this argument for only limited change in the experience of the journey to school over time goes against common sense and everyday observation. Most of us will have experienced urban traffic congestion that appears to coincide with the school run, and we will have noticed the extent to which such congestion reduces during school holidays. However, the data are not incompatible with such common sense observations. First, although the information collected from Manchester and Lancaster broadly bear out trends shown by the much larger NTS, our surveys focused only on children living in two urban areas: travel to school for those living in the countryside is both over a longer distance and more likely to be by car, than by bus or on foot. Thus it can be suggested that much of the increased congestion attributed to school traffic relates to children travelling into towns from surrounding villages (and excluded from our study) rather than the travel of children in towns. Second, it can be suggested that even the relatively small increase in car use shown in the surveys is sufficient to have a significant impact on already overstretched urban traffic systems. Thus increased congestion is not incompatible with only a small proportion of all children travelling to school by car. Those that do are sufficient to make a difference. However, what this does suggest is that urban traffic problems are about much more than school traffic and that arguments that a decline in walking to school has had a significant impact on children's health may be misplaced.

Chapter 6

Travelling to Work

Introduction

Most adults spend a substantial part of their lives at work and the journey to and from work is as ubiquitous for adults as the journey to school is for children. For some adults travelling to and from work can take up a substantial portion of non-work time and convenience to a work place (like being in an appropriate school catchment area) can be an important factor in determining where someone chooses to live. As outlined in Chapter 4, national-level data suggests that, like other aspects of everyday mobility, over the past century the journey to work has got both longer and more complex. Improved access to independent transport for many people has enabled them to commute over longer distances and to combine work trips with other activities such as shopping or taking children to school. It is also suggested that such trips are a major component of urban traffic congestion, with significant implications both for the urban environment and for the amount of time that people spend travelling (Whitelegg, 1992; 1997). It can also be suggested that in the twentieth century the relationship between commuting and residential migration has become more complex. Whereas in the nineteenth century most people lived within walking distance of their workplace, and if they changed their job to a new location they moved house, in the twentieth century commuters have more choice. A longer commute can be substituted for moving home with people choosing to stay in the same location for environmental or family reasons but commuting over a long distance on a daily, or sometimes weekly, basis (Green et al, 1999; Pooley, 2003).

This chapter focuses specifically on the ways in which the journey to work has changed over time in four locations: London, Manchester/Salford, Glasgow and Lancaster/Morecambe. It first assesses overall changes in the distance over which people travelled to work and the time spent commuting, emphasising variations by location and between men and women. Second, it examines changes in the modes of transport used by commuters, focusing again on gender differences and especially on the factors that governed why people used particular forms of transport for their journeys to work. Third, it examines some of the complexities that influence journey to work travel decisions, how commuters juggle different demands on their time, and the impact of this on their choice of transport mode. In common with our analysis of other aspects of everyday mobility, the overall argument advanced is that despite obvious and significant changes in the nature of the journey to work and in the modes of transport used, there has been significant stability over the past century in the structures that govern everyday travel decisions.

Recent research on commuting behaviour and choice of transport mode has been dominated by quantitative analyses that attempt to model travel behaviour and predict future trends (Raju, Sikdar and Dhingra, 1996; Gonzalez, 1997; Wardman, 1997). A number of themes emerge from such research. Some studies emphasise the links between commuting patterns and urban form, focusing on the impact of job decentralisation on the generation of complex cross-city trips (Banister, 1994; Cervero, 1995; Naess and Sandberg, 1996). However, although urban structure has some influence on travel patterns and behaviour, it is generally suggested that in most cities the nature of transport infrastructure is more important than urban form. Much research also focuses on the relative attractiveness of different transport modes and the factors which influence decisions about modal choice. Recent studies, in a variety of locations, have focused on the promotion of bus use (Bentley, 1998), the restriction of car use through parking policy (Parkhurst, 1996; Verhoef, NijKamp and Rietveld, 1996; Mildner, Strathman and Bianco, 1997) and strategies to encourage bicycle commuting (Williams and Larson, 1996). Studies in both the USA and Europe emphasise that regulatory policies to restrict car use, combined with efficient mass transit systems, are most likely to generate high levels of public transport utilisation. In Britain this has been implemented most successfully in London (GLA, 2001; 2004). Decisions about modal choice have also been analysed from a variety of disciplinary perspectives. Whilst some research focuses on the psychology of commuting decisions (VanVugt, Vanlange and Meertens, 1996; Joireman, et. al., 1997; Bamberg and Schmidt, 1998), other studies emphasise economic factors or risk assessment (Noland, 1995; Desalvo and Huq, 1996). However, most such studies again employ a largely quantitative methodology, attempting to model modal choice within a rational decision-making framework. More sociological studies, using survey and related data, have emphasised contemporary gender inequalities in the journey to work (Mensah, 1995; Howell and Bronson, 1996). Though presenting some quantitative data, this chapter focuses especially on the qualitative assessment of commuting decisions.

Historical analyses of the changing nature of the journey to work are relatively rare and concentrate mainly on alterations in the relationship between home and workplace, and the changing structure of the city, rather than on decisions about transport modes and routes (Bloomfield and Harris, 1997). Thus researchers have used census evidence, directories, company records and related evidence to examine the separation of home and workplace in the nineteenth-century city (Vance, 1966; 1967; Carter, 1975; Pritchard, 1976; Dennis, 1984; Green, 1988; Barke, 1991), but the motivations behind such decisions and the impacts on individual lives are rarely revealed (Pooley and Turnbull, 1997). One recent historical study of the journey to work in Toronto 1900-1940 suggests that the decentralisation of employment opportunities tended to shorten the journey to work for men, who lived in suburban locations, but disadvantaged women who continued to work mainly in downtown locations (Harris and Bloomfield, 1997). As outlined in Chapter 3, information on commuting patterns in twentieth-century

Britain comes either from contemporary reports and surveys, which focused on growing problems of traffic in towns from the 1930s (Barlow Report, 1940; Liepmann, 1944; Westergaard, 1957), or from later analyses based largely on limited census evidence (Lawton, 1963; 1968; Warnes, 1972; 1975; Daniels, 1970; 1980; Davies and Musson, 1978).

Changes in the Journey to Work in the Twentieth Century: Distance and Time

It can be suggested that most people will have a reasonably clear view of the amount of time that they are prepared to spend on the journey to work. This will obviously interact with the means of transport available with, in theory, access to faster transport allowing a significant increase in travelling distance. In this section we use evidence collected from a sample of respondents drawn from across Britain to assess the extent to which there have been changes during the twentieth century in the distances over which commuters travel and the time spent commuting. It is important to emphasise that these data relate to all commuting journeys, and not only to the mainly long-distance commutes that cross administrative boundaries that are inevitably used in studies based on census and related data.

Our data suggest that during the century since 1890 there has been more than a three-fold increase in the average one-way journey to work (Table 6.1). In the 1890s the mean travel to work distance was 3.6km whereas by the 1990s it was 14.6km. The latter figure is almost identical to that produced by contemporary National Travel Surveys (see Chapter 4), suggesting that data in this sample are reasonably reliable. Moreover, prior to 1910 over 45 per cent of people had a journey to work of less than 2km and fewer than 10 per cent travelled over 10km. In contrast, after 1950 over 30 per cent of people had a travel to work distance of over 10km compared with fewer than 20 per cent who commuted less than 2km. There have also been consistent locational differences in commuting distances, with variations clearly related to settlement size. Journey to work distances in London (defined as the County of London) were consistently (approximately) double those in places under 100 000 population (in 1951); and large provincial cities over 100 000 population had commuting distances which were slightly larger than most other places, but much more similar to those in small places than those in London (Table 6.2).

In contrast, changes in the amount of time spent commuting have been relatively small. From the 1890s to the 1990s the amount of time spent travelling to work has barely doubled, with most of that change occurring before the 1920s, and with travel times remaining stable since the 1940s. Likewise average travel speeds changed little before the 1950s, but increased gradually over the second half of the twentieth century (Table 6.1). In every decade the modal (one-way) travel time was 10-29 minutes with over 50 per cent of journeys falling in this category 1890-1909, and over 40 per cent in every other decade. However, there were changes at either extreme with the proportion travelling for less than 10 minutes falling from 18.4

Table 6.1   Average Distance (km), Time (min) and Speed (km Per Hour)
Travelled for Journeys to Work Since 1890 by Gender

Decade	Males			Females			All		
	Dist.	Time	Speed	Dist.	Time	Speed	Dist.	Time	Speed
1890-99	4.0	17.0	14.1	1.8	21.3	5.1	3.6	17.7	12.2
1900-09	3.9	21.5	10.9	3.2	25.4	7.6	3.8	22.4	10.2
1910-19	6.2	27.0	13.8	5.1	26.8	11.4	5.9	27.0	13.1
1920-29	6.8	28.2	14.5	6.1	31.3	11.7	6.7	29.0	13.9
1930-39	7.0	30.5	13.8	6.8	31.9	12.8	7.0	30.9	13.6
1940-49	8.2	33.8	14.6	7.3	33.1	13.2	7.8	33.5	14.0
1950-59	10.1	33.6	18.0	7.4	34.4	12.9	9.0	33.9	15.9
1960-69	12.1	34.6	21.0	7.5	32.1	14.0	10.2	33.5	18.3
1970-79	13.1	34.5	22.8	7.6	28.5	16.0	10.3	31.5	19.6
1980-89	15.5	37.3	24.9	8.8	29.4	18.0	12.0	33.1	21.8
1990-98	19.4	39.1	29.8	10.5	30.7	20.5	14.6	34.5	25.4

Source: Details of 12,439 journeys to work taken from 1,834 individual life histories. Statistics relate to all modes of transport and are calculated for the decade in which a particular journey to work started.

Table 6.2   Average Distance (km) and Time (min) and Speed (km Per Hour)
Travelled for Journeys to Work Since 1890 by Location of
Workplace

Workplace	Time period				
	1890-1919	1920-39	1940-59	1960-79	1980-98
London:					
Distance	6.8	11.1	14.3	18.0	20.5
Time	29.0	43.3	50.7	52.2	51.5
Speed	14.1	15.4	16.9	20.7	23.9
Other cities >100,000 population:					
Distance	4.3	5.6	6.5	8.3	10.2
Time	25.3	27.4	28.8	29.3	30.3
Speed	10.2	12.3	13.5	17.0	20.2
Towns <100,000 population:					
Distance	3.7	4.4	6.4	7.9	10.9
Time	20.2	21.7	26.4	25.1	26.1
Speed	11.0	12.2	14.6	18.9	25.1
All locations:					
Distance	5.0	6.8	8.5	10.2	12.8
Time	24.7	30.3	33.7	32.6	33.6
Speed	12.2	13.5	15.1	18.8	22.9

Source: Details of 12,439 journeys to work taken from 1,834 individual life histories. Statistics relate to all modes of transport and are calculated for the decade in which a particular journey to work started.

per cent 1890-1899 to 6.2 per cent 1990-1998, and the proportion travelling for more than an hour increasing from 0 to 18.1 per cent over the same period. Whilst some commuters do spend much longer travelling to work in the late-twentieth century than in the 1890s, this has not been a majority experience. There are also significant variations in travel time by geographical location, with a marked widening in the differential between London and the rest of the country over the century (Table 6.2). Although travel time was positively related to settlement size in all time periods, before 1910 travel to work times in London were no more than 5 minutes greater than in towns of under 100,000 population. However, by the 1920s this differential had increased to 20 minutes and thereafter remained consistently more than double the travel time in smaller towns. This clearly suggests that, especially since 1920, journey times in London have been getting progressively slower relative to other places. Prior to about 1910 London travel to work distances were almost double those in smaller towns, but journey times were only just over one quarter greater. London clearly had a quicker and more effective transport system than most other towns. However, after 1920, whilst the distance differential remained unchanged, the time differential widened. This is demonstrated by changes in mean travel speeds in different locations (Table 6.2). Until the 1970s average travel to work speeds in London were faster than elsewhere, though the differential was slowly reducing. However, by the 1980s and 1990s travel to work speeds were faster in smaller towns than in London or other cities over 100,000 population.

As outlined in Chapter 4, it is known that in the late-twentieth century women have shorter journeys to work than men and that they are more likely to use public transport. However, we do not know how gender differentials have changed over time and how these interact with changing lifestyles and aspirations. Such factors have implications both for women's decisions about residential mobility and for the range of employment available to women after a move generated by the employment of the male household head. Data collected for this project suggest that most men have had longer travel to work distances than women in all periods since the 1890s, with some evidence that the differential reduced in the mid-twentieth century but increased again from the 1960s (Table 6.1). Much the same trend is seen in all locations with both men and women in London having longer journeys to work than elsewhere in Britain. In contrast, there is little difference in the average amount of time spent travelling to work by men and women, and in several decades mean female journey to work times were greater than those for men (Table 6.1). Again this pattern is consistent in all locations but with both men and women spending longer commuting in London than elsewhere. These trends clearly indicate that, in all time periods, women have spent longer travelling over shorter distances than men, and that they consistently used slower forms of transport. Given the fact that many women work part-time (in our sample 85.7 per cent of all journeys to work by part-time workers were undertaken by women), and that they are likely to have additional child-care and household demands on their time, this persistent differential must have had a significant effect on female life-styles and mobility.

Changes in the Journey to Work in the Twentieth Century: Transport Modes

Many of the trends outlined above can obviously be explained by changes in the modes of transport used for the journey to work. It is obvious that, over the twentieth century, there has been a shift away from public transport towards car use. However, the precise timing and extent of such change is not well known and reasonably reliable statistics from National Travel Surveys and census data only go back to the 1960s. There appear to have been three main periods of change in the principal modes of transport used to travel to work during the twentieth century (Table 6.3). From 1890 to the 1930s walking to work was the most common experience, with more than 40 per cent of those in employment walking to work before 1920. Of those using transport, journeys to work were quite evenly divided between trams, trains and buses, with bicycle use increasing rapidly from about 1910. From the 1930s to the 1950s the incidence of walking to work declined rapidly whilst the use of buses and bicycles increased substantially. Train use remained quite stable and trams and trolley buses gradually disappeared. From the 1960s the use of the motorcar became dominant with more than 40 per cent of those in employment commuting by car from the 1970s. Walking to work continued to decline in importance and travelling by bicycle and bus also declined sharply, though train and underground use remained almost unchanged, accounting for about one fifth of journeys to work.

Table 6.3   Main Mode of Transport for Journeys to Work in Britain Since 1890 (Per cent)

Decade					Transport mode			
	Walking	**Bicycle**	**Tram/ trolley bus**	**Bus**	**Train (overground)**	**Under- ground**	**Motor cycle**	**Car/ van**
1890-99	59.4	2.0	16.8	5.0	9.8	5.0	0.0	0.0
1900-09	49.4	11.2	11.6	14.6	10.2	0.4	0.0	1.1
1910-19	40.6	13.3	16.0	9.9	15.4	1.9	0.6	1.9
1920-29	28.5	17.5	10.6	15.3	17.8	2.3	3.9	5.2
1930-39	22.5	19.1	9.7	13.8	18.4	4.1	2.3	9.1
1940-49	17.2	19.6	6.7	23.0	18.3	5.4	2.2	6.0
1950-59	13.4	16.0	2.5	23.3	18.9	4.4	3.0	16.3
1960-69	14.0	5.2	0.2	18.8	16.2	5.3	2.6	35.8
1970-79	13.4	4.5	0.1	15.8	13.2	5.5	1.9	44.5
1980-89	10.3	6.1	0.0	11.7	15.4	5.4	1.8	48.5
1990-98	7.9	6.1	0.2	10.1	17.2	4.5	0.6	52.8
Sample size	2,083	1,379	466	2,073	2,002	564	264	3,108

Source: Details of 12,439 journeys to work taken from 1,834 individual life histories. Statistics are calculated for the decade in which a particular journey to work started.

There were marked and consistent differences in the main modes of transport used in different locations (Table 6.4). Walking, cycling and car use have always been at a very low level in London (though cycling has become relatively more important since the 1980s), with most people commuting in and out of London by underground and main line trains and, especially before the 1940s, by bus. Trams and trolley buses were available, and used most extensively, in other cities of over 100,000 population with walking, cycling and (after 1960) car use most common in towns under 100,000. Use of the bicycle to travel to work between about 1920 and 1950 was particularly notable in smaller settlements, with commuting by bicycle the single most important means of travelling to work in such towns in the 1940s. Such trends obviously reflect the availability of particular forms of transport (with trains, trams and trolley buses more commonly available in larger cities), the morphology of particular urban areas, and the choices of individual commuters who, for instance, found walking and cycling more conducive in smaller places. However, the combination of limited transport infrastructure and lack of traffic congestion meant that it was also in smaller towns that the switch from walking and cycling before 1960, to use of the motorcar after 1960, was most dramatic. Thus in the period 1940-1959 only 14.7 per cent of commuting journeys were made by car in settlements of under 100,000 population, but in the following 20 years this figure increased to 50.8 per cent. By and large those (mostly larger) places with better-developed public transport systems have had consistently lower rates of car use for commuting journeys.

There were both similarities and differences in the main forms of transport used by men and women to travel to work, but with a consistent trend for women to be more dependent on walking and slower forms of public transport such as buses, trams and trolley buses. Before the rise of the motorcar, men were much more likely to commute by bicycle and train (Table 6.5). However, it should be stressed that before 1930, when transport choices were more limited, walking was the single most important means of commuting for both men and women. During the 1930s and 1940s cycling became the most important form of transport to work for men, with women increasingly travelling by bus and (in London in the 1940s, 1950s and 1960s) underground train. Commuting by car became the single most important form of transport for men in the 1950s, but this was not the case for women until the 1970s, though from the 1980s the proportion of men and women commuting by car has been broadly similar. In general, however, women have tended to use both slower and more communal forms of transport (buses, trams) than men who have had access to faster and more individualised means of commuting (cycling, cars). Women have also tended to gain access to newer forms of transport some 20-30 years after their male counterparts.

Table 6.4   Main Mode of Transport for Journeys to Work Since 1890 by Location of Workplace (Per cent)

Mode			Time period		
	1890-1919	1920-1939	1940-1959	1960-1979	1980-1998
London					
Walk	28.7	11.5	6.6	4.7	3.4
Bicycle	5.2	4.0	5.6	1.5	5.8
Tram/trolley bus	14.9	9.5	3.7	0.1	0.0
Bus	20.1	20.6	16.2	10.2	12.5
Train (overground)	24.2	38.9	44.7	45.7	41.8
Underground	4.8	9.9	17.8	23.4	21.8
Motor cycle	0.0	1.2	1.3	1.6	1.7
Car/van	0.7	4.2	3.5	12.5	12.7
Sample size	289	506	954	792	464
Other cities >100,000 population					
Walk	46.6	25.6	13.4	12.3	12.2
Bicycle	11.2	19.6	18.2	5.2	5.3
Tram/trolley bus	26.1	18.4	8.1	0.2	0.1
Bus	7.5	11.6	31.2	27.6	15.4
Train (overground)	7.5	13.1	10.6	7.6	12.7
Underground	0.0	1.1	0.2	0.7	0.4
Motor cycle	0.4	2.9	2.8	2.5	0.9
Car/van	0.7	6.2	14.2	42.9	52.1
Sample size	268	550	1316	1260	755
Towns <100,000 population					
Walk	61.9	34.4	22.2	19.1	10.3
Bicycle	17.5	29.0	24.9	6.2	6.9
Tram/trolley bus	3.8	3.4	1.6	0.1	0.0
Bus	4.5	10.2	20.5	13.0	6.9
Train (overground)	7.0	6.3	8.9	5.4	5.3
Underground	0.4	0.3	0.7	0.4	0.5
Motor cycle	0.7	4.2	3.5	2.3	1.6
Car/van	2.8	11.6	14.7	50.8	67.5
Sample size	286	649	1478	1651	889

Source: Details of 12,439 journeys to work taken from 1,834 individual life histories. Statistics are calculated for the decade in which a particular journey to work started.

Table 6.5   **Main Mode of Transport for Journeys to Work Since 1890 by Gender (Per cent)**

Mode	Time period				
	1890-1919	1920-1939	1940-1959	1960-1979	1980-1998
Males					
Walk	44.3	23.2	12.3	8.0	7.2
Bicycle	13.2	21.6	21.4	5.5	7.1
Tram/trolley bus	13.8	9.0	3.3	0.0	0.0
Bus	9.8	10.8	17.7	11.3	5.8
Train (overground)	14.4	17.5	18.9	17.9	21.9
Underground	1.2	3.2	3.8	3.9	4.0
Motor cycle	0.5	3.5	3.9	3.3	1.8
Car/van	1.6	10.0	16.3	48.1	50.9
Sample size	646	1272	2291	2026	1000
Females					
Walk	50.3	29.3	19.7	20.6	11.6
Bicycle	5.0	9.5	11.7	4.0	5.1
Tram/trolley bus	17.8	13.2	6.2	0.2	0.1
Bus	14.2	22.2	31.7	24.8	16.1
Train (overground)	8.6	20.3	18.1	11.1	10.1
Underground	3.6	3.9	6.6	7.2	6.1
Motor cycle	0.0	0.9	0.6	1.1	1.0
Car/van	0.5	0.7	4.4	29.9	49.0
Sample size	197	433	1457	1677	1108

Source: Details of 12,439 journeys to work taken from 1,834 individual life histories. Statistics are calculated for the decade in which a particular journey to work started.

Modal Choice and the Journey to Work

Respondents in the survey were also asked to record the reasons why they chose a particular mode of transport. Although such issues are best examined at the individual level (see below), it is possible to analyse broad categories of reasons for all 1,834 people in the sample (Table 6.6). Overall the predominant reasons for choosing a mode of travel changed less than other variables over the century, but lack of choice became progressively less significant and personal preference more important as people gained access to a wider range of transport possibilities. Cost constraints also became less significant over time (though increased slightly in the

Table 6.6 Reasons for Choosing a Particular Mode of Transport for the Journey to Work Since 1890 by Gender (Per Cent)

Reason	Time period					
	1890-1919	1920-1939	1940-1959	1960-1979	1980-1998	1890-1998
Males:						
Lack of choice	60.4	41.3	41.4	40.8	38.0	42.2
Personal preference	21.1	31.0	32.5	36.3	38.1	33.3
Cost	9.1	13.0	10.3	4.7	5.9	8.4
Speed	7.0	11.3	11.5	11.2	10.7	10.9
Transport provided	2.4	3.4	4.3	7.0	7.3	5.2
Sample size	497	1065	2074	1849	964	6449
Females:						
Lack of choice	59.6	40.2	46.9	41.9	39.2	43.3
Personal preference	18.0	27.3	27.8	32.9	35.0	31.0
Cost	13.1	9.8	5.0	3.1	2.8	4.6
Speed	9.3	17.9	17.6	16.2	16.9	16.6
Transport provided	0.0	2.8	2.7	5.9	6.1	4.5
Sample size	161	358	1293	1534	1019	4365

Source: Details of 12,439 journeys to work taken from 1,834 individual life histories. Statistics are calculated for the decade in which a particular journey to work started.

inter-war period) whilst the need for fast transport became slightly more important. Locational variations reflect the patterns outlined above. In London, where people commuted over longer distances and spent more time travelling, but also had access to a greater range of transport choices, the speed of travel was more important than in other locations. However, in all places lack of choice was the single most important reason given for choosing a mode of transport in all time periods. People in smaller settlements were most constrained by lack of choice, but transport cost was about equally important in all places.

There are surprisingly few significant differences in the reasons given by men and women for using a particular form of transport. The only large difference is amongst those who consider speed of travel to be important. In all time periods, and especially after 1920 (when male and female commuting patterns diverge most clearly), women were more likely to cite speed as an important factor in determining their choice of transport, although lack of choice and personal preference remained the two largest categories (Table 6.6). These trends suggests that, throughout the century, women have been acutely aware of the fact that they have had to use slower forms of transport than men, and were thus particularly concerned to minimise travel times. This dependence on less efficient, more public and slower transport modes could have significant effects on female job opportunities, life-styles and residential mobility. Women may be constrained to work closer to home, may have less time for leisure activities and may be exposed to higher levels of risk due to a lack of private transport. The greater dependence of women on part-time work also led them to minimise journey to work distances, with travel to work distances for women in part-time employment being on average 75 per cent of their full-time equivalents. It is possible to use qualitative evidence from the case study towns to examine in more detail the reasons why both men and women chose particular forms of transport for the journey to work and how these decisions have varied over time. Attention is focused on the four main forms of transport used: walking, cycling, all forms of public transport and the motorcar.

Walking to Work

Although the frequency with which people walked to work declined rapidly during the twentieth century, many people who commuted by public transport walked short distances (to a bus stop or train station) and the reasons people gave for walking to work were quite similar in all time periods. For those who walked to work most days, the low cost and enjoyment of walking were the main motivations given by respondents. Men and women gave similar responses, although women were more likely to walk to work in all time periods and men were less likely to cite the need to save money as a reason for walking to work. The following responses illustrate these points:

> I soon decided to get up a bit earlier and walk because ... I was paying ... half a crown for tram fares, and I thought I can't even save up to go home. So I started walking to work and walking back (RJ16, Manchester, female, 1930s).

> Well, you were that used to walking you never thought anything about it. I mean you just took it ... I was a great walker then ... I used to like walking, but then again you were saving your pennies and all (RJ54, Glasgow, female, 1940s).

> It was financial. If I walked I was saving a penny/penny halfpenny you know, what I would have spent on the fare I could spend (RJ17, Manchester, female, 1940s).

> Very pleasant, down through houses, residential. Could have got a bus but I preferred to walk cause I like walking (RJ04, Manchester. male, 1950s).

> Half the people got the bus, but I liked walking you see so I always walked it. It took about 15 minutes (RJ03, London, female, 1960s).

Other respondents chose to walk to work because they found it convenient and a number of people stated that walking to work was quicker than waiting for unreliable public transport:

> Yes [there was public transport], but I could walk as quickly then. Those were the days! And they were very infrequent these buses (RJ15, Manchester, female, 1930s).

> Well, you've got more freedom if you walk because getting from where we lived ... we passed through the main shopping street of Woolwich, and you'd often want to look in a shop or pick something up, so it was that simple (RJ43, London, male, 1940s).

> There was a bus route but I didn't depend on it because I knew I could walk in 20 minutes, and that if I waited for a bus, if there's a hiccup in the service, I should be late, and that would mean a loss, in those days a loss of a day's work if you were 5 minutes late (RJ86, London, male, 1960s).

> By walking you could cut across some playing fields so you just sort of walked a diagonal of the route ... it took less time to walk than it did to actually get the bus (RJ65, Manchester, female, 1980s).

For many people walking to work was something they did occasionally when their usual form of transport was not available. Respondents frequently walked to work in thick fog or snow because public transport was not running; or when their car was in the garage, their bike had a puncture or buses and trams were on strike:

> There were times ... when there were very bad fogs. Smogs, smoke and fog you know. And though the tram cars went on lines they did sometimes go off, and you just had to walk home from work you know, that was it (RJ22, Glasgow, male, 1930s).

> Well, again, I think I've probably had to walk home in snow or thick fog or something like that, but it wasn't from choice (RJ37, Glasgow, female, 1940s).

> Well we walked when it was foggy ... Yes we walked all the way home from Manchester, you know from the office all the way. Thought nothing of it in those days (RJ20, Manchester, female, 1940s).

> Well, I walked when they nicked my bike, and possibly if I had punctures, but in the main no (RJ31, London, male, 1950s).

> Yes once or twice ... when it broke down, or the roads were particularly bad in winter. In those cases I walked to work (RJ64, Manchester, male, 1960s).

> We walked if it was very bad weather because we lived down a steep hill and it's, you know, it's difficult if it's snowing and that (RJ76, Glasgow, female, 1990s).

Increasingly, although most people resorted to walking occasionally, this was rarely by choice, with many respondents simply stating that they lived too far from their work place to consider walking under normal circumstances. Even before commuting by car became common in the 1960s there were some for whom walking to work was not an option, though perceptions of acceptable walking distances varied from person to person:

No not [walking] to work because you would have to leave too early in a morning. The subway was so quick and it was so cheap (RJ52, Glasgow, female, 1930s).

Oh no. No it [walking] would have taken too long. Five miles it would have taken an hour and a half ... The bike was so much quicker (RJ24, Manchester, male, 1940s).

Yes far too [far], cause then you were going into the centre of the city and then going to the north of the city again, and it would have been a very long walk (RJ23, Glasgow, female, 1950s).

Commuting by Bicycle

The reasons respondents gave for either cycling or not cycling to work remained almost constant from the 1930s to the present, though those who began work more recently were more likely to show an awareness of environmental considerations. The main perceived advantages of cycling, in all time periods, were low cost, relative speed (especially the ability to undertake complex cross-town journeys quickly, to cut through standing traffic and to avoid waiting for public transport), flexibility and the enjoyment of exercise. These themes are illustrated in a number of quotations from interview respondents:

Well it [cycling] was really the only way. Cause there was such a tremendous detour using public transport ... well the time factor, it was horrendous (RJ14, Manchester, male, 1930s).

Well I had ridden a bicycle to school and it was just slightly easier. I didn't have the long walk to the bus stop ... I didn't have to change buses, it was just easier to go on the bike (RJ03, London, female, 1950s).

... when I started I didn't think I earned very much and by the time I'd paid, well fare to work, I thought this is not on. So if I went on my bike it wouldn't cost me anything (RJ87, London, male, 1950s).

Because ... I could cycle non stop from the house ... but if I, I took the bus, I had to change bus in, in the centre of town and that, that gap in the journey made it, made it longer ... And because the, the buses were travelling along busy roads so it was, it was possible to keep up with the buses basically (RJ77, Glasgow, male, 1980s).

I think ... that there was also the sort of context of health awareness coming in, that it was actually quite healthy to try [to cycle] (RJ99, London, female, 1980s).

Some men and women did not cycle by preference but felt they had little alternative, often because of the nature of their shift work and the lack of suitable public transport:

> Well I used to get up at about, I used to get up at about six o'clock I think
> and I would cycle, it was the only way, there was no other way of doing it
> ... there was no public, there was no buses at that time. I had to cycle to the
> station which was about four miles (RJ82, London, male, 1950s).

> That's when the bicycle came in. It was very handy when I worked night
> shift, particularly if you started late and you finished early in the morning
> and there was no public transport (RJ46, Glasgow, male, 1970s).

However, others chose to cycle because of a positive decision to avoid public
transport because they found it crowded, uncomfortable and smoky:

> I'm afraid I never liked travelling on trams ... they were never very
> comfortable and if you went on the top deck it was very uncomfortable
> because there was smoking on the upper deck. I would sooner ride a bike
> (RJ32, Manchester, male, 1930s).

Whereas men and women gave roughly the same reasons for choosing to cycle
(though as shown in Table 6.5 the number of women who cycled was small), the
reasons they gave for not cycling were rather different. Men were more concerned
about the lack of a secure place to leave their cycle, cited laziness, the weather and
the need to look smart for work; whereas women most often said they did not cycle
because they were afraid of cycling in urban traffic (or in the case of some young
women that their parents expressed this fear and they were forbidden from cycling
to work), that they never considered cycling to work (though they may have cycled
for leisure), or that they could not afford to purchase a bike. Some women also
complained about the effects of the weather and the need to be smart for work, but
women were much more likely than men to avoid cycling because they had to
undertake other tasks after work (such as shopping or collecting children), which
would be difficult to accomplish on a bicycle. The following quotations illustrate a
number of these points:

> If I'd got to look particularly smart for some reason to see somebody, and
> you've got to keep yourself spick and span. Can't always do it on bicycle, it
> depends on the weather, so any things like that would have changed the
> routine (RJ41, London, male, 1940s).

> There might have been the odd days [I cycled] but in the main once you got
> the car you know. It was far more convenient (RJ31, London, male, 1960s).

> Once you get a car it's very tempting when the weather turns bad to just say,
> oh I'm not going to cycle this morning ... I think speed was the essence at
> that time too, and availability of parking. Parking would be alright for a car
> but for a cycle sometimes a bit difficult. It was easy to park the car, and it
> was safe 'cos you can lock it, but with a bike you can lock it and still
> get/still lose it (RJ24, Manchester, male, 1960s/1970s).

> I have always thought it [cycling] was really dangerous and it kind of
> terrified me a bit (RJ97, small town, female, 1980s/1990s).

During the 1930s and 1940s approximately one fifth of men cycled to work
(and around one tenth of women): at this time cycling was seen by many younger
workers as a cheap and efficient means of transport in cities that were small
enough to cycle across easily, and in traffic conditions that were not unduly
threatening. However, even at this time, many women (and some men) were
reluctant to cycle, either because of the traffic or the inconvenience of braving
British weather conditions and having to change clothes on arrival at work. From
the 1950s cycling rapidly declined in popularity and, although some have started
cycling for health reasons in the 1980s, the number of people who regularly cycle
to work remains small. The attitudes consistently expressed by respondents who
travelled to work at different times in the twentieth century, suggest that cycling is
never likely to provide a regular means of commuting for more than a minority of
workers. Given favourable traffic conditions, and appropriate distances between
home and work (in a relatively flat environment), it may be possible to increase
levels of cycling significantly. But for most workers cycling is likely to become
increasingly unattractive as they get older, gain more responsible positions at work
or have to combine commuting trips with other tasks.

Travelling to Work by Public Transport

Attitudes to the use of public transport varied more than those towards cycling and
reasons for using particular modes (trams, trolley buses, buses, trains) varied
depending on the perceived quality of the public transport system available in a
particular time and place. These detailed variations between places and modes
cannot be examined in this chapter. However, in all three cities the overwhelming
reasons given for choosing to use public transport, by both men and women in all
time periods, were consistent: a combination of low cost and lack of alternative.
The following quotes illustrate these themes:

> Well tram cars was ... the mode of transport ... That was the normal mode
> of transport and it was very cheap in these days. That was the only mode of
> transport ... You'd no option (RJ49, Glasgow, male, 1930s).

> In 1955 the area where I lived ... was quite a poor area. I mean we didn't
> have then what we've got now and ... no-one had a car either. The, the best
> facility to get me from like the dock area to the main station, tube station,
> was a bus. There was no other choice, or walk, which I did do quite often ...
> There was no other choice (RJ91, London, male, 1950s).

> I didn't have any other form of transport and very few people, in those days
> anyway, had cars, particularly coming from the council estate where I did, it
> was a rarity. So, I mean, everyone travelled by bus whether it was to work
> or social ... or whatever. I mean it was just a natural thing, everyone
> automatically went by bus (RJ64, Manchester, male, 1960s).

> I was going to continue to work and I thought ... it's uneconomical just ... to run a car for one person, and I thought I can just as easily go by train, it wouldn't cost me anything cause we had free travel (RJ87, Manchester, female, 1990s).

Throughout the period from 1930 there were a number of respondents who could have travelled to work by car but chose to commute by public transport. A number of reasons were given for such choices, including the desire to avoid traffic congestion (cited in all time periods), preferring public transport to driving and the ability to do other tasks whilst being transported by bus or train rather than having to drive. However, there were marked gender differences in such responses with men most likely to leave their car at home because of perceived traffic congestion, but women more likely to state that they enjoyed travelling by public transport. Many women also stressed the value they placed on being able to undertake other tasks whilst travelling (citing reading, knitting and talking to friends as important) whilst men not only commented on this less frequently but were much more likely to work whilst travelling rather than engage in more relaxing activities. These patterns are again quite stable over time and can illustrated by a selection of quotes:

> I could drive, I had the use of my father's car ... when I was in London, but I really found it was too much of a nuisance, because even then it was virtually impossible to find a parking space (RJ83, London, female, 1960s).

> And I think really I, I enjoyed the bus journeys because I could read. I always read on bus journeys (RJ85, London, female, 1970s).

> I drove for about a month and I thought it just isn't worth it, it's quicker to go on the train. I can just work on the train, its more comfortable on the train, I can meet people on the train, and so I, I just opted to get rid of the company car (RJ89, London, male, 1990s).

> I've got quite used to getting the bus now and I've, I've met a few people, who I've known through getting the bus with, and I quite like having a chat with them in the morning (RJ65, Manchester, female, 1990s).

Reasons given for disliking public transport are very much the inverse of the above comments. Both men and women complained that public transport took too long or was unreliable and men, especially, often stated that once they had access to a car they would use it rather than continue to travel by public transport. Both men and women also cited the high cost of public transport as a disincentive, leading to greater use of cycles and walking in the 1930s and 1940s but increased car use from the 1960s. Issues of unreliability were quite closely related to specific locations, with Glasgow respondents especially citing a period of strikes affecting public transport provision which forced them to use other forms of transport. Men, in particular, regularly expressed a general dislike of public transport because of the lack of privacy; whereas many women valued the opportunity to travel with others and saw public transport as part of their social community. Overall, most men placed more value on flexibility, privacy and independence and thus avoided public transport when they could. Thus in the 1930s and 1940s men gained this privacy and independence by cycling, but from the 1960s substituted the private car for the bicycle. Relatively few men or women cited concerns about safety as reasons for not using public transport. Although a small number of female respondents avoided particular locations, the fact that most journeys to work occurred in the day time, when plenty of other commuters were around, meant that safety was not an issue for commuters unless they were on shift work. Again, these themes can be illustrated by selected quotes:

> The days I did have to go on the bus I used to get extremely annoyed and, that was if it was raining, and it, it put me out for the whole day ... I'd got, just an obsession, that I was not going to travel on a [bus] (RJ35, London, male, 1930s).

> Maybe if you were in a hurry, but just more or less walked it cause as I say, well you used to count every penny. You didn't take the tram unless you were in a hurry. You walked everywhere (RJ51, Glasgow, female, 1930s).

> It wasn't a particularly good area then, any more than I think it is now, and shall we say standing about for trains, buses, for the last bus you know at half past eleven, quarter to twelve at night on, on your own, shall we say it wasn't desirable if you could alter it (RJ80, London, female, 1960s).

> Yes, we definitely had two cars at that stage, and the journey/I did try the railway journey to start with, but it ... involved a change which was fairly difficult and it wasn't sensible. Things tended to go wrong on the railways ... and it became a bit unmanageable (RJ81, London, male, 1960s).

> I've never been on public transport since, other than when the car was being serviced. It's a very difficult place to get to on public transport ... but by car it takes perhaps three quarters of an hour (RJ26, London, male, 1970s).

> The trouble is my little eight-minute journey, to do it by public transport would be two buses ... there's no direct route for me from work. ... It's door to door, it's just convenience (RJ92, London, male, 1990s).

Although the proportion of people travelling to work by public transport has declined since the 1980s, for much of the period studied use of public transport has been quite stable and buses and trains continue to be important for many commuters, especially in London. It can be suggested that the switch towards motor vehicles, especially from the 1960s, has been more at the expense of walking and cycling to work than at the expense of public transport. Attitudes to public transport are quite consistent over time. Where cheap and reliable public transport is provided, on routes that link residential areas and workplaces, many people favour public transport. This is especially true for women who not only utilise public transport because they have fewer alternatives, but also express some preference for travelling by bus or train. However, attitudes of men are rather different, with a strong dislike of communal forms of transport expressed by many men. The implications for more sustainable urban transport of such attitudes, which seem deeply entrenched and consistent over time, are clear. Whilst improvements to public transport will win some people back to trains, buses and mass transit systems; amongst some men there is a much more deep-seated objection to public transport which will need to be overcome.

Commuting by Car

Although for most of the period men were much more likely than women to commute by car, both men and women gave similar reasons for using cars, mainly citing speed, convenience and lack of suitable public transport on routes travelled. However, there are important variations over time, and between locations. Car use was much lower in London than elsewhere, but in all three cities in the 1930s and 1940s, many who were car owners chose not to use their cars for work. They took the view that cars were for pleasure activities and public transport was appropriate for commuting:

> If you had access to a car at that stage ... you would have used that for leisure only. It would not have occurred to you to use it for work (RJ04, Manchester, male, 1950s).

> Now taking the car involved driving to the Blackwall tunnel and going round that way, so I would never take the car just to go to work. I would only take it if I was doing something else in the evening (RJ43, London, male, 1950s).

Two principal factors encouraged men (and some women) to abandon public transport and use their cars for commuting as well as pleasure. First, as journeys to work became more complex, due to the increasing suburbanisation of the population and the decentralisation of employment, public transport routes became less convenient. Longer cross-city journeys led some people to switch transport modes:

> Yes I got my first car in 1954 ... I didn't want a car to travel through Manchester to get to Blackley, but I knew when I was offered this job at Alderley Edge that I would have to do it because there was no cross-country transport at all. It was just hopeless, so I decided to have a car (RJ15, Manchester, female, 1950s).

> Yes, I got a car at that point because to travel to x was quite awkward. To do it by public transport would mean ... a bus journey, an underground journey, and another bus journey ... so it really wasn't terribly convenient, so I'd managed to accrue a little capital and I bought a car (RJ39, male, Glasgow, 1950s).

> It's an awkward journey ... you're sort of going into part of London, on to the sort of perimeter, and then move out again across the river ... It's still

London but there's no direct transport. That's really why I use the car. And of course it was still a company car (RJ91, London, male, 1970s).

As indicated above, the rise of the company car (or a car-user's allowance) as a normal part of many jobs was also a key factor in encouraging vehicle use. Many men in the 1950s and 1960s chose not to use their own cars for commuting, but as soon as they had access to a company car they felt quite justified in using it all the time. In many cases the need to use a car whilst at work was an additional factor pushing commuters away from public transport. These attitudes were clearly expressed by a number of respondents who explained why they did not use public transport:

Because I had the [company] car and I would be likely to need the car at any time at work, or one of my colleagues might borrow it (RJ01, Manchester, male, 1950s).

No, if my [company] car rarely had a breakdown. If it was going to be off the road for a day or two, then of course there was another car I could get (RJ38, Glasgow, male, 1950s).

... I went to work by car. Very often you use the car an awful lot because ... you're repeatedly going out to firms ... and you were paid so much for using your car ... so you see you had a good reason for it really (RJ08, London, male, 1950s).

Women were mostly about 20 years behind men in adopting motor vehicles as their principal means of commuting and, although this partly relates to issues of cost and access, there appear to be deeper attitudinal differences between men and women with respect to driving. Whereas men mostly stated that they enjoyed driving, and that it gave them the independence, privacy and control lacking in public transport, many women (including those who drove regularly) said that they disliked driving and only used a car because there really was no alternative. Many women expressed real fear of learning to drive, and concern about traffic, weather conditions and other road hazards:

I did think of learning, I think I did try at some point, but I just really, really hated it and just didn't want to do it. Just, just didn't like driving (RJ67, Manchester, female, 1960s).

Well, I thought about learning to drive, but I thought if my car breaks down and I don't know anything about cars, and if I got a big bill how am I going to pay it, so that put me right off (RJ21, Glasgow, female, 1960s).

Took on driving and one morning it was icy, and the car did just a little skate, and I lost my nerve completely, fortunately near home ... Only got into the car once about three months later and got out within a short time (RJ25, Manchester, female, 1970s).

In contrast, the reasons men gave for not driving related mainly to cost, traffic congestion (especially in London and from the 1970s), problems with parking (again especially from the 1970s), and concern about theft of or damage to the vehicle:

> I could have done [used the car], yes, but the parking was/I would have had to pay for parking all day (RJ64, Manchester, male, 1970s).

> … but as I said earlier it, I find it almost impossible to run a car in London for, for sort of convenience, and it's very difficult to find parking (RJ88, London, male, 1980s/1990s).

> It [car use] was a theoretical possibility, but not in practice. Difficult to use because of the, the road conditions and the, the absence of parking and it, it took as long or longer, and you didn't get any free time to read your newspaper, and it cost more (RJ86, London, male, 1980s).

In general men and women expressed slightly different fears and concerns about driving, and they also had different responses to them. Whereas women who experienced fear of driving often gave up commuting by car, most men carried on despite the irritation of congestion or concerns about car theft. These gender differences are also highlighted in differences in the frequency with which men and women travelled as passengers in cars. Whereas men were car passengers in only 2.5 per cent of all commuting journeys undertaken by car by men, the figure for women was 10 per cent overall and over 20 per cent in the 1960s. Even in the 1990s women were more likely than men to commute as a car passenger, although the differential had narrowed considerably. The development of dual career households also had a significant impact on car use. Whereas in the 1930s and 1940s the majority of married women either did not work, or worked close to home (partly constrained by their limited access to transport), by the late-twentieth century most married women had some form of employment. The need for both partners to travel to work, often over considerable distances, was a major factor in expanding car use by women in the late-twentieth century.

> Well, then I acquired my own car and mainly it was just so I'd got more convenience and could come and go as I wanted. And my husband had a, use of a firm's car, but he was off in opposite directions, and occasionally it was convenient for him to drop me off but not always, and I decided I'd have my own car (RJ87, Manchester, female, 1960s).

Analysis of car use since the 1930s suggests that there have been changes in the attitudes of both men and women, and that, in general, the attitudes of women towards car use have followed those of men but with a lag of some 20-30 years. Thus in the 1930s and 1940s most men who owned cars were reluctant to use them for commuting and were reasonably happy to use public transport (though more critical of it than women). By the 1960s and 1970s these attitudes had changed and although men found some aspects of driving irritating they were reluctant to abandon their cars. However women still had limited access to motor vehicles, partly through income constraints, but also through choice as many women either preferred public transport or feared driving. However, by the 1980s such differentials were disappearing and it would seem that the attitudes of men and women are now more similar.

A Closer Look at Gender Differences in the Journey to Work

Some of the key differences in commuting patterns between men and women are outlined above. However, it is also possible to examine these in more detail and to assess the relationship between commuting behaviour and some of the social, economic and familial constraints that affect men and women differently. Such issues come through quite clearly in the detailed comments made by female respondents, though not all women experienced the same levels of constraint.

Many women did at times feel vulnerable when travelling on foot or by public transport and the basic factors that structure such vulnerability have changed little over time. Thus a woman working in London as a library assistant in the late 1930s made the journey from Ealing to Kew by bus and on foot despite having some misgivings: 'Yes that's right and walking meant going through Acton, not a very nice walk that end of it' (RJ15, London, female, 1930s). Another woman felt especially vulnerable during the blackout in wartime London: 'Well you took precautions you see ... if I was late cause sometimes I worked till about 11 at night, I'd walk in the middle of the road ... I would never have anybody behind me' (RJ29, London, female, 1940s). Public transport could also be threatening as shown by a female respondent working in Glasgow in the 1950s who refused to use the train to travel to work despite living close to the station:

> I never ever liked that station. It was in a quiet area and the streets weren't well lit at the times, and you passed lots of old tenement properties which were really dingy then ... They've all been knocked down now you know, but at that time it wasn't a nice area to walk in. I was frightened. I never used the station unless I really had to (RJ23, Glasgow, female, 1950s).

Some women had complex journeys to work by public transport that ate in to the time they had available for other activities: 'I think I usually did go on that electric train into Manchester and then hike across Manchester and get either a tram or a bus depending on the time of day' (RJ15, Manchester, female, 1940s). But many others deliberately reduced their journey to work to minimize the time and money spent on travelling. One respondent recalled how both she and her husband changed their work after being re-housed in Manchester in the 1960s:

> A wasn't earning a lot and I was only part time. We thought well I could do with getting a job nearer to home so. Anyway we thought about so – cut a long story short – A did get a job at/as caretaker on the estate just about 10 minutes walk from where we lived and then two or three months later I was able to join him at school as/oh initially I'd just started on as a Dinner Lady

> doing dinner duties but then they wanted a cleaner so I gave up the dinner duties and became cleaner so A and I were caretaker and cleaner at this particular school (RJ19, Manchester, female, 1960s).

Although by the 1970s more women were travelling to work by car, they often did so as passengers. Overall, 67.5 per cent of respondents who travelled to work as a passenger were women. Women also used cars in a way that fitted in with their husband's routine. A woman who had part-time clerical work in Manchester illustrates this clearly:

> Well I, I again worked in the afternoons. B used to come home for his lunch by car, we'd have our lunch and he would take me to Christie's and then go onto work himself because it was so near ... Not quite on his route but very little out of his route (RJ17, Manchester, female, 1970s).

The differential journey to work experiences of men and women were also structured by life-cycle factors. Whereas for men the mean distance travelled to work increased with life-cycle stage and career progression in all time periods, for women the reverse was true. In all time periods single women living at home had the longest journeys to work (similar to and, before 1940, slightly longer than that of men), but the distance women travelled to work decreased on marriage and, especially, once they had children. For instance, before 1920, the mean travel to work distance for single women living at home was 4.6 km (compared to 4.3 for men), but for women with children under 15 it was just 1.6 km (compared to 7.0 km for men at the same stage of the life cycle). Moreover, women with children under 15 in the 1960s had a shorter journey to work than single women living at home in the 1920s. Life cycle and family constraints effectively counteracted the impact of new transport technologies in extending travel distances and offering a wider choice of employment opportunities. These constraints also operated on travel times as, despite the fact that women continued to use slower forms of transport, women with children under 15 consistently had the shortest travel to work times.

There were often a whole series of constraints that restricted job opportunities for women, and thus affected their journey to work, though they were not always unwelcome. In some cases a move to a smaller labour market (prompted by a husband's change of job) meant that there was little work available and women had little option but to stay at home with children. One respondent who married in 1944 was forced to give up work as a junior Civil Servant when her husband's work took her to Keswick (Cumbria) in 1946, though she seemed not to resent this fact:

> Well yes they usually/by that time of course married women could stay at work. You know before the war Civil Servants, you had to leave if you got married then but by that time you were allowed to stay on. But it wasn't any option for me because my husband's work was in Keswick you see ... I was quite happy (RJ16, Manchester/Keswick, female, 1940s).

Another female respondent emphasised that a part-time job fitted in best with other responsibilities including caring for sick relatives: 'Yes, I think definitely while the boys were at home and also there was a lot of illness around my family one way or another wasn't there and I was always hopping off somewhere' (RJ17, Manchester, female, 1940s). The same respondent also commented on the pressure that she felt that society brought on married women to return to work in the 1960s - pressure that was not always entirely welcome:

> Well I think in those days there was a lot of pressure for women to go back to work. I was quite happy as a housewife and I was quite happy on my own. I mean if I was all day on my own I could find something that interested me and I'd be quite happy ... Yes a cabbage if you didn't use your brain and do something and the pressure was on there from, from your peers you know – well what are you doing, are you still at home (RJ17, Manchester, female, 1960s).

For many women work that offered hours that enabled them to continue to act as full-time wives and mothers was essential. This usually required work close to home and the careful juggling of commitments and dependence on relatives. A woman with a young family who returned to work as a secretary in Manchester in the 1950s stressed the importance of short hours and local work:

> Yes I worked there a couple of years I know and I was lucky there I managed to get 9 till 3 you see and the boys were at school and I was home when they got home and I walked there ... No I don't think I could have taken anywhere/well I couldn't have gone out of the area, no not with the kids being at school and I had nobody here (RJ20, Manchester, female, 1950s).

Another respondent recalled how she always came home from work to make her husband's lunch when newly married in the 1950s: 'Yes I finished/I had a different lunchtime/so I was able to get home in plenty of time for A./to get him a sandwich' (RJ19, Manchester, female, 1950s). Shortage of money meant that she returned to part-time work quickly after her first child and continued to combine work and motherhood through the 1950s and 1960s, leading to a complex daily routine:

> I would take J to my mothers each morning, 20 minutes walk there, I'd leave J at my mothers etc. then my mother would meet me as I came out of work so my mother had her walk home again and I had my 20 minute walk home again with J ready to be in in time to see to A's lunch when he came for his lunch-time break (RJ19, Manchester, female, 1950s).

Although a lone mother with children did not have to worry about getting her husband's lunch, the financial need to work was much more severe. One respondent in this position in the 1960s stressed how the need to be close to home and to her mother (for childcare) constrained her choice of work place and

sometimes led to complex arrangements whilst she worked in a local telephone exchange on the outskirts of Glasgow:

> Well my mother looked after them for me ... she looked after them during the day and I used to help her at night with any jobs that she had to do, so we worked it between us. And then again I sometimes had a split shift ... and I was able to get home at lunchtime maybe for two hours or so and used to maybe take my baby a walk ... Well sometimes my children stayed with my mother and they were nearer school you know, for if I was maybe going out early in the morning maybe then they'd stay with her the night before and it could be worked out that way (RJ21, Glasgow, female, 1960s).

When the local telephone exchange closed she had the choice of working in either Glasgow or Motherwell and (still with child-care responsibilities) again chose the shortest journey to work: 'I had a choice. I could have gone to Glasgow or Motherwell and I thought well I'll have a big enough (journey) getting from Bothwell to Motherwell, what would it be like if I went to Glasgow' (RJ21, Glasgow, female, 1960s). Such constraints on employment opportunities, linked to financial and social pressures which often pushed women back to work as their children got older, obviously had a knock-on effect on the distance women were prepared to travel to work and where they chose to live. The need to fit work around other responsibilities, together with the fact that some were reluctant to work at all, led to employment and housing choices which minimised travel times despite the fact that women continued to use slower forms of transport than men.

Changes in the Journey to Work Since the 1970s

Travel to and from work forms a particularly large component of the everyday mobility of people in their 30s, and accounts provided by respondents in this age group living in Lancaster and Morecambe illustrate change since the 1970s. They again emphasise gender differences and the extent to which people's travel patterns (particularly those of women) were complicated by family commitments. By the 1970s most men in their 30s used the car to travel to work and Roger summed up the way in which, once acquired, car use became the norm for many people:

> I used to walk to work before I got a car and it perhaps took me 15, 20 minutes, but in a car I can do it in 5, so you know it was, it was a time saving thing as well wasn't it ... And I think once you get that freedom of your own, your own transport you're away aren't you. You're not going to walk to a bus stop and wait in the rain perhaps for a bus when you can just jump in your car and, and off you go (R50, Roger, age 30s, born 1938, Lancaster).

However, not all men became totally car dependent, and Tony stressed that in a one-car family in the 1970s he was able to walk to work and left the car for his wife to use for shopping and the school run. In this case the car was deliberately being left for the more complex journeys that were difficult by public transport:

> I didn't use it for work too much because it was left at home for other half to pick kids up from school and, and yea do her shopping in and stuff like that. She used it more than I did at that stage (R52, Tony, age 30s, born 1939, Lancaster).

However, in the 1960s and 1970s the majority of women in Lancaster did not have access to a car on a regular basis. If they travelled to work by car it was often as a passenger, and many had complex and difficult journeys on foot or by public transport in which they combined a number of functions. Thus Ruth depended on her husband to take her to work, or if he was not available took the bus, and Valerie had a long trek across town to take one child to nursery and one to school before walking back to work.

> D [husband] took me before he went to work, cause I, I started at half past 8 and you know he obviously dropped me off and then went back up to, to work ... Yes, yes unless he had some sort of meeting and then I'd go on the bus from the square, cause there was still sort of quite regular buses then from the square (R8, Ruth, age 30s, born 1936, Morecambe).

> Well I'm sure we left home about, it must have been about quarter to 8, and I would take J/I think he was in/no he wouldn't be in a pushchair then, we would both be walking. We would all walk to N, which is like 20 minutes or so. I would drop J off at N, then take, walk back up to G Road, and take M to B School. And then I would walk into town and go to work (R76, Valerie, age 30s, born 1940, Lancaster).

Very similar themes emerge from the testimonies that relate to travel to and from work in 2001/2. Although some respondents felt that in principle it would be good to travel by public transport, in practice a combination of time and convenience meant that more often than not they commuted by car. Thus Daniel somewhat unwillingly used his car for his long journey to work because of the perceived unreliability of the trains, Craig was deterred by the longer journey time travelling from Morecambe by bus, and Julia avoided the bus because of the inconvenience and long walk to an appropriate bus stop to take her directly to work.

> Well more recently it's/I mean I've gone in the car a lot more often because of the problems on the trains and reliability, but I think in principle I've been going on the trains because I can count that as work time by doing an hour's work (R4, Daniel, age 30s, born 1971, Lancaster).

> Well yea I think about it (using the bus). Um I haven't really/I would like to use it more as I say for coming for work especially but um it just seems to be more hassle, it's easier to come in the car ... Well it would mean setting off earlier than when I come in the car. I think it's because the traffic's so

heavy in the mornings. The bus has to come virtually the same route as the car would come, and it, it's, well it's still very slow (R60, Craig, age 30s, born 1962, Morecambe).

Convenience. It's a long walk from here to the nearest bus stop to get me to (work) 'cause the nearest bus stop is either down at the bus station or at the infirmary. So we're talking a good quarter of an hour's walk and if the weather's nice it's not so bad, nip down the hill onto the canal towpath and you're there. If it's a horrible day with the rain which is more often the case it's pretty horrendous really. And then coming home it's all uphill and you/the last thing you want at the end of the day when you're getting off the bus at 6 o'clock in the evening is then to start trekking up all these hills, especially if the weather's bad. So convenience (R10, Julia, age 30s, born 1968, Lancaster).

Some respondents (especially women) did try to share transport to work with colleagues, and for Nicola this seemed to work well, but often varied and complex routines made it difficult to co-ordinate travel. As in earlier time periods many women combined a number of functions in their journey to work and Diane felt that it was the need to take her daughter to nursery that often prevented her walking or using public transport. In contrast, Jane had little alternative. She did not have access to a car and often walked to work because buses were not running when she had to travel to work for an early shift. Occasionally she would get a taxi, but cost prohibited this most of the time:

I share. I get a lift from A up the corridor, so I get a lift with a colleague … Because it's, it's very convenient, there's only one car coming … and I don't have to pay for parking. That sounds terrible. And it, it is convenient and … we've got into a nice routine of getting a lift … No because the bus route where I live isn't direct. Sometimes I do but it takes me easily, I can leave the house at 8 o'clock and get in after 9 because I have walk towards a bus stop that will take me straight to work and sometimes they go round the houses … you know so I try to avoid a bus if I can (R5, Nicola, age 30s, born 1963, Lancaster).

Because I've got N and if wasn't for my little girl then I probably would walk. Although now having said that not all the time cause if it's a nasty cold day no I wouldn't, I'd probably get public transport. But I did, I walked, and those days I didn't walk I'd catch the bus/But once I came back to work after having N then I couldn't like take her and all her stuff/ And, and now of course it's not particularly that 'cause like some mornings I, I still try and walk with N and she likes it. But I've worked out the only day of the week I can walk is a Tuesday, cause on a Monday I have to take her up to nursery … so I have to go all the way up … and then all the way back down to work and then again at lunch time I have to go and collect her and then come all the way back. Tuesday I don't have to do that, I just come to work and then that's it (R44, Diane, age 30s, born 1971, Morecambe).

When I do an early shift I walk unless it's absolutely chucking it down with rain and then I will give in and get a taxi. And if I'm on an afternoon turn I generally get the bus, but I sometimes walk ... Necessity, there isn't a bus to get me there in time and I object to paying five pounds to get in in a taxi. So I only do it when I'm either very very lazy and need an extra half an hour in bed or if it's, if the weather's really bad then I'll get a taxi then (R21, Jane, age 30s, born 1971, Lancaster).

Thus although rates of car use have increased for women, and mean journey to work distances have increased, the factors that structure decisions about what form of transport to use for this most essential component of everyday mobility have remained relatively unchanged. Many people are deterred from using public transport by a combination of perceived inconvenience and unreliability, and the complex travel patterns of women in particular further constrain their options. Despite almost equal overall rates of car use by men and women today, it can be suggested that gender inequalities in travel still exist, with women more constrained by family and related responsibilities.

Conclusions

This chapter has examined the key changes that have occurred in the journey to work over the twentieth century and, in particular, has emphasised the ways in which gender differentials in access to work and associated constraints on the journey to work have operated since the 1890s. Although some aspects of the journey to work have changed dramatically – linked especially to changes in transport technology and the changing location of residences and workplaces - other aspects have remained remarkably stable. The amount of time that people spend travelling to work has changed little since the 1920s, and most gender-based differences have been very stable over time. Likewise, the factors that structure journey to work decisions have been relatively constant during the twentieth century.

What comes through most clearly is, first, the way in which the journey to work has always been closely linked into a wide range of other aspects of social, economic, cultural and technological change; second, the way in which journeys to work are themselves closely linked to life-style and life-cycle decisions; and, third, the fact that there is a great deal of variability in the ways in which journey to work decisions are taken and preferences expressed. Thus although certain trends are very stable, and there are some predictable and obvious changes over time, at the individual level there is a wide range of complex factors that explain why particular individuals make the decisions that they do. This is especially true with respect to the relationship between residential mobility and the journey to work. Whilst in general, and as hypothesised at the start of this chapter, the ability to commute over longer distances has led to more flexibility in where people lived, and thus a reduction in residential mobility due to job change; and whilst men have, in general, benefited more from such changes than women; there are many individual examples of respondents who put up with long and inconvenient journeys to work because they did not want to move house. Thus one respondent who worked in London as a social worker in the 1950s chose a long and unpleasant journey to work mainly because of a preference for living in a particular part of London:

> Yes, I always intended to (move) but I never got round to it. There weren't that many places to live around Walworth that you know, it was a very working-class area of London and there weren't little flats and bed-sitters in that area, they were all in Earl's Courts, Bayswater in those days and Bloomsbury, and there wasn't, I intended to move and never did, and then I got a boyfriend in Blackheath so there was even less incentive (R03, London, female, 1950s).

Later in life the same woman put up with a long and complicated journey to work because of uncertainty both about her job and other aspects of her life:

> Well I liked the flat really which I suppose is mainly it, and also I was beginning to think I'd had enough of social work and everything by then and I didn't know whether I was, it was all in the melting pot, and my mother was very ill which was one of the things, and I didn't quite know what was going to happen if I was going to be called back home to help out or whatever, and then in the middle of it all I met D and so that was all a possibility, and so I just went on for three years (R03, London, female, 1960s).

The theme of uncertainty, at work or at home, influencing journey to work decisions, and often leading to people undertaking long and inconvenient journeys rather than move their home or workplace comes through in many responses. There is rarely one simple explanation of why particular journey to work arrangements are made and, beneath the broad trends outlined above, there is a range of individual decisions reflecting life-style choices and external constraints, all of which influence commuting behaviour.

Chapter 7

Travel for Leisure and Pleasure:
Children Playing and Hanging Around

Introduction

The previous two chapters have concentrated on those trips that occur most regularly and over which we have least control. Most children have to go to school and the majority of adults below retirement age are in paid employment. Travel to school and to work thus not only take place most days, but also offer relatively few choices regarding where and when we travel and, in some cases, even how we travel. However, total travel behaviour comprises many more journeys that are both less essential and over which the travelling public has much more choice. These range from essential travel like shopping for food that can be scheduled to fit in with other activities, through travel that may be seen as a combination of duty and pleasure (for instance to visit relatives), to trips that are undertaken purely for pleasure, such as visits to a cinema or just going for a walk or ride. In the next two chapters a selection of these trips is examined, particularly with reference to the travel behaviour of children and teenagers, to assess the extent to which travel for what may be broadly termed leisure and pleasure has changed over the past 60 years.

It is difficult to define precisely what leisure time is, and which trips are undertaken for pleasure. First, many journeys, especially today, have multiple purposes and thus travel to or from work may be combined with shopping, dropping in to see a relative, or a trip to the gym. Thus one trip combines both the essential function of getting to and from work and an activity that can be classed as leisure and over which the traveller has some control. Second, there is a large grey area of activities that are both essential for everyday life, but that also fulfil some leisure and pleasure functions. Shopping is the most obvious example. Although it is necessary to buy food and some other items on a regular basis, for some at least shopping can also be classed as a leisure activity that provides access to goods that are seen to improve the quality of life in a society based on high mass consumption. Similarly, although for most people, most of the time, visiting relatives is a pleasure, in some instances meeting the demands of an elderly or infirm relative on a regular basis can become both a duty and a chore that is as much part of an unavoidable everyday routine as the journey to work. Thus distinctions between which activities are for leisure or pleasure, and which are required duties, are indistinct and may vary from person to person and for any individual from time to time. For simplicity, in these chapters we consider all travel that is not for work or education, and focus especially on five categories of trip: young children's play and teenagers hanging around (Chapter 7); travel for entertainment; trips for sport; travel for shopping; and longer outings for pleasure, overnight visits to relatives or friends, and holidays (Chapter 8).

There are many factors that will have affected travel for leisure and pleasure by both adults and children over the past 60 years. In the main these are much the same as the trends outlined in Chapter 2 that have affected all forms of travel behaviour. Most importantly, time budgets show that over the past half-century the amount of time available for leisure activities has increased from around four hours per day (averaged over the whole week) in 1961 to approximately six hours per day in 2001. This change has been experienced by both men and women, but for slightly different reasons. Whilst women have experienced a decrease in time spent on household tasks and personal care, the hours that women work in paid employment have increased. In contrast, working hours for men have decreased, time spent on personal care has also fallen, but the amount of time spent on household tasks has increased slightly (Patmore, 1983; National Statistics, 2004). This is reflected in changes in the reasons for travel reported in National Travel Surveys. As shown in Chapter 4, whereas in 1965 work and related travel accounted for almost 40 per cent of all recorded trips, by 1999/2001 this was less than 20 per cent. Conversely, the proportion of trips undertaken for shopping has almost doubled over the same period, and travel for social activities, sport and other personal business have all increased.

This increase in discretionary or leisure time has been accompanied by an equally important rise in real incomes, as most people have more money to spend on non-essential purchases and activities. Thus total real household disposable income has more than doubled 1971-2002 (National Statistics, 2004) and, although expenditure on most items has increased, the proportion of income spent on essential items such as housing and food has decreased relative to expenditure on travel, recreation, communication and household goods and services (Table 7.1). This trend, fuelled by the increased availability of credit in the late-twentieth and twenty-first centuries, has both changed activities such as shopping from a mainly functional activity to one that is also seen as leisure, and has seen a massive expansion in the demand for entertainment and diversions to fill increased leisure time both at home (for instance through computers, videos/DVDs and other media) and elsewhere. This increased demand for leisure activities outside the home has had an inevitable impact on travel behaviour: not only has expenditure on travel increased, but also expenditure abroad (associated with foreign holidays) and expenditure on virtual travel through computer communications. Whilst increased incomes have led to greater car ownership, new demands for leisure travel have also produced changes in travel modes with consequential effects in terms of urban traffic congestion and pollution.

Although most of the general trends that can be identified over the twentieth century indicate an increase in non-essential travel, there are some contrary arguments. In particular, it can be suggested that changed perceptions of the relative risk of travel around urban areas may have affected both the amount of

Table 7.1   Changes in Household Expenditure in the UK, 1971-2002 (Selected Indices 1971=100)

Expenditure category	1971	1981	1991	2002	% of total household expenditure (2002)
Housing, water and fuel	100	117	138	154	17.8
Transport	100	128	181	251	14.7
Recreation and culture	100	161	283	570	11.9
Restaurants and hotels	100	126	167	199	11.5
Food and non-alcoholic drink	100	105	117	138	9.1
Household goods and services	100	117	160	296	6.5
Clothing and footwear	100	120	187	371	5.7
Alcohol and tobacco	100	99	92	91	3.9
Communication	100	190	306	828	2.3
Health	100	125	182	179	1.5
Education	100	160	199	218	1.3
Household expenditure abroad	100	193	298	715	3.7

Source: National Statistics (2004) p. 94.

travel undertaken and, especially, destinations and times of travel for some people. Most research on the ways in which fear of crime affects the use of urban space focuses attention on the travel behaviour of women, the elderly and children. These are seen as potentially vulnerable groups who are most likely to modify their travel behaviour in response to media reports of crime or violence, even though the greatest risks have been shown to affect young men (Valentine, 1989; Pain, 1995; 1997; 2000; 2001). It can be suggested that over the past 60 years, whereas opportunities for leisure travel have increased greatly for most people, for some groups actual travel behaviour may have become more restricted because of changed perceptions of risk. Thus the elderly may be unwilling to go out at night, some women may avoid certain locations, especially if alone and, especially, parents may place more restrictions on the independent mobility of children (Hillman et al., 1990; Valentine and McKendrick, 1997). It can also be suggested that discretionary travel for leisure and pleasure will be more affected by such factors than travel to school or work: most journeys to work or for education take place during the day time over a well-known route, and often in the company of others travelling for the same purpose. In these circumstances risks are minimised. However, much discretionary travel for leisure and pleasure takes place in the evening, it may entail travelling to parts of town not often frequented, and it may bring the traveller face-to-face with groups that they do not normally confront. Thus, for an elderly couple a city centre may feel safe during the day time when it is full of shoppers, but more alienating at night when it is relatively deserted apart from crowds of youths hanging around apparently aimlessly. Such factors may place significant constraints on travel for leisure and pleasure for some people, and also influence the mode of transport used, driving travellers into the perceived safety of their car rather than using public transport.

The remainder of this chapter focuses on children and adolescents, and on changes in the ways in which they use urban space for informal leisure activities. First, and most extensively, we focus on children aged 10/11 (for whom the data outlined in Chapter 3 provide the longest time series) and examine changes in that most ubiquitous of childhood activities, independent play. Attention is focused especially on the extent to which parental controls have changed, on perceptions of risk, and how this has influenced children's travel for play. Second, we focus on adolescents aged 17/18 and examine changes in their use of urban space for non-essential social travel, focusing on visits to friends and the traditional teenage pursuit of hanging around in town. In particular, we examine changes in adolescent's contact with other youths and teenage gangs.

Changes in Independent Play by Children Aged 10/11

It can be suggested that independent outdoor play is one of the most important activities for young children. Not only does it provide children with fresh air and exercise, but also it provides an unparalleled opportunity to both generate creative play environments and acquire skills of independence and responsibility that are required to negotiate the outside world. Developmental psychologists and others stress the importance of play in developing a wide range of skills and competencies in children (Peplor and Rubin, 1982; Klein, Wirth and Linas, 2003; Sandberg, 2003; Thyssen, 2003) and, increasingly, geographers have begun to focus on the notion of children's geographies. The world of the child is different from that of the adult and the position of children in that world, and the opportunities that they have to explore it, are important formative experiences (Skelton and Valentine, 1998; Holloway and Valentine, 2000; Aitken, 2001). Thus recent research by Matthews, Limb and Taylor (2000) and by Skelton (2000) emphasises the importance of the street for children and adolescents and begins to counter some contemporary assumptions that children have been increasingly forced indoors and no longer make use of outdoor space. These papers provide important contemporary evidence, but present no data on change over time. In this chapter we begin to examine how both play for children aged 10/11, and the use of urban space by teenagers aged 17/18 (see below) has changed since the 1940s and 1950s.

Using data on everyday mobility collected from oral testimonies of four cohorts of respondents (Chapter 3) it is possible to provide both a brief quantitative summary of changes in travel behaviour related to children's play and, most importantly, use qualitative data to explore the experience of outdoor play by children aged 10/11, and how it has changed over time since the 1940s. In this section play is defined loosely as all trips outside the home to play in the streets or surrounding area, either alone or with friends, or to visit friends that live in the locality. We explore changes in the frequency with which such trips were made, the distances over which children travelled, how they moved around the urban area and the degree of freedom that children aged 10/11 had to negotiate their own mobility. In contrast to data on the journey to school, where inevitably the same trip is made twice a day for five days a week and approximately 40 weeks of the year, the pattern of mobility for all forms of outdoor play was much more varied with both the numbers and types trips being made depending on local circumstances.

Table 7.2   Characteristics of Children's Play and Visits to Friends: Children Aged 10/11, Lancaster and Morecambe

Cohort born:	1932-41	1962-71	1983/84	1990/91
Play:				
Mean distance travelled	0.6	0.4	0.5	0.5
Mean time spent travelling	8.4	5.4	6.9	6.9
Mode of travel (% of trips)				
Walk	100.0	99.9	97.8	96.8
Cycle	-	-	-	1.0
Car	-	0.1	2.2	2.2
Bus	-	-	-	-
Companions (% of trips)				
Alone	0.6	2.3	-	2.9
Other children	79.5	80.1	95.1	89.1
Adults/mixed group	19.9	17.6	4.9	8.0
Number of trips	17,250	8,582	4,586	10,278
Mean trips per person per yr	821.4	613.2	229.3	513.9
Visiting friends:				
Mean distance travelled	0.6	0.3	0.6	0.5
Mean time spent travelling	11.2	5.3	7.3	6.4
Mode of travel (% of trips)				
Walk	91.2	90.5	81.4	83.0
Cycle	-	7.1	8.2	11.4
Car	-	2.4	10.4	5.4
Bus	8.8	-	-	0.2
Companions (% of trips)				
Alone	55.2	39.3	40.6	54.9
Other children	32.1	41.7	49.0	38.1
Adults/mixed group	12.7	19.0	10.4	7.0
Number of trips	4,080	4,222	9,466	8,890
Mean trips per person per yr	194.3	301.6	472.3	445.0

Source: Everyday mobility sample, Lancaster/Morecambe, 2001-2003.

Although data are drawn from a relatively small number of individuals, these yield information on several thousand separate journeys for play and related activities when aggregated over a 12 month period, and the pattern of activity recorded for playing and visiting friends is consistent between the two urban areas of Lancaster/Morecambe and Manchester/Salford. Obviously the categorisation of such data is difficult and sometimes playing and visiting friends will overlap. In general, however, playing refers to informal trips made either alone or in company to play outside, whilst visiting friends refers to journeys made specifically to visit a particular person which could then be followed by play either indoors or out. The only real anomaly in the data is from the Manchester sample where one respondent made a number of unusually long journeys to visit friends, thus inflating the mean (Tables 7.2 and 7.3). These differences aside, the data show remarkable consistency over time, but the fact that such outliers exist emphasises the individual and variable nature of everyday mobility.

Table 7.3   Characteristics of Children's Play and Visits to Friends: Children Aged 10/11, Manchester and Salford

Cohort born:	1932-41	1962-71	1983/84	1990/91
Play:				
Mean distancetravelled	0.4	0.5	0.2	0.3
Mean time spent travelling	6.8	5.7	4.2	4.5
Mode of travel (% of trips)				
Walk	99.3	98.8	81.1	90.8
Cycle	-	1.0	18.9	5.8
Car	-	0.2	-	3.4
Bus	0.7	-	-	-
Companions (% of trips)				
Alone	9.6	14.7	-	-
Other children	58.9	57.1	82.1	96.6
Adults/mixed group	31.5	38.2	17.9	3.4
Number of trips	29,310	17,658	8,218	8,700
Mean trips per person per yr	1172.4	1103.6	410.9	435.0
Visiting friends:				
Mean distancetravelled	0.5	1.8*	0.9	0.4
Mean time spent travelling	7.9	7.0	4.9	4.2
Mode of travel (% of trips)				
Walk	94.6	95.1	91.8	93.5
Cycle	-	4.4	-	-
Car	0.1	0.4	8.2	6.5
Bus	5.3	0.1	-	-
Companions (% of trips)				
Alone	51.3	46.4	54.7	76.5
Other children	37.8	44.3	26.8	17.0
Adults/mixed group	10.9	9.3	18.5	6.5
Number of trips	7,266	6,790	4,650	8,950
Mean trips per person per yr	290.6	424.4	323.5	447.5

*Mean distance inflated by one respondent who travels (by car with parents) over 300km approximately twice a month to visit a friend.
Source: Everyday mobility sample, Manchester/Salford, 2001-2003.

With regard to playing, all journeys were short (the mean was 0.6 km or less in all cases and journey time was under nine minutes) and at all time periods the single most important means of transport was travel on foot, remaining at around 90 per cent even for those born 1991-1992. The lowest proportion of travel on foot was for those born 1983-1984 in Manchester where cycling was unusually prominent amongst our sample. Similarly, there has been little change in the level of independence that children aged 10/11 have for outdoor play. In most cases children met up with and travelled with others of the same age (remaining at around 90 per cent for those aged 10/11 at the time of the interview). There is some evidence that in the past children in Manchester were accompanied by an adult rather more than in Lancaster, but this differential disappeared for the cohort born 1990-1991. Overall, there is little evidence of any significant change since the 1940s in the pattern of outdoor play, with children aged 10/11 being allowed to play locally, within 1km of their home, in the company of other children and without adult supervision. However, one change that has occurred is the frequency with which such outdoor play takes place, with fewer trips to play recorded for those born since the 1980s compared to earlier cohorts. It also appears that in the past children had more supervised play than today, perhaps indicating the greater availability of parents to take children to a wide range of play spaces.

Similarly, there have been few changes in the patterns of travel to visit friends though, as noted above, this is more varied as the category includes both friends living locally and those further away. With the one exception noted above, mean distances and times are short (under 1km and 12 min), with travel on foot again the single most important mode (over 80 per cent) in each time period. The only significant change in travel mode is that in the 1940s travel by bus accounted for a significant minority of trips, and that in more recent cohorts this has been replaced by the car. In each time period the majority of children travelled independently (over 80 per cent travelled without an adult in each cohort) with the proportion of such travel that was accompanied changing little from the 1940s to the present. Thus, again, the quantitative evidence suggests that there has been much less change in the everyday mobility of children than might be expected. However, it is notable that whereas the number of trips for play has declined, trips to visit friends have increased. This may reflect the ways in which outings were constructed in the memories of respondents of different ages, but it may also suggest a move away from informal play towards more formal and regulated planned trips to visit friends.

Analysis of the qualitative testimonies given by respondents allows much more detailed assessment of the nature of everyday mobility for play and to visit friends, and also enables consideration of the constraints that were placed on children aged 10/11 and how these have changed over time. It can be suggested that dangers posed by the urban environment to children aged 10/11 can be classified into three main types: first, inherently dangerous places such as open water or derelict buildings; second risks that occur in particular and predictable places due to the activities of people, for instance dangers from road traffic or from railway lines; and, third, threats from other people, either children or adults, that

Box 7.1   Experiences of Playing by Water, Children Born 1932-1941

We would like, like if I was only walking on the canal you know there'd be the logs and stuff like that we'd be jumping on. I know it was dangerous at the time, but you don't think that kind of thing (R325, Derek, aged 10/11, born 1937, Salford).

And one interesting thing, there's a place, it's still there now, P Dam it's called, and it was a mine, a coal mine, and they had pit props in there but they were full of black grease and oil inside, and we used to swim in there and on them, and go home with a big black line right through your body. This was off the tar and the grease and it/but you couldn't let your parents see it 'cause you'd, you'd get told not to swim in there then (R351, Les, aged 10/11, born 1937, Salford).

I don't/well it [the canal] *was always too dirty and you never knew, there was dead dogs and all sorts in it. But some of them did go in the canal. You know these, the, the lads and that* (R328, Hilda, aged 10/11, born Manchester, 1940).

But the dangerous things we did it was horrendous. I mean I wonder how I lived through my childhood ... Well there was a huge pipe and it had to be 50 feet up, um ... A big huge pipe, like a huge water pipe, I'm talking really wide. And I had to walk across that to be in the boys gang. Now if I'd fallen I'd be dead or I'd have broke my back. And then I had to walk across the old ramshackled bridge on the canal and if that had broken I'd have drowned 'cause I couldn't swim. I just, I didn't have any/it was stupid actually, I didn't know it was dangerous. But I wanted to be in the boy's gang (R356, Pamela, aged 10/11, born 1937, Salford).

They weren't keen on us going to the canal really. The canal wasn't very far off and my mother wasn't very keen on us going near there ... One of my mates from school had been drowned there actually so (R110, Charles, aged 10/11, born 1934, Lancaster).

You could always go down there and meet dozens of kids from all around the S area. You'd congregate there and you'd swim around in the, the deep water before it went over the weir. And it was bloody dangerous looking back on it, but you didn't look at it that way then ... We did go on ice. But we sort of frowned on that because we lost a lad, we lost one of our mates in the big freeze of 1948. He went on the ice ... And in fear we kept off it after that, it worked (R52, Tony, aged 10/11, born 1939, Lancaster).

Source: Everyday mobility interviews, 2001-2003.

may in theory occur anywhere but may become associated with particular localities, for instance the impact of gang rivalry or the perceived threat of 'stranger danger'. Both Manchester/Salford and Lancaster/Morecambe contained many of the above environments. Morecambe is on the coast and both urban areas contain many rivers and canals, railway lines, main roads, bridges, viaducts, derelict land and other open spaces that all form attractive but potentially hazardous play spaces for children. In this section we focus on children's play by water, the impact of traffic on mobility for play, and potential threats from strangers, comparing children's encounters with these urban spaces in the 1940s and at the time of interview, and assessing the strategies that children and parents used to negotiate them.

Water provides one of the most fascinating and potentially dangerous playgrounds for young children (Tapsell et al., 2001), and the majority of relevant accounts from the 1940s relate to the risks associated with playing by rivers and canals (Box 7.1). Thus Les recalled swimming in water accumulated in old mine workings, and the problems of trying to get clean afterwards so that his parents would not know where he had been. Most accounts of playing in such potentially dangerous places come from male respondents, but Hilda associated with lads who swam in the canal (though she implied that she would not have done so herself) and Pamela was clearly a tom-boy who would undertake almost any activity to be part of the boys' gang. Thus activities were quite strongly gendered, but some girls were able to cross the gender divide. Both Charles and Tony recalled that friends were drowned in the Lancaster canal and this experience clearly had an impact on both them and their parents, and placed some restrictions on where they could play.

In addition to water, in the 1940s children in Manchester and Lancaster were attracted to a variety of other potentially dangerous environments. Thus Roger played in derelict air raid shelters in Lancaster, whilst Victor (like many other children) frequently played by the railway line in Manchester, though he seemed aware of both the dangers and the extent to which the area was regulated by authority:

> There used to be air raid shelters on there before they were, before they were demolished. We were told to keep out of them, but I mean you used to play in these, you used to play in them ... I think they were dangerous weren't they because I mean they, they were, they were neglected then and I think they'd been sort of boarded up so you couldn't go in, but of course children would get in wouldn't they, and they were dark and that inside and you know, but I mean they were just right for, for children weren't they (R50, Roger, aged 10/11, born 1938, Lancaster).

> There was a siding where they used to put coaches for when they're not being used, and we used to get in those, and running up and down causing havoc. And that'd be one, one favourite place. And slides down the railway banking on the grass was, was another ... Well we never/we, we very rarely went on the railway track itself, only to cross over. We won't play on the lines, no. In fact there was a signal box ... just a few hundred yards away and ... it was illegal to go on railway properties and we had railway police in those days. And the signalman always blooming, he'd play Mary Poppet if he saw us, you know chase us off (R370, Victor, aged 10/11, born 1938, Manchester).

In contrast, children born 1990-1991 recounted very few experiences of playing in potentially dangerous environments. This could have been because they were inhibited at interview, but the majority of children were interviewed alone and there were a number of occasions on which they gave information that they said they would not want their parents to know. However, compared to the generation born 1932-1941, the play space of children today seems to be much more regulated, either by themselves or by parents. In addition, when they did state that they played in what might seem to be a dangerous environment they quickly modified their statement to stress that it wasn't really risky and that they didn't do anything dangerous. Thus having said that he played on a building site, Gareth quickly qualified his statement:

> Mainly/not all the time, cause we have a field, so we play on there, but we don't really go on the dangerous parts of the building site. We may go for bike rides on the dirt paths and everything but nothing too dangerous (R33, Gareth, aged 10/11, born 1989, Morecambe).

In this context Gemma's evidence is interesting. She plays outside a lot with friends, mostly in the street or local parks but stays away from environments such as the river, canal or railway. However, her parents take her (and her young brother) to a local beauty spot by the river, where she swims and plays in the water. Although superficially inviting, this is a notoriously dangerous location where there have been a number of fatalities and there are prominent signs warning visitors not to swim. Gemma's potentially dangerous activities are sanctioned and supervised by her parents, but they are probably no less dangerous than many of the activities undertaken by groups of children in the 1940s:

> It takes about an hour to get down there and about/and then we, we play about there, sometimes take our swimming costume and go swimming in the/it's not that deep but at the end where there's … got a strong current, and sometimes we take up the little dinghy and we go in that with the oars and then when we've had enough or it's getting real cold we cycle back (R42, Gemma, aged 10/11, born 1989, Lancaster).

Some environments are perceived as dangerous not because of what is there or what the individual has experienced, but because of the reputation associated with a location. This is particularly true for children today, many of whom talked about places to which they were either not allowed or would not wish to go, because that place had a reputation of some sort (Box 7.2). In many cases the risk was very unspecific, thus David was not allowed to go alone into a local park 'in case anything bad happens' (R209, David, aged 10/11, born 1991, Salford), but in other cases a more specific risk such as fighting or 'druggies' is identified, although there is no evidence that the respondent has had any direct experience of such risks. These views are expressed by both boys and girls, with some indication that boys were experiencing such constraints more than girls, possibly because boys wanted to go out more but were prevented by the perceptions of risk held by themselves and adults responsible for them. Respondents in the 1940s rarely saw their mobility limited in this way and if they did not go somewhere there was

Box 7.2 Non-specific Reasons for Avoiding Certain Places, Children Born 1989-1992

Because she, she'll think it's/she doesn't, she doesn't like it there [The town centre] *because people, people, people fighting and all that stuff* (R211, Rory, aged 10/11, born 1992, Manchester).

Cause someone could take me if I was with no-one. And it's only down the road, near the park ... I can go in E. But I can't go near the T Centre cause they don't know what could happen to me (R214, Nathan, aged 10/11, born 1992, Salford).

She's afraid like because I don't even know our road very well, that I'll get lost somewhere and I won't know my way back. And she's scared that I might go onto somewhere like the main road, and someone can snatch me (R216, Georgia aged 10/11, born 1991, Salford).

And there's a massive big field to play football, but there's no-one to play football with. And on-one takes me, cause I can't go on my own, too dangerous ... Because someone could nab me. ... Um, we're both [respondent and mother] *worried about that* (R217, Chris, aged 10/11, born 1992, Salford).

Because my mum says there's people hang around who we're not supposed to like ... You don't know what they're doing sometimes ... It's the same reason as I'm not allowed to go down to the field on my own, there's people around that are a bit loopy (R34, Dean, aged 10/11, born 1990, Morecambe).

No we keep out of there [the woods] *in case like there's anyone there. No, we keep near the stream and the park* (R26, Sophie, aged 10/11, born 1990, Lancaster).

And my dad said I wasn't allowed to go [to a youth club] *because there's loads of druggies there. I said that there wasn't and all my friends go* (R28, Loren, aged 10/11, born 1989, Lancaster).

And then/because the guide leader/I am allowed on my own but because my guide leader said that a couple of bad things have been happening late at night then she normally takes me home in her car (R42, Gemma, aged 10/11, born 1989, Lancaster).

Source: Everyday mobility interviews, 2001-2003.

usually a very specific reason. One exception was Tony who talked about how he found a particular footpath threatening, even though nothing bad had happened to him there. However, it did not stop him from using that route:

> One place I was always wary of was a footpath, you know ... And on one side of it you'd got high privet hedges at the back of the council houses and on the other side you'd got a solid fence and they had railway sleepers, vertical railway/railway sleepers, and it was black. And it was how soon can I get to the end of here sort of thing ... Yea it was always unnerving ... It was just you were always nervous and you're thinking how can I get along here, how fast can I do it (R52, Tony, aged 10/11, born 1939, Lancaster).

One aspect of the urban environment that is often blamed for reducing the independent mobility of children is the increasing traffic volume on urban streets. This has been associated with more indoor play, greater restrictions on where children can go, and an increase in the degree to which children are escorted, especially on the journey to school (Hillman et al., 1990). This is, of course, not a threat posed by the environment itself but by the activities of people (notably motorists) in the urban environment. Although traffic volumes have undoubtedly increased over the past 60 years, leading to greater concern about the risks that vehicles pose to children, worries about traffic did figure in the responses of those who were aged 10/11 in the 1940s. Thus Christina recalled how her otherwise relatively unconstrained mobility was affected by the main road: 'The only thing that restricted you then was the main road at the top of the street, and I wasn't allowed to go up to the main road on my own. ... No restrictions apart from the main road' (R57, Christina, age 10/11, born 1940, Morecambe). However, the key theme that emerges is that whilst residential streets were relatively safe in the 1940s because of low rates of car ownership, children were aware of the potential risk from traffic in main roads but, like other dangerous play spaces, they learned to handle these dangers as part of their everyday life and they did not unduly restrict mobility (Box 7.3). Thus Victor was aware of children killed on the main road, but he was not prevented from playing out. In contrast, for children aged 10/11 today parental concerns about traffic impose much greater restrictions on many children. Some do still play on the road but, like Gabriel and Lorna, they stress the care that they take and the fact that they only play on relatively quiet streets.

In addition to the threat posed by motorists, in the twenty-first century there is also extensive concern about the potential danger posed to young children by strangers (Pain, 2000; 2001). To what extent are such concerns really new, and have there been changes in the ways in which children and parents handle such threats? Both male and female respondents who were aged 10/11 in the 1940s recounted encounters with potentially threatening strangers that today would have generated major concern (Box 7.4). However, their testimonies suggest that although clearly sticking in the memory, at the time the incidents were not viewed with particular alarm, parents and the police were rarely informed, and the children simply handled the experience as part of their everyday life. They may have modified their behaviour slightly, but the incidents did not unduly restrict their play space and everyday mobility. In contrast, as outlined above, few children aged 10/11 today have actually encountered any danger from strangers, but there is a strong perception that such dangers exist and restrictions are placed on mobility both by parents and by the children themselves (Box 7.4). Thus Lorna restricts her

Box 7.3   The Changing Impact of Traffic on Mobility, Children Aged 10/11, Manchester and Salford

---

I don't play on the road. I play on the pavement ... Cause it's dangerous to play on the road, cause you might get run over (R217, Chris, aged 10/11, born 1992, Salford).

No, cause like it's just like in our street and there's like, it's just a busy street and there's all cars and then there's the road and then there's the pavement and the houses and houses. There's not really no place for you can play, but unless you're on the pavements ... So we're not allowed to play on the road most of the time cause it's dead busy (R213, Laura, aged 10/11, born 1991, Salford).

Yea. But we sit on the pavement and throw, like play kerby and we play dodge ball and stuff ... when we throw the ball and then we all get off the road and then one, the person whoever gets the ball they just keep hold of the ball and then they're on. We/and then when the car's gone past/but we/what is we do is whoever gets the ball they're on, so when someone gets it we say/oh someone get the ball, wait till they grab hold of it, ah you're on now, cause you've chased the ball. And we play tiggyball, and if you tig, give someone, some/one person has to throw the ball at someone and if they catch it they're on wi' you. And you throw, wait till a car comes and then let the car, wait til a car's coming down then we let them grab the ball before the car gets to/near you. And when they touch the ball they're on, so (R202, Gabriel, aged 10/11, born 1992, Manchester).

Well we go to, on the street, her street and, and my street, and S Road, just round there and places like that ... it's quiet ... I've got an area. I'm only allowed/yea I've got one area that I'm allowed to play. That's like S Road and her street and everythin (R215, Lorna, aged 10/11, born 1991, Salford).

Mum was frightened of us being on the road on a bike. My brother didn't/was about 15 when he got his (R367, Beatrice, aged 10/11, born 1937, Manchester).

Well there wasn't a lot came down our streets really. There's not as much as there is today ... I think there was only one person, and he had a television shop, Mr E, he was the only one in the street that had a car (R328, Hilda aged 10/11, born 1940, Manchester).

We'd hear of kids getting run over, coming off bikes and things, but there was nothing/it was not/it was sort of an event of very minor significance. I mean we knew we had to watch cause we knew cars, well we saw cars quite frequently running along and we/but we knew about vaguely careless drivers who perhaps should have taken more care. But I don't remember any accidents particularly no. No, no accidents to the people I knew (R323, Harry, aged 10/11, born 1942, Manchester).

Well the main Liverpool road runs past ... There's one or two lads got killed on there crossing ... we were just told to watch what we were doing you know (R370, Victor, aged 10/11, born 1938, Manchester).

Source: Everyday mobility interviews, 2001-2003.

Box 7.4   Threats from Strangers in the 1940s, Children Aged 10/11

The only fears we used to have was in the park. There would be men, and probably from the Moor Hospital [Asylum], *and we would be wary of them, so if any men approached us/we were often flashed at, even in those days ...Well, you knew it was wrong and you kept well away from them, but we would be half-frightened and half laugh[ing]. We knew to keep away from them ... An RAF chap stopped me and offered me money to go down on 't/ this was when I was going down into town shopping for me mother/offered me money to go down onto the canal with him. I didn't know what for, but I knew it was wrong. But I still got the shopping, and took it back home. So I wasn't so frightened, but I just knew it was wrong ... And I don't think that I ever told my parents, because sex wasn't ever talked about* (R55, Teresa, age 10/11, born 1937, Lancaster).*

An odd time we had a funny man in a car asking us to get in the car with him, which of course we knew we hadn't to do, but I mean we were only young then And there used to be a swing on the bottom of the hill and we used to play on this swing, but you know that was just a/and we came back, told my mother and/well they didn't do anything about it, you know I mean the police weren't informed or anything in those days you know (R111, Rosemary, aged 10/11, born 1936, Lancaster).

Only once did I come into contact with anything like that, and that was a flasher ... it was round my granny's area ... And he was on this sort of railway bridge looking down on, on us kids. And I think I was one of the eldest there, and I remember feeling, funnily enough, that he was admiring me cause he was staring at me. And I was kind of quite you know flattered this was happening. And I mean I've often thought about this since. And he then exposed himself, and of course it scared me to death and I went home ... I don't think I ever told them [parents], *someone/no I didn't no ... I think because subjects like that were taboo* (R339, Elizabeth, aged 10/11, born 1940, Manchester).

I think the only time it every happened to me ... a man exposed himself, and we just followed him ... We wanted to find out where he was so we could tell someone, but we lost him. [I: And did you tell anybody?] *I can't remember whether I did. No I don't think I did ... But no I don't remember anything nasty in my childhood. Or being nervous of anyone* (R356, Pamela, aged 10/11, born 1937, Salford).

And the thing that we were warned most against was flashers, you know being woodland areas. And one of the great pursuits was to go out and find courting couples, we'd spy on them. But the, the queer characters used to be out as well looking for the same thing. And, and we were warned not to speak to strange men, because we were actually, three of us were actually accosted like one/at one point ... Exposing himself. But nothing much other than that happened luckily. But the police were called (R370, Victor, aged 10/11, born 1938, Manchester).

Source: Everyday mobility interviews, 2001-2003.

own play space due to fears about vague threats from strangers, but she did not recount any actual incidents that had occurred:

> I, if my mates go I don't go, because like sommat could happen to me and all my mates, and that's why I don't go cause I don't want to be part of it. ... Well they go to the Canal and that's why I don't like like what could happen, and the people round there and the men and everything round there (R215, Lorna, aged 10/11, born 1991, Salford).

Evidence cited above suggests that whilst quantitatively there have been relatively few changes in the everyday mobility of children aged 10/11 for outdoor play and to visit friends, qualitatively there have been some changes. Although there are similarities in the ways that children perceive risk, there is some evidence that children aged 10/11 are today more constrained in the areas over which they can play, and that they are given less freedom to learn how to negotiate the urban environment for themselves. This can be further explored by looking explicitly at the strategies adopted by parents and children to regulate urban play space. Although, as outlined above, children in the 1940s had rather more freedom than children today, even 60 years ago most children aged 10/11 were constrained by clear rules about what they could or could not do. These related to the identification of boundaries outside which they should not stray, times when they should return home and who they were allowed out with. Thus Maurice was not allowed to play by the river, Beatrice's mother expected to know exactly where she was playing, and Valerie had quite a high level of mobility, but only because she was allowed out with her elder sister, sometimes to activities that she did not enjoy. There was also a high degree of variability in individual experiences: whilst some children were given considerable freedom others in the 1940s (such as Beryl) had very restrictive and protective parents. It can thus be suggested that the strategies that children and parents adopt have changed relatively little over time:

> There was no regulations you know ... you just didn't stray so very far ... But some areas were out of bounds ... [if you went] over the railway bridge and in the [river] Lune. It was semi out of bounds ... If you got caught you were in trouble (R59, Maurice, age 10/11, born 1934, Lancaster).

> I played in the back garden. And occasionally I went to friends' houses, but not very often ... I played out, just outside for a little bit in the evenings in the summer. We weren't allowed to go off out anywhere in the evening. Oh no no. Mum wanted, mum wanted to know where we were (R367, Beatrice, age 10/11, born 1937, Manchester).

> I was in the care of my sister a lot, who was a teenager, and everywhere/well it was a shame really because everywhere she went I had to tag along beside her, so when she was out with her friends so was I (R76, Valerie, age 10/11, born 1940, Lancaster).

> My mother there was so many things she sort of would not let me do. You know she would not let me go to the swimming baths because she didn't

think they were very clean, and if I was sort of/I couldn't have a bike or anything like that because I might fall off and hurt myself. That was one thing you know, and I sort of went on anybody else's. I did fall off and so I was in trouble you know (R353, Beryl, age 10/11, born 1935, Salford).

This can be further illustrated with reference to the extent to which children aged 10/11 were allowed to cycle on the road. Cycling was relatively uncommon for children aged 10/11 at all time periods, and bicycles were perceived more as play things than as a means of transport. Although traffic volumes were lower than today, respondents born 1932-1941 recall being restricted in where they could go on their bicycle due to fears about traffic. This is illustrated by the evidence of Beatrice (Box 7.3) and a number of other (mostly female) respondents. Children born 1989-1992 and aged 10/11 at the time of interview reported very similar constraints, but they were more widespread and affected both boys and girls equally. In most cases parents restricted cycling to parks, dedicated cycle lanes and pavements and did not allow their children to cycle on the road. Ben and Chris both stated their fears and strategies quite clearly:

I normally ride where it has the green and then if it stops I go on the pavement, or if there's somebody there I go onto the road and then I'll go back onto the pavement (R206, Ben, aged 10/11, born 1992, Stockport).

Even though I've passed my Cycle Proficiency Test I still ride on the pavement, 'cause there's a risk of getting run over. When you're going one way and a car could be coming another way and you won't be able to brake so, that fast, and the car could come into you (R217, Chris, aged 10/11, born 1992, Salford).

The degree to which children today are subject to more parental control than those 60 years ago is also demonstrated by the extent of their freedom to roam and the strategies that parents now use to protect children. Thus Janet recalled being able to move freely around her local area on her own without any parental restrictions. In contrast, although Rory is allowed out alone, he has to follow a well-defined strategy when crossing the road outside his house and is watched by his mother when doing this.

I've, I've even walked to H Park, which was about four or five miles away … On my own yea … they [parents] were quite used to me just wandering off … Also I had a grandmother who lived probably about ten minutes walk away, so I could be there for all they knew you know … I had an awful lot of freedom (R320, Janet, aged 10/11, born 1936, Salford).

On Z Street the cars speed up a bit but when, when, when I cross over I look both ways before I even cross … My mum watches us going over the road (R211, Rory, aged 10/11, born 1992, Manchester).

The mobile 'phone has also allowed parents to keep in much closer contact with their children than they could in the past. A number of children mentioned that when they went out alone or with other children they were required to take their mobile with them and in some cases parents checked up on their children regularly. How, precisely, being watched from a window or carrying a mobile 'phone improves safety is never made explicit. A parent watching from inside the house or on the end of a 'phone cannot prevent a child being hit by a car. However, compared to the 1940s, it can be suggested that increased surveillance by parents both increases parental power and reduces the degree to which children feel responsible for their own actions (Fotel and Thomsen, 2004). Whether this actually helps children to grow into independent adults is debatable. Ben clearly felt a victim of such parental control when he was allowed out alone at the age of 10 so long as he took his mobile:

> I take my mobile with me ... Yea, 'cause I have to warn her [mother]. The first time I went I had to go – I'm on a bus – I'm going – I'm coming out, where I got changed, and all that (R206, Ben, aged 10/11, born 1992, Stockport).

Children are also well aware that mobile 'phone theft is common, and that possession of a mobile can increase the risk of being attacked. Thus, paradoxically, the device that parents increasingly see as a way of exercising some control over their children can itself become the cause of potential danger. Layla was well aware of this and had devised a strategy to minimise this risk:

> But I've decided now that I take my mobile out in my pocket, but I keep it in my pocket and zipped up. And when it rings I stand with my, my back against a wall so I can see what's going on around me and answer the phone ... So you're not stood in like a wide open space, that somebody could come from behind you, or at the side, or anything ... so I just play safe with it (R234, Layla, aged 10/11, born 1991, Manchester).

This analysis has focused on long-term change from the 1940s to the late-twentieth century. Using qualitative evidence it is hard to pin down precisely when such changes occurred, but the testimonies remain largely unaltered until very recently. There is a little evidence of increased restrictions (especially for girls) in the cohort born 1983-1984, but it is really only the accounts of those born 1990-1992 that are significantly different from those of earlier cohorts. Although children today are still allowed to play outside, and they still mostly undertake such play on foot and unaccompanied by an adult (and thus quantitatively change is limited), they do appear to be more tightly regulated in where they can go and more aware of potential dangers than children were 60 years ago. Few children today have experienced danger and the ways in which their play space is regulated restricts the likelihood that this will happen. In contrast, those born in the 1930s appear to have had more exposure to a range of potential risks in the urban environment and they learned to cope with these without allowing them to restrict their everyday play.

It has been suggested that one of the major influences on such trends is the role of the media, with present-day television and newspapers giving sensational coverage to the relatively small number of serious incidents that arise and thus heightening the fears of both parents and children (Williams and Dickinson, 1993; Kidd-Hewitt and Osborne, 1995; Soothill, 2003; Peelo et al, 2004). It is perceptions of risk rather than actual experiences of risk that are affecting behaviour. The changed role of the media is borne out by an analysis of the coverage of crime and related incidents in newspapers local to the two study areas. In Lancaster, sample months (January and July) were compared for 1948 and 2003 from reports in the main local newspaper, *The Lancaster Guardian*. This showed that the coverage of crime and related dangers increased more than four fold from 41 incidents over two months in 1948 to 188 in 2003. Moreover, whereas in 1948 most incidents were reported when the case came to court, and appeared under a separate court section, in 2003 in addition to court reports incidents of crime were covered on most pages of the newspaper. However, in each time period the number of serious offences was small and, as indicated in the oral testimonies, there is no evidence that children today actually experience more danger than they did in the past.

In Manchester and Salford we compared issues of the *Manchester Evening News* and the weekly *Salford Advertiser* for the months of January and July 1948 and 2003. Results of this brief analysis were more inconclusive than the analysis in Lancaster. Whereas in 1948 the *Salford Advertiser* (like *The Lancaster Guardian*) rarely carried reports of crime (less than one report per issue), in 2003 such reports occurred regularly and prominently with over six per issue. However, the *Manchester Evening News* showed a different trend with a reduction from 57 to 40 in the crimes reported over a two-week period in 1948 and 2003. It is likely that such figures reflect changes in the editorial policy of individual papers as much as any real trends, but two tentative conclusions can be suggested. First, based on evidence from the *Manchester Evening News*, incidents were reported as frequently in the past as today and, second, that reporting of rare high-profile crimes in national media may be as, or more, important than what appears in the local press.

Overall, it can thus be suggested that both in the 1940s and today serious crime is rare, but that a combination of national and local media reporting of those incidents that do occur has raised the public perception of risk to children. Although many children are still allowed to play out, and their overall mobility has changed little, children aged 10/11 do appear to be subject to more constraints than they were in the past. Children today are not being allowed to experience everyday risks and potentially this is harming their ability to negotiate urban space and to deal in a rational manner with risks that do occur. We are not suggesting that children should be exposed to unnecessary danger, but there is little evidence from the accounts of children aged 10/11 today that such dangers have been experienced by many children. However, most think that risks exist and this affects their behaviour. Other studies have suggested that the main perpetrators of this high perception of risk are the media, giving undue prominence to a small number of very high profile cases, or blowing out of proportion those incidents that do occur (Furedi, 2001). Our limited survey of the local media in Manchester and Lancaster support this conclusion. It can also be suggested that experience of danger may be greater in large urban areas (such as Manchester) compared to smaller places.

Hanging Around in Town: Adolescents Aged 17/18

In contrast to children aged 10/11, teenagers had far fewer restrictions on their leisure mobility. Adolescents aged 17/18 are at an age when they can expect a high degree of independence, but most do not yet have access to a car. They are midway between the world of childhood and adulthood and, although they have left behind the concept of play, hanging around with friends can form an important part of their everyday life. More formalised activities such as sport and entertainment are examined in Chapter 8: here we focus on the more informal trips to meet friends and socialise that were recorded by respondents in Manchester/Salford and Lancaster/Morecambe. Of course, such activity does not go unnoticed by other users of urban space and the extent to which groups of teenagers in town are perceived to be problematic is explored in more detail in Chapter 9. This section, first, briefly reviews quantitative evidence on the pattern of everyday mobility linked to informal leisure and, second, uses qualitative data to explore the extent to which teenagers aged 17/18 experienced constraints on their mobility, and especially the degree of conflict that existed at different times between youth gangs in the two case study towns.

Taking data for the broad categories of visiting friends and social activities, that incorporate a wide range of informal recreational activities and that were reviewed in Chapter 4 (Tables 4.10-4.13), there is again considerable similarity between the two towns and consistency over time. Mean distances travelled for social activities are short (under 5km in all time periods) but with a slight lengthening of trip distance from the 1950s to the present. Although there were a small number of long journeys recorded, over 40 per cent were less than 1.5km in each time period. Mean journey times were also short (under 20 minutes) with a reduction in travel time from the 1950s to the present. This matches changes in total mobility patterns. Walking was the single most important form of transport for such trips in all cohorts. In Manchester the bus was widely used in each time period, but in Lancaster it was replaced by the car. This reflects differing public transport systems in the two towns, but overall there is no evidence of a significant decline in walking over time. Thus for those born 1983-1984 walking continued to account for at least half of all trips for social activities. Most travel was undertaken in the company of other teenagers of the same age, though where car travel was involved most teenagers of this age travelled as a passenger with an adult. These data thus suggest that for much discretionary social travel the pattern of activity has changed little for those aged 17/18 since the 1950s. Most trips are over a short distance, walking continues to be important, and association with other teenagers is a significant part of the activity.

Qualitative evidence emphasises the relatively high degree of independence experienced by respondents aged 17/18, though in the 1950s and today many parents stipulated specific times that their teenage offspring (especially girls) should return home. The comments of Teresa, Christina and Beatrice were typical, and to some extent these are echoed by Becky (aged 17/18 in 2001/2). She says that although she is not bothered about walking home alone, her boyfriend's father expresses concern and insists that she is accompanied. However, many teenagers (and most males) in the past and the present experienced few controls on their mobility. Thus Susan stressed that she had no controls imposed on her by parents but that her shy personality limited what she did alone, and Nisha (aged 17/18 at interview) stressed that she experienced no restrictions when moving around Manchester and Salford today. Thus, again, the data stress individual variability, with some more constraints for females than for males; but overall neither the pattern of activity – with a high degree of independence – nor the factors that impose constraints have changed radically over the past half century (Box 7.5).

Much of the activity that those aged 17/18 undertook entailed little more than meeting up with friends. The purpose of the mobility was group sociability. Often this occurred during the daytime at weekends, and in the early evening after school/college or work, and is a theme that recurs in accounts from each age cohort. Thus Joe recalled meeting up with friends in a coffee bar on Morecambe promenade on a Sunday and then parading as a group along the promenade, and Christina recalled travelling from Morecambe to Lancaster to meet friends and do nothing but wander aimlessly around. In this case her parents' prohibition on bars placed some further restrictions on what she could do:

> We, we used to meet up at, at/on a Sunday at B's Coffee Lounge on Morecambe promenade, and things like that. But again that would be there'd be a group of you, you wouldn't be, wouldn't be boy girl boy girl you know ... and then a walk along the promenade and all that sort of thing ... after having a coffee part of the ritual was sort of this promenade walk you know (R9, Joe, age 17/18, born 1938, Morecambe).

> I had one or two friends in Lancaster that I used to meet up with and, and we just used to walk around. When I think about it now it was silly because there wasn't as many places to go to in Lancaster. I went/I wasn't allowed in bars. My parents weren't exactly temperance, but they were almost, so I wasn't allowed in bars. And we used to walk up and down the streets, which were two way traffic then, just looking in the shop windows basically, or just hanging about (R57, Christina, age 17/18, born 1940, Morecambe).

These accounts are not at all dissimilar to the testimonies of adolescents aged 17/18 today. Few are restricted from going in bars, but lack of money often means that they spend most time just wandering around, talking and generally passing the time. Thus after school rather than going straight home both Caroline and Tom will meet up with friends and spend several hours just hanging around or sitting talking.

Box 7.5 Constraints and Freedoms of Adolescents Aged 17/18

I had to be in for half past 10, but apart from that I could go where I wanted ... And no questions asked (R55, Teresa, age 17/18, born 1937, Lancaster).

We were allowed anywhere so long as we were back in the house by 10.00 at night, and I think that was mostly to stop my parents worrying where we were (R57, Christina, age 17/18, born 1940, Morecambe).

Even when I started work my mother wanted to know that/who I was with. And if we were having a night out, sort of a late night, I think I had to be in by half 9, 10 o'clock, even when at 17. And if we wanted to/occasionally we'd go to say the Locarno dancing and it was a case of either daddy came and picked us up in the car or we had to be in by a certain time, there was none of this/we didn't have late nights as such unless we were all out together as a family (R367, Beatrice, age 17/18, born 1937, Manchester).

I used to [walk home] but Neil [boyfriend] never lets me walk home by myself now. He always walks me home ... I didn't mind walking home by myself that much but it was his dad really ... that had a go, it was his dad that had a go and said that he should be walking me home but ... With it being a bit of a rough area but also, but Neil knows that if I walk home I walk down the cycle path and he doesn't like me walking/well he ... He'd rather I walk down the main road, but he always walks me home now because/and I don't mind that, it's just that I feel bad for Neil you know cause he's got to walk back afterwards. But at the end of the day I've got to walk there in the first place so (R12, Becky, age 17/18, born 1983, Morecambe).

Um nothing really restricted me apart from my personality ... I was very shy ... I wouldn't go to the, the cinema by myself, and I preferred not to do things by myself. So that was the only restriction (R371, Susan, age 17/18, born 1962, Salford).

What we want yea, I get a lot of freedom ... Quite easy for me. I don't have like regulations of what time I've got to be home or anything, so (R223, Nisha, age 17/18, born 1985, Manchester).

Source: Everyday mobility interviews, 2001-2003.

Such activities do not sit easily with classifications of journey purpose in travel surveys, but they form an important part of the travel behaviour of many adolescents:

> Then some days I'll go straight, I'll walk straight from school into town and meet my friends in town and I'll hang around for, till about half four or even half five if we're very bored. And then I'll walk home from town (R23 Caroline, age 17/18, born 1983, Lancaster).

> Sometimes I hang around here talking. I'll go home on the bus if I'm with R or someone. We'll maybe pop into a shop or something. And then we'll, we sometimes we sit on a wall and just talk crap and stuff or usually get into big philosophical debates for a long, for, for some time. Usually like sit

there for about two hours and then realise we've been there for that long.
And then, then, then we'll walk home yea (R220, Tom, age 17/18, born
1985, Manchester).

Most such activity posed few risks either to teenagers or to others, though
some residents may view groups of youths hanging around with suspicion; but
there were times in both the 1950s and today when adolescents encountered
potential dangers that affected where they went and how they travelled. Using the
qualitative data it is possible to examine the risks that adolescents perceived when
moving around Lancaster/Morecambe and Manchester/Salford, how these have
changed, and how they compared to the risks perceived by younger children and
their parents. It can be suggested that moving around town in the 1950s was
certainly not risk free, but that the perceived risks for those age 17/18 were rather
different from those affecting younger children. Whereas children aged 10/11 (and
their parents) were concerned mainly about the dangers of traffic, risky play areas
and, increasingly in the late-twentieth century, 'stranger danger'; for teenagers
aged 17/18 threats were more likely to come from other groups of youths or from
the dangers associated with being out much later than their younger counterparts.
However, it can be suggested that at all times most teenagers had a clear view of
the areas through which it was safe to travel; they recognised the dangers and
negotiated their own safety. Moreover, there is a high degree of variability in the
data, and at all time periods some adolescents were much more adventurous than
others.

Several respondents, recalling the 1950s, were aware of possible threats in
potentially dangerous areas, especially fights late at night around dance halls and
the territoriality that existed between gangs in different parts of the towns. But this
did not unduly restrict their mobility, and respondents stressed that the violence
rarely became serious (Box 7.6). In the small town of Lancaster and Morecambe
respondents aged 17/18 today gave few accounts of real violence or fears that
affected them when travelling around town, though two female respondents
expressed concern about travelling around Morecambe late at night, though in both
cases this related more to reputation than to actual experiences. In this sense it can
be suggested that, as with children aged 10/11, the reporting of crime and violence
rather than actual experiences may be a much more important factor in structuring
travel around Lancaster and Morecambe today than it was in the 1950s. In contrast,
some present-day teenagers in Manchester and Salford reported experiencing real
threats of violence and in a few cases (for instance Sunil, Box 7.6) respondents
reported racist incidents that affected where they went in Manchester and Salford.
This is one factor that has changed substantially since the 1950s. The other factor
that has changed, and one that many of the older respondents commented on, is the
perception that whereas in the past violence was relatively low level with nothing
more than fist fights, today it is much more likely to involve knives or guns thus
giving a much greater likelihood of serious injury. In this sense the risks that
teenagers are exposed to may be theoretically greater than in the past, but there is
little evidence that this has fundamentally altered behaviour for this group.

Box 7.6   Mobility Restrictions Imposed by Other Adolescents on Teenagers Aged 17/18

It was very territorial, you didn't come over S Bridge and turn right onto M 'cos there'd be fights ... That was totally out of bounds. If you were on there you were in a fight ... It was the people there, the potters, the tinkers ... It was their area. It was notorious. That was one place you didn't go ... You used to have a bit of a banter with the lads off B. It's territorial ... I wouldn't say we fought with them, we used to play 'em at football and kick hell out of each other. But M was the only dangerous one with fighting ... You just knew where not to go (R59, Maurice, age 17/18, born 1934, Lancaster).*

You used to get odd fights in the dancehalls and, and outside afterwards you know, simple because people had had too much to drink or they'd be falling out over a girl or something like that. You never got any/I mean you never got anybody with knives and things like that you know. But yea there used to be fights, there used to be them (R50, Roger, age 17/18, born 1938, Lancaster).

Yea. Sometimes you'd go and torment other gangs. But there was a lot of gangs, not well warfare, but rivalry you know. And you'd sort of ten of you'd ride up on your bike and sort of pick a fight or pick an argument ... I suppose it was serious at the time yea. [but] *we didn't have weapons ... There was hardly/very very rare there were police about ... it was a rivalry, but it wasn't so vicious really* (R351, Les, age 17/18, born 1937, Salford).

Well I think how I could put it is every, every area sort of had their own gangs didn't they, their own mates you know. And sometimes, it just depends where you was, you could, you could get some people like don't like that gang, gang, we'll go and fight 'em, and that was it you know (R327, Ken, age 17/18, born 1938, Manchester).

Even though I live there probably not, I don't know, I suppose It's a lot better than it used to be but with all the past fights and rumours ... I wouldn't really like to walk round (R15, Andrea, age 17/18, born 1984, Morecambe).

Yea. And my brothers go there as well, I see my brothers. And K is just a place to go, just a quiet place. Places where trouble don't get started cause one thing I can't deal with is fighting, I don't like fighting, I can't deal with it (R37, Joel, age 17/18, born 1984, Lancaster).

I wouldn't like to go in Salford cause ... No, it's racist. I wouldn't like going into Moss Side ... No. I wouldn't like going into Longsight either. I just stick to my area ... it's like/I, I, I used to go, I used to get it done to me all the time ... Even people who know me and I know that if I go down there they won't hit me or anything like that, but there's one odd people that would shout the odd comment about you. And if you say anything back and then they'll all just gang up and all this and/so I still won't go no (R230, Sunil, age 17/18, born 1984, Manchester).

It's the kind of people you hang around with, everyone sort of wears that sort of thing, so yea it is seen like you know us and them. I mean we don't really see it like that, but they do. And yea they cause like, like big fusses about it often. And they'll just simply you know start something simply because of that say (R220, Tom, age 17/18, born 1985, Manchester).

Source: Everyday mobility interviews, 2001-2003.

In summary, it can be argued, first, that overall travel behaviour for play and social activities by children and adolescents has changed little over the past half century. Journey distances and times have remained short, travel on foot continues to be important, and much of such travel takes place without an adult. However, whereas for children aged 10/11 there is some evidence of increased constraints imposed by adults, despite little evidence of any real increased risk, for adolescents the opposite appears to be the case. Few adolescents have any real restrictions placed upon them, but the risks that they face (especially in the larger urban area of Manchester and Salford) may be greater than in the past.

Chapter 8

Travel for Leisure and Pleasure: Entertainment, Sport, Shopping and Holidays

Travel for Entertainment

Entertainment can be defined in a variety of ways and can include a multiplicity of activities. In this section we focus on a selection of specific and fairly consistently recorded activities that can be compared over time. The main activities included are visiting cinemas, theatres, concerts and similar events, eating out at a restaurant and related activities. Quantitative data reviewed in Chapter 4 demonstrate clearly that although the frequency with which such social activities are undertaken has changed over time, the distances over which people travel, and the characteristics of trips, have altered relatively little (Tables 4.10-4.13). Moreover, changes in frequency are not consistent. Thus whilst some forms of entertainment, such as eating out, have become more common, others such as visits to the cinema have declined, especially for the young. The frequency with which people undertake travel for entertainment is also strongly linked to the life course, and the activities of adults with young children are especially constrained in this respect (see Chapter 9). Data on travel mode and travel companions mirrors evidence presented elsewhere. Whilst there has been a decline in the use of public transport, an increase in car use, and a decrease in young children travelling alone, it remains the case that many trips are over short distances, are undertaken on foot, and that young children and adolescents have not completely lost their independence.

Qualitative evidence provides more insights into the changes that have occurred. We focus first on visits to the cinema and second on eating out. For most children aged 10/11 in the 1940s going to the cinema was a regular occurrence. Both towns had a wide range of venues and most respondents could easily walk to the cinema from their home. There were two main patterns of activity. Many respondents attended Saturday daytime screenings aimed specifically at children and usually a group of children would take themselves to the cinema alone. In contrast, evening screenings were usually attended as part of a family outing and in these instances children aged 10/11 would have been accompanied by an adult. It could be that parents were less willing to allow children to travel to the cinema alone in the evening, but it can be suggested that the main reason for being accompanied was the social nature of the family outing. However, even in the

Box 8.1 Travelling to the Cinema Aged 10/11

Um usually my, my pals. One, one of, one of my pals. And, and probably the thing we did most with my mum and dad was go to cinema I think when, when they weren't working at night (R9, Joe, aged 10/11, born 1938, Morecambe).

Well you went to pictures. You went to Odeon on a Saturday morning when you were kids ... More often than not Saturday morning when I was about 10 yea ... Walked it ... [with] my mates. Maybe some from school, some from round there. There'd be a few of us you know (R3, Mary, aged 10/11, born 1935, Lancaster).

Well my mother took me to the/you see I think/I don't think we went to the cinema by ourselves. I think my mother took me to the cinema. There was a local cinema also about 5 minutes walk away. My mother used to take me (R357, Olive, aged 10/11, born 1937, Manchester) .

We would cross the main road, the A, the main A6 road, and go to the local bug hut ... Yea the cinema. ... Especially on Saturdays you know when it was, when it was children's matinees. They had a children's matinee. But also I can remember going with my mother. I must have been in that age to remember going with my mother and it must have been the end of the war because obviously in the war you, you/it was very difficult to go out in the dark ... Ooh I would say at least once a week (R348, Margaret, aged 10/11, born 1934, Salford).

I suppose it was just like I was just starting to go to the cinema on my own. There was one in the middle of Urmston really ... The Curzon cinema ... Friends really. And we usually get dropped off and we go in and watch ... (R231, Colin, aged 10/11, born 1984, Manchester).

Sometimes I go with my brother. And my sister said that I can go with her to see Harry Potter whenever it comes out, the film. And I rarely go with my mum cause she doesn't really want to watch any films. So it's mainly just me and my brother and sometimes friends. ... Mum just drops us off and ...we work out when it's going to finish, cause it tells us when it starts, and then she comes at that time (R33, Gareth, aged 10/11, born 1989, Morecambe).

Nearly every week if there's a film I want to watch and there's a coupon in The Visitor that gets you in for 99p, it's usually £1.50 ... If my brother wants to watch the film then I go with my brother otherwise my dad takes me in the car, and mum, and drops me off ... We ask what time the film finishes or if my dad's not there then me and my brother walk down to the, my mum's shop cause it's not far away (R34, Dean, aged 10/11, born 1990, Morecambe).

Yea I go there loads of times, like on like a Saturday. Me and my mum go sometimes on like on a Saturday. Like all our family have gone (R213, Laura, aged 10/11, born 1991, Salford).

Source: Everyday mobility interviews 2000-2003.

1940s there was considerable variety, and whilst some respondents frequently travelled to the cinema alone aged 10/11 others (such as Olive) said they were almost always accompanied (Box 8.1). Some, respondents aged 10/11 today also go to the cinema quite regularly, but although they often watch films alone or with friends their own age they rarely travel to the cinema independently. Usually a parent or elder sibling takes them to the cinema and collects them after the film. However, it can be suggested that one of the main reasons for this change is the alteration in urban structure that has taken place since the 1940s. Whilst older respondents mostly had a cinema within close walking distance of their home, today there are far fewer cinemas and a trip to see a film requires a longer and more complex journey for most people. As Dean explains (Box 8.1), he is allowed to walk alone the short distance from the cinema to his mother's shop. It is the increased distance to a cinema, rather than other concerns, that has caused a shift to more car use and thus more children aged 10/11 being accompanied on trips to the cinema.

Adolescents aged 17/18 of course have much more freedom and in both the past and present the cinema formed an important part of their entertainment, linked to many other activities, usually involving meeting friends of the opposite sex, as indicated by Roger and Joe. Roger also explained how he had a wide range of entertainment opportunities in Lancaster and Morecambe in the 1950s, certainly more than adolescents in the area have today. For this group there have been few changes over the past half century, but as with children aged 10 adolescents now have to travel further to the cinema than in the past, and although they often travel independently the increased distance means that they often look for a lift, especially late at night. The testimonies of Nisha and Colin from Manchester illustrate this:

> I used to go to the cinema most Wednesday afternoons and then probably go to the cinema again Wednesday night, yea, and I think I'd got round to taking a girl, a girl by then, I think so (R9, Joe, aged 17/18 born 1938, Morecambe).

> Well the cinema/I mean, I mean there was plenty, there was plenty of cinemas in Lancaster. And plenty of pubs, but of course at 17 you did/you had to be careful where you went if you're drinking there. So I mean if you wanted, if you wanted to go to the cinema you would, you would stay in Lancaster, but if you wanted a bit more entertainment like trying to find a young lady or something like that or, or going dancing then, then you went to Morecambe, especially in, in the summer months (R50, Roger, aged 17/18, born 1938, Lancaster).

> There's one in the Trafford Centre which is where we go, and we usually, like I said one, one of my friend's drives, so I might get a lift with him [or] I'd probably get a bus or maybe get a lift with my dad or mum, whatever's easiest or available (R231, Colin, aged 17/18, born 1984, Manchester).

> With my friends it's probably/they'll probably/we probably go Trafford Centre mostly, cause that's where most of the things are. So probably just

like cinemas, eat out. And probably go Rusholme. That's about it really ...
We go/I go, probably go by bus. And then either someone will come and
collect us, and if not then we get the bus back ... Oh that'll be probably
once a week really. Cause that's when we get like time to meet up properly
and then like have a bit of fun, so we go once a week (R223, Nisha, age
17/18, born 1985, Manchester).

Life course constraints on entertainment are clearly illustrated by Margaret
who felt that travel for entertainment more or less ceased in her 30s because of the
constraints of a young family. These themes are pursued in more detail in Chapter
9:

Well we just/it, it just didn't come into our lives at that time and I can't
remember. You know it, it was just busy with the children. They weren't
old enough, the children weren't old enough. When the children were old
enough we'd take them to the cinema occasionally. Very occasionally
though, not regular. When they were tiny no the, the cinema didn't come
into it no, no (R348, Margaret, aged 30s, born 1934, Manchester).

A similar pattern emerges from the accounts that respondents give of eating
out. At each time period there was a considerable variety of experience, with some
people rarely eating out (usually due to cost or family constraints) and others
eating out regularly. Although going out for a meal has increased in frequency by
no means all respondents today eat out frequently, and in each time period fast
food was common. The only difference is that to some degree a trip to the fish and
chip shop has been replaced by a meal at McDonalds or a similar fast food chain.
In most cases eating out was a sociable activity, undertaken with family and
friends, and most travel was either relatively short distance to a local restaurant or
café, or undertaken as part of another trip, for instance a meal after an outing to the
cinema or shopping. Thus as an 18 year old in the 1950s Elizabeth would visit a
café in Manchester when shopping but only rarely ate out in a restaurant in the
evening. Likewise, at the time of interview, Vicki (also aged 17/18) saw eating out
as an occasional activity. In contrast Saeeda regularly ate out with family and
friends, and Barbara explains how, in her 60s, a combination of more time and
money enables her to eat out much more than in the past. However, for Beryl, with
a young family in the 1960s a meal out was a rare event due to the difficulty of
getting a babysitter. Thus although there have been changes in the availability of
food, and the ease with which people can eat out, the basic factors that structure
such activities have changed little over the past half century. Experiences are
varied, many people were constrained, and most trips were short and often linked
to other activities:

We used to go/they were, they were mostly cafeterias such as in Lewis' or
you know wherever. If we went shopping. I don't ever remember going to
any, any restaurants in Manchester as a, you know round about 18 ... But I
remember we did go to the Ping Hong. And I remember going to some other

restaurant, but I can't remember what it was. But it was very very rarely (R339, Elizabeth, aged 17/18, born 1940, Salford).

No no, maybe, well maybe once every couple of months or something, if we could get a sitter you know. But you see we were stuck because we couldn't always find anyone to babysit you know. And then of course you had to/also it was, it was quite expensive eating out, especially you know if you only had one wage coming in (R353, Beryl, aged 30s, born 1935, Manchester).

Um well of course the point is I think, I think you eat out because I like to be in company, right. And also it's a change from cooking yourself. And I think you've got a bit more money to spend (R369, Barbara, aged 60s, born 1936, Manchester).

I mean I have been out occasionally, like the other night I'd not seen my friend P for ages so we went out for a nice Italian in town just as a treat. But not really consistently … I got the bus into town and met her in town, because she lives in Withington. And then we went out to eat, and then got the bus back (R221, Vicki, aged 18, born 1985 Manchester).

We go, we do that every weekend now mostly, every Saturdays, and my parents … All the family, my parents yea. With friends we always go/whenever we go out we always end up eating anyway. But with family we go like every Saturday we're going out … We go to, sometimes we go to McDonalds to take a take-away, take-out. Or sometimes we go to that same place in Rusholme, yea. There's loads of restaurants there (R226, Saeeda, aged 17/18, born 1985, Manchester).

Travel for Sporting Activities

In comparison to many other activities, for instance travel to school, to work, or visits to friends, trips to either watch or participate in sport are usually undertaken less frequently. However, for males in particular sport can form an important part of leisure activities. Compared with the more frequent activities outlined above, we might also expect there to have been much greater change in the nature of travel to sporting activities over the past 60 years. It can be suggested that, whereas in the past most people either played for or supported a local team, and travelled only short distances for fixtures, today many sports fans will follow a national league team to fixtures all over the country, or will play matches in a wide variety of locations. However, overall, the mean distance travelled to sporting activities has not increased consistently, and the mean time spent travelling (as with other aspects of mobility) has mostly reduced (Tables 4.10-4.13). Not surprisingly, there has been an increase in the amount of travel by car and in the extent to which young children are accompanied. In this respect too, travel for sport conforms to the pattern of other travel behaviour. The last 60 years has seen some increase in

Box 8.2   Travelling for Sport in Manchester and Salford

> *No there was no reason to go further because Cringle Fields was, it was a big park, 55 acres, and plenty of places where you could play cricket ... That's the only thing I ever played, cricket. I used to play a little bit of/on the school field in the winter/but in those days it was absolutely seasonal* (R331, Arnold, aged 10/11, born 1936, Manchester).
>
> *Definitely. I played football, basketball, at that time ...Thursday nights I trained at Peel Moat which is like the astra turf near North Area ... And on Saturday mornings I play/home games were at White Hill near the Ash, near the fire station in Heaton Chapel. And away games were, we were taken to various places, like Glossop, Chapel-en-le-Frith, and all over the place* (R222, Rob, aged 10/11, born 1985, Stockport).
>
> *I used, I used to play football quite a bit ... It used to be on that street* [Who did you play with?] *... It was like the boy I said I walked down with, he's got/there are 5 brothers, so there's them lot, and there's some more people, other people who lived near there, so we always used to have a kick-around.* [How often would you do that?] *... It depended on the weather. If/whenever the weather was good we used to play* (R239, Hassan, aged 10/11, born 1985, Manchester).
>
> *I play netball at the Velodrome, basketball at the Velodrome. Football with our old teacher ... And I do um, what else did I say now ... Tennis I do and I play it at home with my friends. And swimming I go sometimes with my cousin and I go with my mum and my auntie.* [How often to you go to the Velodrome?] *About ... seven times a month ... Me, my brother/me, my cousin, another cousin, my brother and a friend.* [How do you get there?] *Walk ... About 20 minutes, half an hour I think* (R202, Gabriel, aged 10/11, born 1992, Manchester).
>
> *But it/on a, on a Saturday, on a Saturday and/on a Saturday I used to play* [football], *you know not professional but for the local, you know the, the youth club or whatever ... But if I was/on a Sunday morning they used to have the, the old pub games, but there used to be quite a crowd got, got there you know ... You, you, you know well you didn't have to pay, they just used to come round with the hat after. But you could get, you could see some good games you know ... Oh yes, yea, it was only round the corner yea* (R325, Derek, aged 17/18, born 1937, Salford).
>
> *On Saturdays mornings I get, I get up at about, really early. And I get the 192 to where the Apollo is. I walk through Ardwick into Hulme, where I get picked up by my friend's mum, who's like done a round journey. She picks up someone from Sale then/they live in Chorlton, and one of the other people who play badminton live in Chorlton, so she drives to Sale and then back into Manchester, and picks me up from Hulme. And then/I wait at a bus stop/and then we drive into Moss Side, and play badminton from 9 o'clock till 10 o'clock at Moss Side Centre* (R222, Rob, aged 17/18, born 1985, Stockport).

Source: Everyday mobility interviews 2000-2003.

the total amount of recreational travel, and much greater car use. However, such journeys still occur relatively infrequently compared to other local trips, and many such trips are undertaken on foot.

It is also important to stress the individual variability that exists within the data set (Box 8.2). As with other types of everyday mobility in both the past and the present individual circumstances and personal preferences produce a high degree of variation, and generalisations can be misleading. Thus in the 1940s and 1950s Arnold (aged 10/11) and Derek (aged 17/18) mostly played and watched football or cricket locally, whereas in the 1990s Rob travelled much further afield at the age of both 10/11 and 17/18. However, also in the 1990s, Hassan's sporting activities were restricted to kicking a ball about in his local street. Gabriel, aged 10/11 at interview undertakes a good deal of sport but is quite independent, walking alone some 20 minutes to the Manchester Velodrome, and thus challenging the assumption that today all young children are ferried to their everyday activities by parents. It can thus be suggested that even for sporting activities, where on the face of it there has been more change in travel behaviour than for some other categories, it would be wrong to assume that all experiences are the same. Whilst, overall, more people travel by car over longer distances than in the past, there are many exceptions to this. It can also be suggested that such variability needs to be given higher priority in contemporary transport planning, a theme that is returned to in Chapter 11.

The fact that some everyday travel for sporting activities has changed relatively little over the past 60 years is emphasised if we compare the testimonies of Joe and Dean as 10 year olds in Morecambe some half a century apart. Joe was very keen on football and played whenever possible in the school yard and on local waste ground. However, at the age of 10/11 he rarely watched a match, and remembers his first visit to the local football ground (Christie Park) as a nine year old as a one-off event. Dean, aged 10/11 at interview, was less enthusiastic about sport, but played football and other games on land adjacent to his home both with friends and when necessary on his own. Like Joe, he rarely watched sport and also remembers a recent visit to Christie Park as a one-off event. Despite the passage of time the experience of everyday travel for Joe and Dean is very similar:

> The priority was to get to the school yard to play football before school started ... Oh dear it was a terrible year thinking back cause I used to just play and play and play and sometimes my parents used to come and drag me out of the playground ... I can remember, I can remember very clearly the first football match I ever went to, it was 1947 at Christie Park but I didn't, I didn't start watching football regularly until, until later (R9, Joe, aged 10/11, born 1938, Morecambe).

> There's somebody who lives across the street from me and then there's/there's two people who live across the street from me. And then there's/Max is sometimes hanging around there. Yea that's about it ... Sometimes I play football on my own. But there's/we've got a piece of land and it's got a gate and I play against the gate ... Football, Frisbee and sometimes we play baseball but with a tennis ball and that's it ... I went to

watch Morecambe Football Team and they beat Southport five four/four three, yea four three ... That was just a one off (R34, Dean, aged 10/11, born 1990, Morecambe).

Travelling to Shop

Shopping is one of the most ubiquitous of activities, undertaken partly out of necessity and partly for pleasure. As outlined above, it can be suggested that shopping has both increased as a proportion of all travel over the past 50 years and that in particular shopping as a leisure activity has grown substantially. However, although there has been some increase in car use, alterations in the mean distance and time travelled, and in the characteristics of trips, are in line with other types of mobility. Overall, change has been neither large-scale nor consistent, though children aged 10/11 today spend rather more time shopping than they did in the 1940s, suggesting that they are more often expected to accompany their parents on shopping trips (Tables 4.10-4.13). Qualitative data again stress the variability of individual experiences. It would be wrong to suggest that everyone has changed their shopping behaviour in the same way, and not all respondents recorded substantial increases in shopping-related travel over the past 60 years.

For children aged 10/11 most shopping consisted of either running errands to collect goods from local shops, or being taken on shopping trips with a parent. Most children aged 10/11 do not have a great deal of individual agency over their shopping and this has not changed substantially over time. However, for the more independent children of this age window shopping, or just hanging around in town looking in shop windows, was an activity that a small number of respondents in each cohort undertook. In the 1940s girls in particular were expected to run errands for their mothers and popping out to the local shop on their own was a normal part of everyday life. At this time in both Lancaster/Morecambe and Manchester/Salford most shopping was done locally with the majority of neighbourhoods having easy access to a range of local services. Lack of a refrigerator, together with limited income, meant that fresh foods such as bread, milk and meat were bought almost daily. Daughters aged 10/11 were often given the task of doing this shopping. However, the travel this entailed was very limited, moving in a well-known territory, and dealing with neighbours that were part of the local community. Janet, Mary, Pamela and Ruth all remembered these activities well (Box 8.3).

By the 1970s much of this neighbourhood shopping had disappeared and although children might still pop out to a local shop for sweets or a newspaper, most food and other shopping was done in a supermarket or town centre. This altered the pattern of shopping trips for children, with most shopping done as a family group usually on a Saturday. Jackie, Becky and Julia (all from Lancaster and Morecambe) provide typical accounts. Many boys, such as Toby and Marty avoided shopping when they could, but Marty's account also emphasised that some children aged 10/11 still retained considerable independence. At the time of

Box 8.3   Travelling to Shop Aged 10/11

> *The co-op, co-operative. It was just up the road. And yea you know you'd usually shop there on your own, and my mother would like run out of something and you'd go up the road for it ... and I used to collect the bread on my way home sometimes* (R320, Janet, aged 10/11, born 1936, Salford).
>
> *Everything was very handy, not far. It was halfway between home and school. I used to go and get bread every night. Cause you didn't shop like they do now. We didn't have a fridge* (R356, Pamela, aged 10/11, born 1937, Salford).
>
> *I'd nip to shop for a loaf or I'd got to bake house I'd say to go for, get bread or summat. I'd go like that but I wouldn't go into town for it you know* (R03, Mary, aged 10/11, born 1935, Lancaster).
>
> *Well the thing, again you see the thing was with it being so close I'd nip out of the back gate then I'd cross the back street and I'd knock on the back door and I'd go in and sort of into the back of the shop and say you know my mummy wants this that and the other you see* (R8, Ruth, aged 10/11, born 1936, Morecambe).
>
> *We would shop with the family on a Saturday, we'd go into Morecambe and we'd do shopping* (R10, Julia, aged 10/11, born 1968, Morecambe).
>
> *Not really, I hated going shopping when I was 11. No I'd do anything to get away from mum's dress shopping. Going round spending endless hours looking round Marks and Spencer's* (R18, Toby, aged 10/11, born 1984, Morecambe).
>
> *I'd have gone with my mum to that ASDA just there ... Once a week ... Would have walked, it's just a five minute walk, not even that, it's just around the corner. But we used to go to Sainsburys as well, which is in Lancaster and then we'd go, you know, more into the town centre, Lancaster town centre with mum. That would be with my mum, we'd walk there ... Yeah, 'cos we didn't have a car. I think occasionally biked it there. That would be to go to Sainsbury's to do like the main/well main bit of shopping would be there but occasionally we'd get stuff from Sainsburys and you know there'd be individual shops she'd want to go into in Lancaster* (R12, Becky, aged 10/11, born 1983, Morecambe).
>
> *Yes I do. I sometimes go shopping for my mum at Sainsbury's, so I cycle to Sainsbury's ... Yea, go along the cycle, the cycle track ... Normally I go out if they're going shopping, unless they need me to carry things, and I'll go out into town or go and call on someone* (R45, Marty, aged 10/11, born 1990, Lancaster).
>
> *Well some/we usually go to ASDA. We go in the car. And we sometimes stay at ASDA and have something to eat. And then come back in the car* (R43, Jackie, aged 10/11, born 1990, Morecambe).

Source: Everyday mobility interviews 2000-2003.

interview he was cycling alone to Sainsbury's (along a cycle track) and although he tried to get out of going shopping in town with his mother, he frequently went into town alone or with a group of friends, and went shopping for music or games for himself if he had money to spend (Box 8.3).

This pattern of activity is mirrored in the accounts given by other age cohorts, with those in their 60s at the time of interview experiencing the most change. Pamela, born in Salford in 1937 and still living in Salford aged about 66 at the time of the interview, had stressed her family's use of local shops for most things in the 1940s, when she either walked or used public transport for all trips (Box 8.3). However, in 2003, her pattern of shopping had changed completely. She mainly used the Trafford Centre in Manchester or ASDA, was very price conscious, always travelled by car, and often turned a shopping trip into a leisure outing including stopping (with a friend) for something to eat. Indeed, she sometimes chose the shopping centres she went to by the quality of the restaurants that they had:

> I do everything by car. Um well the buses are just not reliable, I wouldn't dream/I mean I have a breathing problem anyway, so you know if I walk too far and it's uphill I get out of breath. So the car stops all that ... And wherever I go I need a car. If I want to go to the Trafford Centre I need to have a car ... I mean I know I can get the bus, but God at my age I'm not getting a bus ... Well they're not reliable and I, and I just don't like public transport now ... I just prefer the independence of my car. I can leave when I want, I'm not tied to times ... I've never been on it for years ... Well I do yea. I go to ASDA because it's/I just believe the Americans bring the prices down. I don't go to Tesco any more cause it's a rip-off, and I don't go to Sainsbury's any more cause it's a rip-off. I'm really conscious of prices deliberately because I just think they're making tons of money at my expense aren't they. I buy/you see I don't eat fast food, I cook everything, so. And because I'm off work, you know I don't work any more, I/you can watch the prices ... Depending on what the restaurant's like, well the, the cafés. You know we always stop and have something to eat half way through the day. So depending what we feel like really (R356, Pamela, aged 60s, born 1937, Salford).

Pamela's account also emphasises another common theme in attitudes to public transport. She was adamant that she did not like travelling by bus, and cited ill health as one reason for using her car, but when pressed to explain what she disliked about public transport had to admit that she did not know because she had not used it for years. Such attitudes are not only very different from the majority view of public transport half a century ago, but have real implications for the development of sustainable transport policies. This theme will be explored further in Chapters 10 and 11.

Day Trips, Outings and Holidays

Holidays, outings and visits to relatives are an important part of the social life of most people and are one of the aspects of everyday mobility that we might expect to have changed most over the past 60 years. Although this study has focused mainly on everyday travel within Britain, one of the most notable general changes in holiday travel has been the expansion of air transport, especially low-cost airlines, that have allowed many people to journey abroad for leisure and, especially, to supplement a long summer holiday with a city break in Europe. Nationally, this is an aspect of mobility that has changed out of all recognition (Urry, 2002). Even for travel within Britain it can be suggested that the combination of more leisure time, higher disposable incomes, greater car ownerships, and a network of friends and relatives that are much more widely scattered that in the past, has led to an expansion in both the frequency and distance of outings and weekends away. However, although it can be argued that there has been a massive expansion in this type of travel, as a proportion of all trips such trips remains tiny. Travel to school or to work takes place almost daily, trips to shop or to visit nearby friends are regular and frequent, but outings and weekends away remain for most people a special event that occurs only a few times during a year. Thus the total impact of this sort of travel on overall mobility behaviour should not be overstated.

Quantitative data derived from the interviews confirm some of the above assumptions, but also again emphasise the difficulty of generalisation with respect to individual travel behaviour. The distance travelled to relatives or for outings depends as much on life-course stage as it does on the decade in which it took place, and there are examples of both long and short trips in each cohort. Overall, there is a trend towards longer journeys, especially for holidays, but even these changes are not completely consistent across all cohorts. Inevitably more travel for leisure is now undertaken by car, but many local outings are undertaken using public transport or on foot (Tables 4.10-4.13).

Qualitative accounts again emphasise the different experiences of respondents and also show that although mobility potential has increased considerably over time, not everyone has been able to utilise that potential. If we focus on the day trips undertaken by children aged 10/11 and teenagers aged 17/18 there is as much evidence of stability as there is of change. Thus in the 1940s and 1950s, Derek, Irene, Les and Ken all remembered day trips to local attractions both in the Manchester area (Belle Vue) and further afield (Blackpool or Southport). The only real difference between the two age groups was that children aged 10/11 were mainly accompanied by parents whereas adolescents tended to travel alone, often by bike. This could pose problems for some teenage girls, for instance Barbara's father objected to her wearing shorts whilst cycling, but most respondents recalled trips around the local area on a regular basis in the 1940s and 1950s. Evidence from those aged 10/11 today suggests that many families travel little further for day trips now than was common in the 1940s, and that some experience quite

Box 8.4   Day Trips for Respondents Aged 10/11 and 17/18, Manchester and Salford

Like I mean Blackpool now is, is very very near, but in them days when I was 10 we used to kind of, my gran and my granddad used to get on, there used to be a coach. There was no heater on, but I remember they used to take a travelling rug, but was that like a full day out to Blackpool (R325, Derek, aged 10/11, born 1937, Salford).

But on Bank Holidays he'd be usually home. And he, my dad would take us children, not the babies, the older ones, to Belle Vue for the day. Or he, he was very fond of horses, he came from Burnley and they had horses, and he'd take us to Knutsford to the May Day Show. He would take us all over ... Oh we, always on the bus, or buses ye (R333, Irene, aged 10/11, born 1937, Manchester).

Only I go to the beach with my Mam and Dad in the summer ... Southport or Blackpool or there's one that's dead far away and it's got like sand hills and, and the sea's not that far out and you can go in your car to the sea ... And then in Blackpool you can/we park the car up and then we run to the beach with a spade. And then in Southport we take the car with us cause the sea's a long, long way away (R218, Charlie, aged 10/11, born 1992, Salford).

Yea we go Knowsley Safari Park, Chester Zoo, and places like that and like Blackpool and stuff ... Well we'd get a taxi ... Yea. Or someone would drop us off. If we're going Knowsley Safari Park we'll have to like borrow a car that they're probably going to/that's a bit broke because it won't get, it won't get sand in and everything, so ... Yea my dad and my mum can drive, but they just don't/my mum had a car, but I don't know what happened to it (R215, Lorna, aged 10/11, born 1991, Salford).

Belle Vue Zoo was very popular yea. And then there's, they're might be a boating lake at Platt Fields at Manchester, you know which we thought was miles and miles away ... Well it would be about 5 mile. Now you get in your car and you're there in 10 minutes. But as a kid we used to think it was half a day to get there like ... Well we'd go on the bus, and well we did a, quite a lot of walking (R351, Les, aged 17/18, born 1937, Salford).

I mean sometimes if I wasn't working a weekend I'd be on my bike, I'd be cycling, I'd, I'd go to New Brighton ... Oh yes. Southport, I used to go there quite often. You know in the summer months ... It, it was hard work mind you, but I mean we was young and full of vigour, vim, or whatever you want to call it you know (R327, Ken, aged 17/18, born 1938, Manchester).

And I joined a cycling club when I was 16 I think, and I used to go cycling on a Sunday. Yea. Cause I got told off by my dad because we/I used to wear shorts and we weren't allowed to wear shorts you see, so I put my shorts on under my trousers and then when I got to the meeting place where everybody met I took my trousers off, and rolled them up and put them in my, in my, in my bag (R369, Barbara, aged 17/18, born 1936, Salford).

Source: Everyday mobility interviews, 2000-2003.

severe constraints to their mobility. Thus, though travelling by car, Charlie visits the same resorts in North-west England that earlier generations did, and Lorna's family depend on taxis or a borrowed car for their days out (Box 8.4).

For those in their 30s with young children day trips could prove difficult. Thus Beatrice, in her 30s in the 1960s, remembers that she had very few outings and then mostly just to the local park because of family constraints; and Warren, in his 30s at the time of the interview, highlights the tensions that can exist in a family when each member does not have the same priorities:

> I didn't miss not doing things on my own. But because they were very young children at/when I was 30 they were sort of young, and sort of they kept me busy. And my husband, who worked nights, he was on the papers, well I was a lot on my own in the evening. And he, he would have days off during the week which was good cause in holiday time we could go out to Heaton Park, take the kids for the day for a picnic. But I was/I did spend a lot of time with just the children (R367, Beatrice, aged 30s, born 1937, Manchester).

> I mean my wife likes going to the theme parks with my son obviously and I don't like doing that because usually there's loads of queues and you can stand an hour and a half waiting to go on a ride, I just don't see the logic. However for the love of my son and the love of my wife I put up with it cause they like the day out you know. And so if I had my way I wouldn't go anywhere where it's too busy. I, I much prefer maybe walking and going on holiday to the country, just taking in a quiet life, whereas my wife's a little bit opposite, she likes shopping and busy busy busy, lots of people. We try and get a happy medium you know (R380, Warren, aged 30s, born 1966, Manchester).

Respondents in their 60s at interview also gave a wide range of responses. Some, like Hilda, were enjoying a very mobile retirement and were able to take their grandchildren regularly on outings (though mostly to exactly the same places that children had been taken to 60 years previously), but Irene admitted to having lost interest in trips out and to doing very little despite being a moderately healthy 66 year old, largely because she had no-one to go out with:

> Everything I say, like say at weekends we'll get up Saturday morning and I'll say let's go and get the kids, we'll take 'em to Blackpool. So we just go up, get the car seats and shove 'em in there. Play football on sands with em, granddad does, while I watch. And we take 'em on Pleasure Beach or whatever (R328, Hilda, aged 60s, born 1940, Manchester).

> Well that's simply because I haven't got anybody to go with, yea, yea. I did use to do things like that until I finished work yea. But … No. I'm not, it's very strange really, I'm 66, but I'm not an old 66. There, there are thing that I'd go on. You see, you see I've just no interest in them, yea (R333, Irene, aged 60s born 1937, Manchester).

Box 8.5   Holidays Aged 10/11 for Respondents in Lancaster and Morecambe

Yea we had really extravagant holidays. We used to go to Ulverston. For a week. I think I was 10 when I, when I went there and I think we went to Windermere when I was round about 10 ... Well I went to/gosh went to Windermere in ... my dad's car ... we went as a family. I don't know how the heck I got to Ulverston when I think about it ... with my mate from the chippie. Well his family lived at Ulverston and we went there (R9, Joe, aged 10/11, born 1938, Morecambe).

The only place I remember going on the train regularly was um, when I was that age, was to Blackpool to visit an uncle and, and aunt who lived there. We used to/now if I went there obviously I went with my parents That was a sort of little family holiday. Oh once, only once a year, sort of ... Yes, like the summer holiday you know yes, yes ... A week I should think. Yes a week (R8, Ruth, aged 10/11, born 1936, Morecambe).

We would walk down to the Castle Station carrying cases and then we'd get a train from Castle/not from Castle Station, Green Ayre Station ... So we walk down from F, down the back ways, down to Green Ayre Station, get a train to Heysham and then get the boat from Heysham to Belfast, and then get a train from Belfast to Londonderry, and get a bus from Londonderry out to where we lived. And I remember once us having a taxi, only once. You, you would walk sort of um two or three miles from where we got off the bus to, to where my aunt lived (R55, Teresa, aged 10/11, born 1937, Lancaster).

Well when we got to the station it was a long walk from the station up to the house, but we always walked it to there ... Well we ... went every year, probably just a week at a time and we stayed at different houses, different family houses. He had a lot of brothers and sisters, so. Same days every time, Wednesdays to Barrow cause it was market day, Thursdays to Ulverston cause it was market day there, and, and so ... We usually always went there for holidays (R111, Rosemary, aged 10/11, born 1936, Lancaster).

Last year I went to Florida in/we went to Orlando. And then we just went on to the ... Universal Studios, I went to Disneyland, Wet and Wild Water Park place and well we did lots of things really (R33, Gareth, aged 10/11, born 1989, Morecambe).

No we haven't, but we're going in July. Yea we're going to Cornwall ... we're going for a week. We normally go every year but last year we were going to go abroad but we tried to save up but we couldn't cause it's that much for all of us ... And the year before we couldn't make it cause [sister] was born that year and we were going to go in August but then my mum started to have pain and that lot and then she was born the second/third of September so ... we couldn't go and so (R26, Sophie, aged 10/11, born 1990, Lancaster).

No we haven't been on holiday. But I go to my nana's, for like in the six week holiday I go to my nana's for a couple of weeks ... in Middlesbrough ... Well if my dad's got a couple of weeks off work he'll drive us there But if my mum's feeling okay she'll drive us up. If she's not we'll probably/my sister will take us and then she'll drive back (R32, Jessica, aged 10/11, born 1990, Morecambe).

Source: Everyday mobility interviews 2000-2003.

For most people the annual holiday is the most important trip away from home and, as outlined above, it can be suggested that changes in the ease with which long distance travel can be undertaken have fundamentally altered the pattern of holiday travel over time. However, as with other aspects of everyday mobility the picture is very mixed, and in many respects the extent to which change has occurred in reality is rather less than theory or popular perceptions might suggest. Although increased incomes and access to cheap package holidays, especially since the 1970s, have revolutionised overseas travel for many, even today not everyone has access to this degree of leisure mobility. Similarly, even in the 1940s and 1950s, whilst most families were quite constrained in their holiday arrangements, some did travel over considerable distances.

Thus if we compare the accounts of travel for holidays provided by respondents aged 10/11 in the 1940s and at interview, the similarities are as notable as the differences (Box 8.5). In the 1940s, those families that went away on holiday frequently visited relatives, both to reduce cost and to combine a holiday with keeping in touch with family. Most such trips were undertaken within about 100km of home with, for respondents in Lancaster and Morecambe, holidays in Blackpool and Furness particularly common. Thus both Ruth and Rosemary regularly holidayed with relations in Blackpool and Barrow/Ulverston respectively. However, some travelled further afield, for instance Teresa's family visited relatives in Ireland and Joe both holidayed with a friend's relatives in Ulverston and went with his parents to stay in a hotel in Windermere. Although Joe's parents had a car, for most respondents at this time travel was by public transport. Many children aged 10/11 today do have both more frequent and more exotic holidays than the cohort born in the 1930s – Gareth's trips to Florida are not untypical – but not all respondents are so fortunate. As in the 1940s, some families were constrained by cost and other factors, and for many relatives still play a major part in holiday plans. Thus Sophie had not had a summer holiday for two years because of cost and the birth of her baby sister, and for Jessica her holiday was two weeks with her Nan in Middlesbrough.

Similarly, the accounts of those aged 17/18 in the 1950s, and respondents that age at the time of interview, also show many similarities (Box 8.6). Although overseas travel is obviously now much easier, many (especially male) adolescents were quite adventurous in the 1950s, and some teenagers today are quite constrained in their mobility. In both the 1950s and today, schools and other organisations also played a significant role in organising trips for adolescents aged 17/18. As a 17 year old in the 1950s Joe, who had quite adventurous holidays when aged 10/11, was able to take himself off with a friend to Northern Ireland for a holiday in a hotel. His account suggests this was the 1950s equivalent of a teenage holiday in Ibiza or Cyprus today. Bob also undertook a substantial amount of holiday travel without his parents, his work on the railways enabling him to travel to Penzance with a friend, however for Ruth organised trips to the Lake District provided through her youth club were her only access to a holiday. Lee is typical of the well-travelled teenage respondent at the time of the interview, with organised trips (through choir and school) to Germany and France and a summer holiday

Box 8.6   Holidays Aged 17/18 for Respondents in Lancaster and Morecambe

---

Oh yes, yea I went to, I went to Northern Ireland for a holiday when I was ... Yea when I was 17, to a place called Whitehead just outside Belfast ... There used to be a ferry from, you know the, the Heysham Belfast Ferry ... it was with Derek Robin, they guy from the chippie and another, another guy, there was three of us ... It was a week ... We stayed in a hotel, one of those things you do when you flex your muscles a bit and ... it was fabulous. I remember it was beautiful. I went to Antrim and the Giants Causeway and places like that. Absolutely fantastic. Fantastic, I loved it. That was the holiday of a lifetime up to then. You know it was brilliant, I loved it ... Got drunk for the first time in my life ... Probably when I was 17 I, I went with my mum and dad to London for a few days I remember ... We used to, we used to stay with/no we didn't used to stay, we used to see people in London and we used to go and see a show ... In my dad's car ... It, it was a, it was like a boarding house. There were two Morecambe guys who ran it and it was near Euston Station (R9, Joe, aged 17/18, born 1938, Morecambe).

On the railways you got free rail travel, so that's why I went to Penzance ... And it was a lad I knew from school, he worked on ... so we got these free passes, and went down to Penzance. That was one big holiday we went on ... I would never have thought of going/paying the rail fare down to there (R113, Bob, aged 17/18, born 1940, Lancaster).

No youth club weekends yes we used to go up into the, as I said before into the Lakes and stay, you know camp out in church halls and things, not under canvas, we used to sleep in the church hall ... Oh we'd only have two a year, one in, at the beginning and one at the end of the year (R8, Ruth, aged 17/18, born 1936, Morecambe).

Quite a lot. I went, I went to what was it called, I've forgotten the name of it, Germany. I went to Germany with the choir in February. And I went on a French Exchange the month afterwards. And then I went to Greece in the summer holidays ... that was with my friends, but not with/not my girlfriend cause her parents wouldn't let her go ... Cause they're, they're quite protective and there wasn't any, any adults there, just, just all of us lot (R48, Lee, aged 17/18, born 1984, Lancaster).

But we don't/Blackpool really is the first holiday I've been on in God only knows how long which hasn't been a relative holiday do you know what I mean, cause I count a holiday as going to see my sister, but I haven't done that for a bit and that used to be my holidays (R12, Becky, aged 17/18, born 1983, Morecambe).

Last summer we went to Samos in Greece. Yea it's an island in the Mediterranean. Fantastic, 42°C ... It was, it was incredible. That was in June. Yea, it was brilliant, T they're really good, fantastic holiday. I mean they take you there, when you get off the plane they don't leave you, they talk to you and they tell you like, like this is where you're/they take you on a big coach, the lady tells you like, gives you like sheets out of all the activities that they've got planned if you want to take part, if you want to do them, which is great (R16, Dan, aged 17/18, born 1983, Morecambe).

Source: Everyday mobility interviews 2000-2003.

Box 8.7   Holidays for Adult Respondents in Lancaster and Morecambe, 2001-2003

Yea. We went to Malta, we had a week in Malta and we had a fortnight in Tenerife in November and, and this holiday in Cornwall ... Feel decadent ... Well I finished work in the/at the end of December 1999 and we just felt that we wanted to have a break so we went to Malta and we've, and we've never been to Malta before and it seemed likely that there'd be a bit of sunshine in, in April so it was ... lovely ... It was yea self catering apartment. And then we did the same thing in, in November. We've never had any winter sunshine and there was a cheap offer came up in/you collected tokens for, for a flight and so we collected these tokens and we got a flight to Tenerife for £75 each return ... It was through a newspaper yea, yea, yea So we, we did that and it was brilliant, it was (R9, Joe, aged 60s, born 1938, Lancaster).

We/I mean this/obviously we have more holidays now. I mean we're going to the Algarve/we always go to the Algarve, have done for about, well for 10, 12 years with Bob and Pam. We always have a villa and go self catering and this year we're going in, again of course in May and, and then we're going to the Algarve again which is about five weeks later with some friends and then we're going, we're going with the family to Disney later in the year. So we fortunately, we're, you know we, we have more trips like that which is/so really summer is, is just, is just to relax and do as we like you know time (R8, Ruth, aged 60s, born 1936, Morecambe).

Holidays in the last 12 months. We always every year/for about the last 5 years we've had a family holiday in Devon with Mark's parents and brothers and the wife and the three nephews and we always have a house and we all travel down separately, we all go in our cars. Me and Mark travel down usually a day or two before and stop half way down the country. Last year we stayed in Hereford and we had a couple of nights in Hereford and broke the journey and then drove on to Devon to meet the family on the Friday ... And that's usually for about 10 days and that's how long we're away cause we always stop a couple of days before and a couple of days after ... This last year other than that we didn't have any other holiday other than our long weekends away with our friends at the farm or/they're not really holidays, they're just a break ... About, about six or so a year, six or eight a year with them (R10, Julia, aged 30s born 1968, Lancaster).

No we don't, we don't go anywhere. It's probably why I'm knackered. I haven't the energy to actually go anywhere. But also having I it's not been that practical and also anywhere that might be child orientated up until now hasn't really been appropriate because like baby she's not really going to appreciate it, we don't want to go and do baby things with a child that's not going to appreciate it (R44, Diane, aged 30s, born 1971, Morecambe).

Source: Everyday mobility interviews, 2000-2003.

with friends in Greece. However, it is notable that some girls in particular still experience significant constraints: Lee's girlfriend was not allowed on the trip because there were no 'adults' present. Dan, like many teenagers holidayed abroad with his parents, stressing the ease of the package holiday in which everything is provided. In this sense it can be suggested that although today's teenagers may travel further than those in the 1950s, organising an independent holiday to Ireland or Penzance half a century ago required much more initiative and skill. Not all adolescents today enjoy frequent overseas holidays. Becky had just returned from a weekend in Blackpool at the time of the interview, but apart from occasional visits to her sister this was the only break that she could recall. Like many in the 1950s her leisure breaks were local and often depended on relatives.

The group that have probably seen the biggest change in holiday travel are those aged 60 today. As we have seen, in their youth most leisure was relatively local and 60 year olds in the 1940s would rarely have holidayed far from home. Today, many of this cohort have both the time and money to take multiple holidays overseas: Joe and Ruth (whose trips when younger were described above) are typical (Box 8.7). Joe in particular, has taken the opportunity of retirement to take three holidays in a year, to Cornwall, Malta and Tenerife. However, he was always quite adventurous in his travel and he and his wife were also able to make use of special offers for cheap flights that tempted them to travel frequently. Respondents in their 30s today were in many ways the most constrained by family and cost, for Julia the annual holiday was a trip to Devon with many other family members: creating a large party both reduced costs and enabled a family reunion. However, for Diane, the birth of her daughter has temporarily at least curtailed all holidays.

Conclusion

Both theoretical and popular writing about mobility, culture and society tends to emphasise change rather than stability. In particular, it is usually assumed that over the past half century there has been an unparalleled increase in leisure travel: a mobility revolution creating a completely new pattern of recreational activity. Although to some extent this is true, with many today enjoying frequent leisure travel both at home and overseas, the extent of these changes is not universal. Half a century ago many people were quite adventurous and teenage boys in particular had considerable freedom to travel independently. Moreover, the constraints that limit travel for recreation have been quite stable over time. In general, girls have less freedom than boys to travel independently for leisure, and for many adults a combination of cost constraints and family commitments severely restrict the amount of recreational travel that can be undertaken. In other words, although there has been change, this has not been experienced by all. In both the past and the present there is a great deal of individual variability in the experience of leisure travel, and many of the accounts that our respondents provided of recreational travel today were remarkably similar to their recollections of non-essential mobility half a century ago.

Chapter 9

Mobility, Family and the Life Course

Introduction

There is an extensive literature on residential migration that demonstrates how migration is closely related to the life course, with most movement being undertaken by young adults, and with many moves precipitated by key life course events such as marriage, birth of a child, divorce, children leaving home, retirement or death of a partner (Rossi, 1980; Champion and Fielding, 1992; Pooley and Turnbull, 1998). It seems reasonable to suggest that everyday mobility will also be affected by life course factors, and the ways in which family commitments can constrain mobility have already been alluded to in earlier chapters. In this chapter we focus on two aspects of the relationship between mobility, family and the life course. First, we examine the ways in which the mobility of children aged 10/11, those most dependent on adults for their mobility, is affected by family circumstances, and the ways in which this has changed over time since the 1940s. Second, we focus on respondents born 1932-1941, and examine the ways in which the mobility experience for this group has altered over their life course: what are the key changes in mobility experience that they have encountered during their life time? This is achieved by combining some quantitative evidence with the use of detailed case studies to create vignettes of mobility life histories.

During the twentieth century, there have been a series of well-documented changes in the composition and organisation of Western families (Haraven, 1978; Anderson, 1980; 1985; 1994; Davidoff, 1990). Most obviously, over the last half century in England and Wales there has been a reduction in mean family size (3.2 in 1951 and 2.4 in 2001); the dispersal of kin produced by greater long-distance residential mobility; longer education and delayed entry into the work force (in 1951 19 per cent children aged 16 and 9.8 per cent of children age 17 were in education whereas in 2001 77.6 per cent of children age 16 and 17 were in education); related but complex changes in the age of leaving home (van Poppel, Oris and Lee, 2004); increased rates of separation and divorce leading to more lone-parent families (in 2001 6.5 per cent of households were lone parents with dependent children, there is no equivalent figure for 1951); and a higher proportion of working mothers (in 1951 35 per cent of women worked either full or part time, whereas in 2001 the figure was 57 per cent). At the same time most families have experienced rising real incomes and better health, with fewer periods of mobility-restricting poverty or illness. However, in terms of both income and health the gap between those best and worse off has widened (Shaw et al, 1999). It can be argued that these changes will have had some impact on the ways in which families negotiate mobility and on the impact of mobility constraints on individual family members.

Mobility and the Family

There are many ways in which family structures and circumstances can influence the mobility of children and other family members. As already illustrated in other chapters (and explored in more detail below) marriage and motherhood can severely constrain female mobility. In this section we focus especially on the ways in which family structures and attitudes can influence the mobility of children age 10/11 and explore the extent to which these factors have changed over time since the 1940s. We focus on this age group both because we have the longest time-span of data for children aged 10/11, and because this is the age group that will be most dependent on family members (parents, siblings and other relatives) for their mobility. It can be suggested that family structures and attitudes may influence mobility in a variety of ways. For instance, mobility may be restricted in lone-parent households or in a family where there is prolonged illness. The lack of an adult with free time may constrain where a child aged 10/11 is able to go and the things they are allowed to do. Conversely, a child with elder siblings, or with a co-resident or nearby extended family, may enjoy greater mobility due to the availability of a wider range of adults. However, such trends may not be straightforward and the relationships postulated above may in some instances be reversed. Thus a child in a lone-parent household could be given greater freedom due to other demands on parental time, and the child living in an extended family may be subject to greater control due to the presence of more adults. In some cases an ever-present grandparent or sibling could impose significant constraints.

Just as family structures and relationships between household members are complex, and relate mainly to personal and familial attitudes and beliefs, so too changes over time are far from straightforward. Although there has been an increase in divorce and separation in recent decades, higher mortality in the past (especially following the impact of the Second World War) also produced lone-parent households. In our data set the proportion of lone-parent households increased from 6.5 per cent for children age 10/11 in the 1940s to 15 per cent in the most recent cohort. The figure was highest (25 per cent) for the cohort born 1983/4. Co-resident extended families were uncommon in all four cohorts, with just 6.5 per cent of children age 10/11 living in an extended family in the 1940s/50s and none in our data set for later periods. The sample is too small to provide quantitative data on mobility by different family types, but the variety of ways in which mobility responded to family structures and circumstances is clearly reflected in the qualitative evidence provided by respondents.

Several interviewees in all cohorts commented on the extent to which others influenced their mobility. This could take a number of forms, ranging from the mundane (such as unwanted shopping trips) to the impact of serious illness of a relative. The effects also varied from simple inconvenience to potentially serious absence from school. Thus Beryl resented frequent shopping trips with her mother in the 1940s, and in the 1990s Saeeda missed school due to her father's illness and the perceived need for her to be at the hospital with other relatives:

> My mother was a shopaholic even in those days ... Yes she loved shops yea. She'd drag me round, which I hated ... Oh I did, well you know being/at 10 you don't want to be going round shops looking at clothes, you want to be out playing with your friends don't you (R353, Beryl, aged 10/11, born 1935, Salford).

> But like sometimes, cause like when we/when he used to have like operations, cause he had/he went once and this operation wrong and then I had to miss a full day off school cause I had to be at the hospital with my mum and everyone, and I didn't go to school, school that day. So like I don't/I think I missed quite a few days in primary yea, yea (R226, Saeeda, aged 10/11, born 1985, Manchester).

For many children aged 10/11 their social and leisure activities were to some extent determined by what others around them were doing. Where parents or siblings had a time-consuming hobby or interest, the respondent often felt that they had no option about participating, irrespective of whether the activity matched their interests. Beryl's unwanted shopping trips are one example, but there are many more and in some cases (for instance Rob) this feeling of being included in activities against one's will could even extend to their parents' choice of route when travelling. Thus in the 1970s Nick resented being dragged into church-related activities, especially the Whit walks, and Peta remembers that she had little option but to attend the church youth group her father ran in the 1980s. Respondents from all age cohorts expressed very similar concerns:

> My sisters were part of it [the Whit walks], I never really got on well with Sunday School, so. I was more interested in running about. But my sisters used to take part in the Whit walks ... So we/yea well my dad was you know pretty well into that sort of thing, so it was a, it was a duty rather than a pleasure at that age for me you know. The whole family went walking out (R337, Nick, aged 10/11, born 1969, Manchester).

> Yea, yea. Both my parents were involved in the running of that group [church youth group], so that was one of the reasons why we all went there. We weren't exactly forced to go but you know we all, we all sort of went there. But we had friends from, from school and from our street who went as well (R389, Peta, aged 10/11, born 1971, Manchester).

> But my parents like scenic routes, so they might take you down country roads and get lost and you end up getting home really late ... I hated it. I refuse to go on any journeys with them now cause they just ... I tell them, 'right I'm not coming again if you go on a scenic route', but they still do it (R222, Rob, age 10/11, born 1985, Stockport).

Most commonly, children aged 10/11 were entrusted to elder siblings or other relatives for at least some of their everyday mobility. Usually this was beneficial, in that it enabled children to undertake activities that they would not otherwise do; however on occasion (as with their family's social activities) having to accompany a brother or sister could prove annoying and lead to unwanted mobility. Valerie's experience of being entrusted to an elder sister in Lancaster in the 1950s is especially telling, and she clearly resented the fact that she could not control her own mobility and had to 'tag along' with a sibling. However, for others such as Ruth, Louise, Sandra and Nisha having an older relative (usually a sibling but sometimes a cousin) to look after you was empowering in that it allowed mobility that would not otherwise have taken place. Again, respondents in all cohorts related these experiences, and it is perhaps revealing that most such accounts come from females. Girls age 10/11 were probably more protected by parents than boys, and thus negotiating mobility via an older sibling was an important way in which they could make journeys and do things that would not otherwise be possible:

> Geoff, my elder brother, would take me but even then you could you know sort of go on the bus from, from Morecambe to Chorley (R8, Ruth, aged 10/11, born 1936, Morecambe).

> I was in the care of my sister a lot, who was a teenager, and everywhere/well it was a shame really because everywhere she went I had to tag along beside her, so when she was out with her friends so was I (R76, Valerie, aged 10/11, born 1940, Lancaster).

> We had older cousins as well, 'cause my mum had older sisters. So we all had the younger cousins, and they'd all come to our house or my gran's, because I had an older brother, but the older cousins that were his age, used to come to our house as well, so we, we just all, we just all looked after each other (R358, Louise, aged 10/11, born 1963, Salford).

> Every August we'd go up there for a whole week my and my brother. And when we used to go up there for a week we used to go by train. My parents used to stay at home and we'd go up by train ... 'cause my brother's two years older than me, so he would look after me and everything (R38, Sandra, aged 10/11, born 1984, Morecambe).

> I think they'd let us/I think they would be like let us go wherever we wanted to go. But if it was like a bit too far from where we were living so I think my mum wanted a sister to come with us or we maybe take one of my cousins with us and they usually come. But yea so it has to be like it would have to be someone older than us that that would take us (R223, Nisha, aged 10/11, born 1985, Manchester).

The availability (or unavailability) of a particular parent is obviously also a factor that influences the daily mobility of children aged 10/11. This may simply relate to pressure of work, preference, or other circumstances that meant that only one parent was available. This could then influence what was done and the mode of transport used. Such constraints affected all cohorts to some degree, but most of those born in the 1930s lived in relatively large families and thus there was usually an adult around to escort a ten year old where necessary. However, increasingly in the late-twentieth and twenty-first centuries family separation and divorce has meant that children have to negotiate living in two places. Many fall quite easily into what appears to be a complex routine, but what they do and where they go can vary depending on whether they are living with their mother or father at the time. This complicates travel and can mean that a child may do different activities, and use different travel modes depending on which parent they are living with at the time. Whilst many children adapt to this quickly, or even see it as empowering because activities that one parent denies may be allowed by the other, for some the lack of a single base can be disruptive and cause insecurity.

Thus, amongst our respondents, both Ashley and Claire had quite complex routines that involved shuttling between parents and ensuring that the appropriate possessions were in the right place, whilst for Becky her activities were affected by which parent she was with as only her father had access to motor transport. Susan, too, mostly did activities with only one parent even though they lived as a family. Her account of growing up in the 1970s suggests a highly gendered pattern of activities with shopping and local trips undertaken with her mother, whilst longer outings were with her father. During such outings, usually her mother stayed at home because she wanted time away from the children. Thus, it can be suggested that although the increased incidence of divorce and separation over the last two decades has also inflated the extent to which children aged 10/11 undertake activities with only one parent, even in two parent households it is possible for activity patterns to be highly gendered and usually undertaken with only one parent:

> That, that was, that was a factor. If we went out for the day generally my mum didn't come because she wanted peace away from the kids ... That, that was her decision yea. And I don't really remember my mum coming out with us very often, no. Not unless we was visiting a relative, usually one of hers, not my dad's. And so consequently if we would go further afield it would be in the car with my dad. And if we were going somewhere locally, usually to involve shopping, it would be with my mum on the bus, or walking (R371, Susan, aged 10/11, born 1962, Salford).

> When I was 10 and 11 that was about the time my mum and my dad got divorced so I either done things with my mum or with my dad and going to Newcastle and that, would have been with my dad, because he had the van so we will have gone in the van (R12, Becky, aged 10/11, born 1983, Morecambe).

> It, it does depend where I was coming from. If I was coming from my mum's it sometimes, you know my mum would give me a lift here or she'd walk me and sometimes my dad would come over and, and walk me here, pick me up but sometimes I'd come here [to Dad's] straight from school so I'd just walk down the hill to here and then I'd go back up to school the next

morning, so in that case I'd just be walking to here from school (R7, Claire, aged 10/11, born 1983, Lancaster).

Yes I go and stay there [with Dad]. But it was sort of after/I think sort of around that time we got more organised with that, and sort of set up a rota where I'm with him Monday nights and Thursday nights and then whose ever weekend it is. But on Sunday nights I'd always be back here to get ready for school and get things sorted out (R49, Ashley, aged 10/11, born 1983, Lancaster).

For some children it was simply parental attitudes that affected mobility. Where parents were unwilling to travel either due to their own experiences, financial constraints or simply personal preference this could severely constrain mobility for a young child. Thus Warren felt that what he saw as his father's old-fashioned attitudes to travel and expenditure severely restricted his mobility as a child in the 1970s at a time when for many people increased incomes and greater car ownership were extending mobility. This also emphasises the way in which restricted mobility in an age when most people travelled only locally was accepted, but that as mobility horizons have extended children have found it more difficult to accept the restrictions placed on them:

But my father ... He is very Victorian ... he was very strict in a sense that you know you'd come home from school and you couldn't interrupt him while he was watching the news. And you know he wasn't a very touchy or lovey father. His priorities were different. You know anything, any treats or that, was all by my mother you know and she/I think in my whole life really I've only had one holiday and that was in Blackpool for two days you know till I actually left home ... And we didn't/he didn't really spend a lot of money, well he spent no money taking us anywhere really, so. But he had a very poor upbringing and he thought well you know the fact that he's actually putting food on the table for us is enough, yea. So no we didn't do a lot, didn't go anywhere really (R380, Warren, aged 10/11, born 1966, Manchester).

Mobility and the Life Course

Family constraints on mobility are obviously closely related to life course events. Most people go through periods of their life when mobility is restricted, possibly by lack of income, family commitments, illness or infirmity and other periods when they are able to travel freely and enjoy a high degree of everyday mobility. This section, first, uses quantitative data to explore the extent to which mobility change over the life course mirrors the well-established relationship between migration and the life course (outlined above) and, second, uses qualitative evidence to examine in more detail the ways in which everyday mobility has changed over individual life courses. In this section we examine in some detail the lives of a series of respondents born in the 1930s, and assess the interaction between changing mobility opportunities and personal life course events.

Using National Travel Survey data analysed in Chapter 4 it is possible to make limited comparisons between age groups between 1965 and 1999/2001 (Table 4.3). These data show some significant shifts in the distances travelled for everyday mobility over the past four decades. In summary, first, in every category except young people aged between 16/17 and 20 there has been a substantial increase in the total distances travelled for everyday mobility. Second, whereas in 1965 the most mobile group were males age 21-29, in 1999/2001 men age 40-49 had the greatest everyday mobility. Third, although adult women had lower levels of mobility than men in both time periods, the differential has reduced between 1965 and 1999/2001. Fourth, whereas in 1965 female mobility decreased steadily with age (from age 16); in the later survey it remained much more constant (and even increased slightly for women age 40-49). Fifth, whereas in 1965 mobility decreased markedly for those over 65, in 1999/2001 the reduction was much less and only the very elderly experienced reduced mobility. Overall, this suggests that constraints of both childcare and ageing are substantially less today than they were in the 1960s.

These data thus show that over the past four decades these has been a shift from a pattern of everyday mobility that broadly mirrored that of residential migration (with most mobility amongst young adults), and with a combination of age and life course constraints the major controlling factors, to one in which life course constraints have become less significant (especially for women) and that high levels of everyday mobility have continued into relative old age. It is perhaps significant that the group for whom everyday mobility has changed least is adolescents aged 16/17 to 20. It can be argued that, apart from financial considerations, at each time period this group has experienced the fewest constraints on their mobility, and that increased opportunities for mobility in the late-twentieth century have been offset by the fact that a much higher proportion of the age group are still in education with both limited time and income for everyday travel. In contrast, in the 1960s most young adults over 16 were at work but still living with their parents. They probably undertook a longer daily journey to work than most students travelled for education in the late-twentieth century, and they enjoyed a relatively large disposable income without any of the financial and other constraints of a home and family to support.

Using data collected from Manchester/Salford and Lancaster/Morecambe, it is possible to examine in more detail the ways in which everyday mobility changed over the life course for a particular age cohort. Quantitative data were analysed in Chapter 4 and are summarised briefly before focusing on qualitative evidence that explores the ways in which attitudes towards everyday mobility have changed over the life course. For respondents born 1932-1941 changes in the pattern of everyday mobility over the life course broadly reflect national trends (Table 9.1). The mean length of trips increased steadily over the life course, car use increased as both walking and the use of public transport declined, and at each life course stage women tended to travel over shorter distances and use slower means of transport than men, though gender differences were least amongst the young and he old (i.e. those without family constraints). Teenagers aged 17/18 were most

Table 9.1   Summary of Mobility Change Over the Life Course: Respondents Born 1932-1941, Manchester/Salford and Lancaster/Morecambe (Percentage of all Trips)

	Manchester/Salford				Lancaster/Morecambe			
	Age 10/11	Age 17/18	Age 30s	Age 60s	Age 10/11	Age 17/18	Age 30s	Age 60s
Distance								
<500m	56.5	20.7	16.8	21.4	50.4	24.2	23.7	11.8
500m-1499m	27.1	21.4	25.8	16.4	32.9	36.6	29.6	23.2
1500m-4999m	12.7	38.2	30.8	33.6	12.0	29.1	35.3	46.8
5000m+	3.7	19.7	26.7	28.7	2.9	10.1	11.4	18.2
Mean distance (km)	1.3	4.2	4.5	6.1	1.2	2.6	3.5	5.8
Total annual travel (km)	3,526	8,602	7,375	10,025	3,358	6,344	6,841	9,111
Time								
<10 min	42.7	21.9	14.5	22.4	36.5	21.0	18.9	17.5
10-19.9 min	32.8	24.0	34.1	30.2	40.9	38.8	57.8	40.5
20+ min	24.5	54.1	51.4	47.4	22.6	40.2	23.3	42.0
Mean time (min)	12.8	25.1	27.3	22.7	13.2	21.1	16.1	21.7
Mode								
Car	0.3	4.7	31.8	58.3	0.3	0.5	46.5	74.6
Walk	88.0	48.7	33.8	29.4	89.1	56.7	40.5	21.1
Bus	9.6	35.3	20.1	10.0	8.2	28.4	9.1	1.5
Cycle	1.4	10.8	1.2	1.8	1.7	13.2	0.0	1.1
Other*	0.7	0.6	13.1	0.5	0.6	1.2	3.9	1.8

Data relate to all journeys recorded aggregated over a 12-month period. *Includes travel by train, taxi and motor cycle.
Source: Everyday mobility sample, Manchester/Salford and Lancaster/Morecambe, 2001-2003.

likely to make unaccompanied trips whilst, unsurprisingly, women in their 30s were most likely to travel with children. Overall, a combination of life course factors and societal trends has shaped the everyday mobility of this cohort over the past 60 years.

The ways in which everyday mobility evolved and changed over the life course can be illustrated most effectively by the detailed examination of the life history of five respondents at four cross-sections of time. We have randomly chosen two males and three females to examine mobility change over the life course in more detail. They have been chosen not because of anything unusual or dramatic in their accounts, but rather because of their ordinariness. The accounts clearly illustrate the ways in which life course factors constrained mobility for some, and reflect the influences of broader societal trends in transport and behaviour, but they also demonstrate substantial continuity in individual everyday mobility.

Janet was born in 1936 and lived in various parts of Salford all her life. She was an only child, her father was a labourer at a local chemical works and her mother was a housewife. At the age of 10/11 (in the mid-1940s) she lived at home with both parents and attended the local school. She usually undertook the five minutes walk to school alone. The local area provided her play space: the street, a local park (five minutes walk away), or sometimes a larger park some four miles distance. She also regularly visited her grandmother who lived 10 minutes walk away. All these journeys were undertaken on foot and mostly alone. She recalls few constraints on her mobility and never felt unsafe:

> I've, I've even walked to H Park, which was about four or five miles away ... On my own yea ... they [parents] were quite used to me just wandering off ... Also I had a grandmother who lived probably about 10 minutes walk away, so I could be there for all they knew you know ... I had an awful lot of freedom.

The only place she did not go was some local woods that were close to an asylum. Longer trips into Manchester were taken by bus or tram (usually with her mother when aged 10/11, but alone very soon after), but most activities were local. The family shopped at the local Co-op and at the age of 10/11 Janet often ran round to the shop alone to collect things for her mother. Entertainment was usually at one of several local cinemas. Most weeks she went to the cinema one evening with her parents, and she attended a Saturday morning children's programme at another cinema with friends at least every other week. Holidays were usually spent in rural Cheshire. The extended family owned a 'cottage' there (Janet described it as a 'converted hen coop') and she travelled there by bus from Manchester quite often during the school summer holidays, often meeting up with her many aunts and uncles.

By the age of 17 Janet still lived at home and was training to be a nursery nurse, attending college half the week and working the rest of the time, though from age 18 she worked at a Manchester children's hospital as a children's nurse and lived in whilst on duty. All her travel around Manchester in 1952/3 was undertaken on foot or by bus (trams were withdrawn from Salford in 1947 and from Manchester in 1949) and she still travelled freely and usually alone or with her boyfriend (whom she married at the age of 21). She never owned a bike and had no access to a car. Social activities revolved around Guides and helping out with Brownies (activities that also provided camping holidays in the summer), a church youth club, dances organised by the church and the occasional visit to the cinema. She never went to pubs 'Well it's just something we just didn't do ... And no we didn't, we'd just had no interest' and rarely ate out, largely because it was too expensive. Although her work required her to travel further than at the age of 10/11, most of her other activities remained local and she continued to walk alone round Salford with no sense of threat.

In her 30s (1960s) Janet was married with two small daughters. She had given up work when she married and her life revolved around her home and family. Although her husband had a car Janet could not drive 'I never wanted to. And I wouldn't have access to the car during the week anyway ... My husband used it for work' and her independent mobility was still undertaken on foot or by bus. Family outings were usually by car, but when her husband was at work she mostly walked. The main reason she gave was cost:

> I mean I used to walk to see my friend who lived probably three miles away. I'd walk there with the two children in the pram ... Yes, and walk back ... Uh huh, we couldn't afford it [the bus]. But we'd got one salary and that was it. We managed to pay the mortgage and everything like that, but there wasn't much spare money.

However, in addition, travelling by bus was difficult with a pram and two small children. Janet usually saw walking several miles as preferable to using public transport and she frequently undertook long walks for pleasure. Most shopping was still done locally at the Co-op (again to which she walked and came back with the pram loaded with groceries), and she would never consider using a taxi because of cost. At this stage Janet rarely went out in the evening, and almost never alone. She explained this by a combination of family commitments and constraints imposed by her husband: possibly because of his concerns about safety, or maybe just because he did not like her to be out in the evening. Janet accepted these constraints to her mobility as a normal part of life:

> No because well I wouldn't, I didn't go out much in the evening on my own then because we'd got the two young children. And my husband didn't like me to be, to being out at night on my own ... Well it used to be a bit different then. Wasn't quite as easy I suppose ... It didn't bother me. As I say I like sewing, I like knitting. And my husband was still studying one thing and another. So it was just norm, you didn't question, I mean that was life.

Summer holidays were usually undertaken as a family in the Lake District either camping or staying in a friend's caravan, continuing a tradition of rural holidays started as a small child.

At the time of interview Janet was in her mid-60s, both she and her husband had retired, they still lived in the same locality in Salford, but her mobility was in many ways much greater than it had ever been. They now own two cars (Janet had learned to drive when she went back to work when her children were older) and they live a full and active life. However, Janet rarely goes out alone (and then only locally) and most activities are undertaken with her husband: 'there's always two of us together. I go and see my friends who live nearby and that on my own yes'. Much of Janet's time is taken up with visiting her daughters and grandchildren who live elsewhere in Lancashire, shopping (mostly at edge of town shopping centres) and going to the gym. All these activities are normally undertaken by car with her husband and Janet rarely drives: 'I don't like driving ... 'cause I could do, but I don't like it ... I'm not particularly interested'. The couple rarely use public transport, the only exception being that they sometimes travel to central

Manchester by train or metro (tram) because they perceive parking to be so difficult and expensive in the centre of the city:

> We use the train. Going into Manchester we go on the train now. He drives down to the station and then we get the train. Well it's a reduced rate anyway. And parking in Manchester is very abominable ... So it's easier to catch the train, which goes directly into Manchester ... And if necessary we can even get the Metro, Metrolink and do it like that at the station ... Very convenient once we get down to the station in Swinton.

Other trips out (for instance to Southport) are by car, they rarely eat out (Janet likes cooking) and they rarely go out in the evening except to quizzes at the local cricket club when (unusually) they walk:

> I don't need to [go out in the evening] 'cause I've been out all day and I like to stay at home at night. Unless there's something special we're going to or something like that. No we don't go out at night time much ... We go to the local cricket club, it's just up the road. We go to all these quizzes on a Tuesday night. We always walk there and walk back again.

Holidays are still taken in the countryside and they own a static caravan in Shropshire which they visit every two to three weeks. This second home has greatly extended their mobility and they have a separate network of friends in the Shropshire area that they visit regularly.

This unremarkable case study of the way in which one woman's mobility has changed over the life course provides clear evidence of both continuity and change. The constraints imposed by marriage and family responsibilities, together with increased fears about safety, have restricted Janet's everyday mobility; but at the same time increased real income and access to a car have enabled her to extend both her mobility and range of activities undertaken in her 60s. Throughout her life Janet has enjoyed walking and rural holidays run through her life from her childhood. Her life history is probably typical of many women of her generation for whom marriage and motherhood quite severely restricted mobility and opportunities, but who are now able to enjoy greater mobility than they have ever done in the past.

The extent to which changed perceptions of risk can influence everyday mobility is illustrated especially clearly by the example of Roger who was born in Lancaster in 1938 and lived in the same town all of his life. In many ways his mobility profile resembles that of Janet, with a transition from mainly local mobility to much greater freedom produced by car ownership, but without the constraints of motherhood. However, here we concentrate on the extent to which Roger's perception of risk changed over time. At the age of 10/11 (late 1940s) Roger lived at home with both parents (he was an only child) and his play space was centred on the local area constrained only by his parents' perceptions of risk from traffic and other dangers, which he did not always heed:

> ... we were, we were told we had to play on the back street rather than the
> front street because traffic, although I mean traffic then was/but the buses
> used to come up and down D Street then, so we were always told to play on
> the back street. And of course we went onto the B waste ground because
> that was you know somewhere that/I think it used to be allotments at one
> time ... Well, well we, we were allowed/yea we used to go up onto/the next
> street up from D Street is P Street, we used to go up and play on there at one
> time I can remember, cause there used to be, there used to be air raid
> shelters on there before they were, before they were demolished. We were
> told to keep out of them, but I mean you used to play in these, you used to
> play in them.

At the age of 17/18 (in the mid-1950s) Roger still lived at home, but was
working as a railway fireman. His activities were still mainly local and reflected
the usual interests of teenage boys at the time: pubs, dances, the cinema, cafés and
girlfriends. Much of this took place in Lancaster, but he also travelled a little
further to Morecambe for dances. When not walking he travelled by bus or train.
Although he was aware of some dangers from fights, these seemed not to affect his
mobility and his activities were relatively unconstrained:

> No I think, I think when you're 17, 18 you don't, you don't see the same as
> you would now perhaps. No I mean there, there were odd fights, you used
> to get odd fights in the dancehalls and, and outside afterwards you know,
> simple because people had had too much to drink or they'd be falling out
> over a girl or something like that. You never got any/I mean you never got
> anybody with knives and things like that you know. But yea there used to
> be fights, there used to be them.

In his early 30s Roger was married with a young son and now worked as a bus
driver. He was also a car owner and this considerably extended his mobility with
regular trips to Preston and Blackpool and most shopping done by car at large
stores in the town centre rather than at local shops. Despite being a bus driver he
never used public transport. He does not recall any particular constraints on his
mobility produced through fear or perceived risk, but recognises that this may have
reflected the types of places that he and his wife chose to go to in their 30s:

> Yea I, I don't think we felt unsafe walking the streets then, no. I mean we
> probably didn't go to the, to the places where the younger ones went then. I
> mean as you get, when you're in your 30s I mean you're ... I mean we
> were, we used to be a member of L Sports Club then, you know the, the
> Social Club there ... So we'd perhaps go down there more than visit a pub
> in the town or something like that you know, so you probably weren't
> getting where the younger ones were getting. But you didn't/I don't think
> you feel/felt threatened.

In his 60s in 2001 Roger and his wife each run a car and he has become totally
dependent on this means of transport. He enjoys driving and only walks 200m to
the local paper shop. Even short trips into town are undertaken by car and he hates

public transport. However, what has changed even more than his mode of transport is his attitude to risk. He now finds the centre of Lancaster threatening at times, especially late at night, and is glad to have the means to get away quickly. Even though he recognises that his fears are probably unfounded, this perception is another factor encouraging use of the car rather than walking or using public transport:

> I wouldn't like to be, and my wife is, is the same opinion, now we wouldn't like to be walking round Lancaster now on a Friday and Saturday night. I mean we've driven through a few times when we've, when we've been out, and you see all these young ones around here now you know. Em I mean it's full of students isn't it. Well I mean, I mean the students don't cause problems and it's very rare we get any trouble with the students, but the young locals ... I don't know. You, you/I think you feel more/I think you would feel threatened now you know. I mean you read all/I mean it's probably unfounded, I mean they tell you it's unfounded statistically ... I think when you get a bit older you tend to, to see more danger than perhaps that at you know 18 you wouldn't bother about it would you. I mean we'd been out the other night, it's a fortnight ago, we went out with some friends and ... it was about well ten thirty, quarter to eleven when we came out, and we walked back up into the Square and it was absolutely heaving with, with youngsters ... and you know my wife was glad we got in the car and away you know, yea.

Like Janet, the mobility changes that Roger has experienced over the life course reflect both his altered personal circumstances and broader societal influences. However, although he now travels much further and more frequently than he did when he was younger and more constrained by income and a lack of independent transport, in some respects his mobility has become more constrained. Whereas when 18 or even in his 30s he moved around Lancaster freely and did not perceive any significant risks, today he is much more aware of potential threats (real or imagined) and alters his mobility to take account of these factors.

For some respondents the pattern of everyday mobility that they established as a child has changed remarkably little over half a century or more. The account of Mary, aged 66 at interview in 2001, illustrates this clearly. In 1945, aged 10, Mary lived at home in Lancaster with her family. She did not attend the geographically closest school, but her parents sent her to the nearest school that did not require a main road to be crossed. She could thus travel safely to school alone, either on foot or occasionally on her bicycle. This choice of school, based on parental decisions about where it was safe for her to travel, had a significant effect on Mary as this was a Catholic school and even though she did not come from a Catholic family this school choice determined her religious beliefs for the rest of her life:

> The only reason we were Catholics it was the nearest school when we were born that they didn't have to cross roads. If you went to B School you'd a busy road to cross but at C it was straight down. You'd only like your own school/your own roads to cross. So they were put to C.

Most of Mary's everyday activities were contained within her local neighbourhood: she played safely in the street with friends who lived nearby; occasionally travelled (with other children) to play in the local park; ran errands for her mother to the local shops; went to the cinema in town most Saturday mornings (a 20 minute walk); and bought fish and chips from a shop close by. Longer distance travel was rare, partly constrained by her mother's ill health, but also by cost.

> Oh yea when we come home from school you'd have your tea and then you'd go and play out yea … No no you could play, you could run across road. You'd be playing in middle of road, ball and that and you wouldn't have no/there might be but very occasional/breadman going to end at street … At times we'd go up to/well Moor as we called it, wi' swings and all that and through t'park. Yes if there was a crowd of us were going we'd go up and we'd take a bottle of pop wi' us you know and a few sandwiches and we'd go up yea.

By the age of 17 in 1952 Mary still lived at home and worked at a shop in Lancaster town centre. She walked to work, which took about 20 minutes, and often met up with a friend who worked in the same place. Her pattern of everyday activities remained very local, using neighbourhood shops for most everyday items and supplementing this with trips to town. Most girl friends lived nearby and she met up with them regularly just to talk, to play with younger relatives and sometimes to go swimming. Her boyfriend lived on the other side of Lancaster so courting took her out of her immediate neighbourhood. With her boyfriend she walked to the cinema, sometimes to the pub, occasionally they ate out at a café, and she visited his home. Longer trips, for instance a day out to Morecambe, would be undertaken by bus. The overall picture, however, is of a relatively self-contained world with limited travel and where most needs could be met locally.

> Well you'd only down hill hadn't you, there's a little hill and there. I mean you'd/on/then I mean we had a butchers, we had Co-op, we had a dairy at bottom of D Street. I don't know whether/you know P at all, well at bottom of it there was a dairy. Ooh it was great yea. You'd go down, take a jug and they'd fill it up wi' milk. Did that thing. And then down C Street again, where you're talking, just after you come off H Street, on the right hand side across the road there's like a little passage/before you start the houses on the left hand side going up there's like a little ginnel thing, well there was a bake house there and oh it was lovely.

In her mid 30s Mary was married with two children and living on the opposite side of Lancaster to the community in which she had grown up. However, her everyday activity patterns had changed relatively little. Her children were old enough to take themselves to school and Mary always worked at least part time. She travelled to work by bus (about 10 minutes) but most other activities were undertaken locally. Everyday shopping was done at the neighbourhood Co-op, she used a nearby fish and chip shop, occasionally visited the local pub and most of her friends lived close by. Her main entertainment outside the home was bingo once a week in Lancaster, but the closeness of friends in the local community was obviously important to her. The family did not have a car and occasional longer trips were undertaken by bus or train:

> Oh yea, in the morning after kids had gone to school if I wasn't at work I'd go [to a neighbour's house] and have a cup of tea and/tea and toast and then another morning she'd come in/cause we had a marble fireplace, tiled fireplace as they called it then and S still had the old fashioned black one you know and the open fire and everything and we used to have toast done on it and it was lovely, you know so yea.

At the time of interview Mary was retired, widowed, and lived alone. However, the pattern of her life had changed relatively little. She maintains close contact with her family and from time to time looks after her grandchildren who live nearby. She still plays bingo in Lancaster, and sees friends and neighbours locally. However, her mobility is constrained by her inability to walk long distances, and what she perceives as a poor and inconvenient bus service. She relies heavily on family members and friends for lifts or, when necessary uses a taxi. She can also no longer easily get her shopping locally and usually goes to a local supermarket once a week with her daughter:

> For simple reason the buses are bad and there wouldn't get a bus there and it was too far wi' me legs to walk so we just got a taxi. It's easier ... It's a disgrace. To say that we get little buses, two little buses every hour and I mean/well you've probably been in them buses haven't you ... You get on, you're alright going into town but I mean you come home wi' two bags of shopping on them little buses and let's face it there's a few well endowed people in't there ... you can't/there's no way you can get on them buses and we/it's/we did have three buses before they took this wi' bus station, well that wasn't too bad, so obviously if you've missed one bus and you're waiting for/there's going to be more people and it's a disgrace, yea. Yes I think it's a disgrace the way it were done.

Whilst Mary's account stresses continuity over a long time period, other accounts from women growing up in a similar area place more emphasis on change. Meg (born in 1937) grew up in Heysham and recalled that her childhood consisted of fairly unconstrained mobility around the local area. She could play in the fields and on the seashore, and although she remembered a friend being killed on the road that did not affect what she and her friends did:

> We were completely free. It's just amazing. When I think about it we used to go down to Half Moon Bay. We used to play in the field. There was a farm field behind the house. We used to go haymaking. We played with bees, frogs ... and nobody ever seemed to check on us. We never seemed to come to any harm ... And we used to go on the railway side picking cowslips. We used to go to the bobbin mill and they used to let us play in

there with the bobbins. And we used to go down to the harbour. And it was complete freedom.

However, Meg rarely travelled far from her local area, largely because her father did not like travelling away from home and her mother seemed always to be busy. She was allowed to travel alone some distance by bus to visit her grandmother, but rarely went anywhere with her parents. At the age of 10/11 her mobility was local and largely self-contained:

> My father wouldn't sleep away from home so we never had a holiday. My mother was always busy. She used to take people in for bed and breakfast in the summer cause they were always desperate for people to have somewhere to sleep when the hotels were full. I mean that was the days when it was a boom place. And so we never went out of course. I don't remember ever being taken out by my parents ever anywhere.

At the age of 17 (in 1954) Meg still lived at home in Heysham and worked in Morecambe. She recalled that she walked almost everywhere, partly to save money and partly because she enjoyed walking. Her social life with friends was extensive, including sports such as badminton and swimming, shopping, the cinema, theatre and concerts. Almost all activities were in Morecambe, and Lancaster was perceived very much as a separate urban area that was rarely visited. Again, she had few restrictions on what she did or where she could go, excepting that her father was quite strict in that he expected her to be in by 10.00pm and he also objected strongly to her going into pubs:

> No I always had to be in at 10 o'clock at night. My dad started putting his foot down then. I met this, this young man at the youth club and he used to walk me home. And if we stopped talking at the gate my father would come out and say 'it's time you were in lady'. He used to call me lady. So when I was/he was very strict about that coming in at a certain time, yes … I know once I'd been in a pub for a drink, that was the only thing, um and my father blew his top 'cause he didn't think women should go into pubs … I'd only gone in for a shandy with somebody. So that was the only thing.

By the time she was in her mid-30s Meg was married, with two young children, and living in Morecambe. Her horizons had broadened considerably: she had a car and at the time was studying as a postgraduate student. Despite the demands made on her by her family she undertook a wide range of activities which were no longer confined to Morecambe. She travelled to Lancaster regularly and Lancaster town centre became part of her everyday action space. One substantial addition to the pattern of her social activities was that by the early 1970s she was eating out much more frequently than in the past, but she also engaged in more home-based entertainment: 'And it was becoming a popular thing you know to go out for a meal at night with friends. I also did a lot of entertaining at home. I used to make dinner parties'.

At the time of her interview in 2002 Meg was almost 65. She is divorced and lives alone in Morecambe. She works part time and still runs a car. In comparison with Mary, whose everyday mobility seems constrained by age and has changed little over time, Meg now has a busier social life and travels more widely than at any of the other cross-sections of her life for which we have information. She not only undertakes frequent trips to see her children and grandchildren, but also travels widely for leisure and pleasure all over the North West and further afield. Despite being a car owner she is not car dependent and frequently chooses to use public transport:

> Well it depends where I'm going. If I'm going out in the country I take the car. If I'm going to Lancaster or Preston I go on the train. And even if I'm going to Windermere I go on the train because it's easier and I don't have to worry, I've no responsibility. And it's cheap, I've got my Senior Citizen Rail Card, so it's quite cheap to go to Preston. And it's quick. I can go straight through from here in a morning at quarter to 10 and be in Preston at about 20 past.

However, the one thing that does restrict her mobility slightly is, like Roger, an increased sense of fear when out at night in public places. This was not something that she commented on at all for earlier time periods, but now in her 60s she is increasingly concerned about walking at night in either Lancaster or Morecambe. She has not actually experienced any danger, and admits that it is fear based upon media reports of incidents but, as with many children and adults, this is a factor that has progressively constrained her mobility at a time when in other respects it is greater than ever before:

> No, no. I wouldn't/at one time I'd have even walked into Lancaster along the canal, but I felt so uneasy last time I did it, I was looking behind me. And even at Lancaster late at night, or Morecambe late at night, I wouldn't dream of walking around. I feel/and I'm not a cowardly person ... Well in case anybody's following me. I mean you read of these people who are set upon. Even on the cycle path. I wouldn't even cycle down there late at night.

Howard, born in 1934, has also seen quite a lot of changes during his life, but in many ways his mobility has altered very little over 60 years. At the age of 10/11 he was living with his parents and brother in a semi-rural suburb on the western edge of the Manchester/Salford conurbation. He went to a primary school about a mile away at which his father was head teacher, and he usually cycled to school each morning with his father. In 1944/5 public transport was still affected by wartime restrictions, and although his father had a car before the war he disposed of it due to petrol rationing and did not get another one. It can be argued that Howard's early introduction to cycling had a lasting impact on his attitude to travelling around the Manchester conurbation:

> Well my dad was quite keen on using his bike so he bought me one and well, well it was easier, in fact when I think about it it was rather easier, sort of war time bus services and so on. There was a bus once an hour, so apart from bad weather times it was/most of the time it was more convenient to go on the bike. It was about what, about a mile.

Like Meg, Howard remembers playing freely in the local area with the streets and adjacent fields his normal playground. Occasionally he would travel into Manchester with his parents for shopping, for a meal or for a treat such as the circus, but most activities were undertaken locally:

> When I said playing in the street, opposite where I lived was like a long cul-de-sac with a garden at one side of it, so we played around there and sort of in and out of that street.

> I mean if I went there [Manchester] I was usually going for sort of nice things if you like. You know perhaps have a meal in a café while I was there you know. I'd probably get bored doing shopping and things. But we'd probably have a meal in a café and that sort of thing, or going for a drink ... And going to a circus at Belle Vue once a year, that, and that sort of thing ... So I think I would see Manchester as somewhere quite exciting.

At the age of 17/18 in 1951/52 Howard was still living at home (his father had just died) and he worked as a laboratory assistant in Manchester, with one day and two evenings at a local technical college. He normally took the bus to work because it was too far to cycle, but he still used his bike for local trips and sometimes for longer leisure rides into the country:

> Well I should think it would have taken too long at that time in a morning. And you/the working day was half past 8 to half past 5, so if you think to do a 10 mile journey either end of that on a bicycle it would have been a bit much.

> And I was using it [bicycle] mostly just local stuff. Sort of if I was going up to W from B, or across B, that kind of thing. You're only talking about a couple of miles either way, that sort of journey. So I'm probably only using the bike for at the most four or five mile specific journeys.

He knew Manchester well because to get to work he had to change buses and walk across the city centre, and he felt comfortable walking around the city alone. This was part of his normal action space and there were few places that he avoided:

> Well because I was travelling through it and working in it I knew the, you know obviously the city centre I knew virtually every inch of it. You know it was familiar territory, I was there five days a week ... So, so you know I was moving around just by myself more or less as I wished within reason.

By his mid-30s in circa 1972 Howard was living alone on the edge of Salford, only a few kilometres from where he had grown up. He had been married and had a five year old daughter but was now separated from his wife and only saw his daughter once a week on a Saturday. He had swapped his pedal cycle for a motorbike which he used to travel the 2km to his work as a primary school teacher in Salford, and also used it for most other trips including shopping (2-4 times a week) in a local supermarket and to visit friends. Family and life course factors affected his mobility in that what he did on a Saturday when his daughter visited was very different from his travel during the rest of the week. He would take his daughter on outings around the local area, or to visit her Grandmother, always travelling by bus as he did not trust a five year old on a motorbike. His mobility pattern was very different when he was alone in that he went to the cinema about once a month, regularly met up with friends in a pub or restaurant in Manchester or Bolton, and often bought fish and chips from the local shop when he could not be bothered to cook for himself:

> Yea, well at that stage she was [five] she used to come to me every Saturday. They delivered her to me Saturday morning and I took her home at night, that was the usual practice ... that was, that was by bus. Sometimes I'd take her out to places, parks, picnics, that kind of thing. And quite often we went down to visit my mother, and in which case we might have gone out, we might have spent the time at my mother's house. And more often than not we went down to my mother's and all sort of had the day together. And/but you know if I wanted to take her out somewhere by myself for a treat I could do you know there was no, there was no problem about that.

At the time of interview, aged 68, Howard still lived in the same part of the city (but at a different address). He was retired and lived alone, but led a very active life heavily involved with local voluntary organisations. Although he did graduate from a motorbike to a car whilst he was working (largely due to two accidents he had on his bike); for financial reasons he sold his car when he retired and at the time of interview walks frequently, sometimes still uses his pedal cycle locally, and uses buses for longer trips around the city. He is very conscious of the health benefits of walking and is active in promoting walking locally:

> I mean, I mean I walk/I'm retired now so I walk, I mean I walk down to the middle of the town and walk in for shopping, which is you know 10 minutes walk either way. I do a lot of walking now/have you come across the Health Walks programme ... that's being promoted nationally. Um that's the thing, I call it the anti couch potato programme. It's getting people off their bottoms to do a bit of exercise, telling people if they walk so many miles a week fairly quickly it does them good, this sort of thing you know. And I'm involved with that. I'm help to organise that in our local area. So I'm going on sort of fairly brisk three mile walks once a week or so. And again sort of walking down to the centre, either for shopping or to catch a bus into Manchester.

He visits his daughter regularly in Rochdale, a journey that requires three separate buses, but although he complains mildly about the length of time it takes compared with using a car, in general he is happy with the public transport provided and his decision, mainly for financial reasons to sell his car. However, he did state that if he could afford to run a car he would do so.

> I've to get a bus for that, I've to get a bus into Manchester and then the bus up to Rochdale, and then a local bus from there. And it's not too bad ... Yea. Two quite long ones and then one short distance one ... It takes a long time, it's sort of about two hours travelling. Whereas when I had a car I was doing it in about 40 minutes. So it's, that's the main thing. If you're doing anything like that with a bus it's more fiddly. Calculating times and waiting in-between times and so on makes, makes that longer, but that, that's the inconvenience of it.

In general Howard remains confident in moving around the Manchester urban area, though is aware of localities that he would avoid. He admits to some concerns when travelling around in the evening and mixing with gangs of youths on the streets, but recognises that his fears are probably unfounded and affected by media reports. However, despite this very rational view, like Meg and Roger, his mobility is now more affected by concerns about safety than it ever was in the past:

> Once I was walking up/I'd been out late, coming up the road with the bus there was a gang of teenagers and you know you sort of watch them and they were probably perfectly alright, it's just that I watched them until we'd passed each other. So you know you think of these thoughts going through your head. But I don't want to be an old man who distrusts all the kids in the area ... No. But there are problems. I mean there's, there's one gang of lads at the moment keep meeting in this area and I, you know I know nothing desperate, but they're sort of damaging bus shelters and you know petty vandalism type things and I'm happier, I'm happier not to stand near, too near to them just in case they, they do anything a bit worse ... The only time that's really affected me was that there were/I was waiting for a bus and they were hanging around the bus shelter at the same time so I was, I was glad when the bus came. I don't think anything would have happened to me, but you just sort of felt uncomfortable and I was glad when the bus came. In fact the bus driver saw them, and when I got on he said do you mind if I drive a hundred down/drive a hundred yards before I take your money. You know he wasn't happy. So you know just you get odd little bits of atmosphere like that yea. How much is true how much is perception I'm not sure.

Conclusions

Like residential migration, everyday mobility is closely related to the life course and is affected by family composition and behaviour. Women, in particular, are affected by the constraints of marriage and motherhood. Although to some extent this has occurred throughout the period studied (from the 1940s), there is also evidence that the influence of life-course factors on everyday mobility may be changing. Increased real incomes and greater access to the car have begun to erode mobility differentials and, in particular, there is now little evidence of a decline in mobility amongst the active elderly. Although obviously those who are ill or infirm have reduced action spaces, looked at from an individual life course perspective many people in their 60s today are enjoying greater mobility than ever before. In this sense the mobility revolution that has taken place in the last half of the twentieth century has made real changes to the everyday mobility of many people and has to some extent altered the factors that structure this mobility. However, there is also evidence that some people, especially the elderly, increasingly restrict their mobility due to fears that did not exist two generations ago.

On the other hand, examination of the ways in which family size, structure, behaviour and attitudes affect everyday mobility, suggests that there has been less change over the past 60 years. For many children, in particular, mobility is still constrained by the activities and preferences of other family members. To some extent this is simply part of a process of negotiation that always occurs when people live together, but at each time period studied it can be suggested that whilst some children aged 10/11 found their family structures enabled mobility, others found that other family members imposed unwelcome restrictions. Thus, whilst mobility potential has certainly increased since the 1940s, this is not necessarily converted into mobility experience. Moreover, some societal trends have increased the likelihood that family attitudes and activities will constrain mobility. When perceptions of risk are heightened by the high media profile of rare cases of child abduction, then this can provide another brake on mobility with some children in the late-twentieth and early twenty-first centuries allowed rather less independent mobility than their grandparents (Chapter 7). Moreover, the impact of time-space compression in which parents increasingly fit a greater number of tasks into the daily routine means that children are increasingly likely to be taken on unwelcome trips because of parental activities, whilst family dispersal has meant that children are also less likely to have relatives close by who can provide adult company to enhance their own mobility. As with other aspects of mobility studied in this book, detailed examination of the links between mobility, family and the life course reveals a high degree of individual variability in the experiences of respondents.

Chapter 10

Transport Policies, Technologies and the Experience of Everyday Mobility

Introduction

We have so far focused on the ways in which people structured their everyday mobility, on the degree to which there have been changes both in the extent and nature of mobility, and especially in the factors that influence mobility. We argue that although there have been some obvious and important changes, the underlying factors that influence everyday mobility have remained remarkably stable over the twentieth century, and that changes in the amount and nature of mobility have been much less than is sometimes suggested by theoretical literature and general statements. Changes in both transport policy and transport technology obviously have a major influence on everyday mobility in cities. So far these have been left relatively implicit. The main dimensions of transport change over the twentieth century, and the key changes in public transport provision in the case study towns, have been sketched in earlier chapters (2 and 4). We now focus more explicitly on the interaction between transport policy, transport technology and individual everyday mobility. Two questions are pursued. First, how did individuals experiencing new transport technologies for the first time react and adapt to them? For instance, did the experience of new technologies alter travel behaviour or were new technologies easily absorbed into established or routine travel behaviour? Second, how have past policy debates about urban transport affected the provision of intra-urban public transport and what impact has this had on the travelling public? These questions are examined in two main contexts. First, examination of policy debates in Manchester and Glasgow since the 1920s, focusing on conflict between trams, trolley buses and motor vehicles; and second, assessment of how travellers in these two cities reacted to changes in public transport provision.

It can be suggested that the interaction between individual travel behaviour, urban transport policies and new technologies will relate to a number of different factors. These include the choice of transport available in a town, personal factors relating to income and family circumstances, societal pressures and preferences that might influence expectations and alter travel behaviour, policies that may restrict the use of particular transport forms and personal preference and whim. Thus someone may prefer to use public transport to travel to work but if there is not a convenient route they may feel constrained to utilise more individualised forms of transport. Such factors often emerged as significant variables in the case studies that examined the reasons why people used particular transport forms

(Chapter 9). They were also highlighted in Chapter 4 in the context of one individual's everyday mobility around London in the 1930s. This chapter contends that, despite experiencing new forms of transport technology, and to some extent being manipulated by transport technology, people's travel aspirations have changed little over the twentieth century. It is argued that, at all times, people aspired to use the quickest and most individual forms of transport available. However, differential constraints on mobility hindered some and led to significant mobility inequalities.

Trams, Trolley Buses and Motor Vehicles in Glasgow and Manchester

Debates about intra-urban commuter traffic in Manchester and Glasgow from the 1920s to the 1950s centred around two related themes: competition between different forms of public transport – especially trams and motor buses – for passengers; and competition between private and public transport for road space. Eventually the motorbus came to dominate public transport provision and the private car reigned supreme as the single most important form of commuter transport in provincial cities. However, throughout the study period there were heated debates about the merits of each transport mode and about ways of easing urban traffic congestion. These debates about urban transport policy fundamentally influenced the travel choices available to urban residents. Given the importance of walking in the twentieth-century city, as demonstrated in earlier chapters, it can also be suggested that the policy debates that took place ignored the form of transport that was used most often and by most people.

In both Manchester and Glasgow the well-established and extensive tram networks were very popular with commuters in the 1920s, 1930s and 1940s. They were perceived as a cheap and convenient form of transport, linking working-class residential areas to the city centre and industrial areas; and because their fixed lines enabled them to run during the frequent thick fogs and smogs they were seen as both more reliable and safer than other forms of transport. Many interview respondents expressed such views, and detailed information with regard to the journey to work was given in Chapter 6:

> Well, there was only one way in those days and that was by tram which was excellent, it were always, there was one along every 10 minutes into the city centre. A very good service (RJ04, Manchester, male, 1930s).

> I mean the trams were very, very frequent, all from Altrincham through to Manchester. I mean it was a tremendous tram service. There was one every two to three minutes (RJ14, Manchester, male, 1930s).

> We used to get a lot of fog in those days and the buses would maybe be off, but the trams used to still run cause they were on rails you see so it was easier for them to you know ... (RJ21, Glasgow, female, 1940s).

Tram fares were especially low in Glasgow where they continued to be heavily subsidised until the service was withdrawn and a study in Manchester in the 1930s argued that the subsidy for tram fares should be increased to the Glasgow level (Simon and Inman, 1935). This was never achieved but Manchester Corporation did heavily subsidise certain routes – such as that from the new council estate of Wythenshawe to the city centre – to encourage suburbanisation and cut the travel costs of those moving to peripheral estates in the 1930s. Consequently in both Manchester and Glasgow the tram networks enjoyed a high volume of use throughout their period of operation (Tables 10.1 and 10.2). According to survey respondents the only reasons why people did not use the trams were either because they lived in locations not served by the tram network, or because they chose to save a few pence by walking or cycling.

Table 10.1   Utilisation of Corporation Public Transport in Manchester, 1902-1965

| Year | Tram | | Trolley bus | | Motor bus | | Total |
	%	(N)*	%	(N)*	%	(N)*	(N)*
1902	100	(24)	-	-	-	-	(24)
1906	100	(134)	-	-	-	-	(134)
1911	100	(166)	-	-	-	-	(166)
1916	100	(210)	-	-	-	-	(210)
1921	100	(278)	-	-	-	-	(278)
1926	97.0	(318)	-	-	3.0	(10)	(328)
1931	84.0	(293)	-	-	16.0	(56)	(349)
1936	59.1	(201)	-	-	40.9	(139)	(340)
1941	23.9	(83)	11.5	(40)	64.6	(224)	(347)
1946	21.1	(89)	15.4	(65)	63.5	(267)	(421)
1950	-	-	14.5	(71)	85.5	(417)	(488)
1955	-	-	16.2	(73)	83.8	(378)	(451)
1960	-	-	10.4	(42)	89.6	(360)	(402)
1965	-	-	4.3	(14)	95.7	(313)	(327)

*Millions of passenger journeys. NB: Data only refer to Manchester Corporation transport and include journeys for all purposes.
Sources: Manchester Corporation Tramways Department, Annual Reports, 1902-28; Manchester Corporation Transport Department, Annual Reports, 1929-65.

Despite their popularity with the travelling public, the tram networks in both cities had substantial critics. These voices were already present in the 1920s, and became much stronger as the century progressed. A number of specific objections were raised against the trams with very similar points being made in both Manchester and Glasgow. First, it was argued that trams were old fashioned and that they presented an inappropriate image for a modern city (Simon and Inman, 1935; Simon, 1938). Thus as early as 1924 one Glasgow councillor – a proponent of the motorbus – argued that trams were 'an obsolete system for a city with the requirements of Glasgow' (*Glasgow Herald*, 30th May 1924 p. 7), and some 20 years later similar sentiments were echoed by the 'Progressive' group on the city council who proposed that 'the trams had served the people of Glasgow well, but they were now an outmoded form of transport and should be eliminated' (*Glasgow Herald*, 31st December 1955 p. 4).

Table 10.2   Utilisation of Corporation Public Transport in Glasgow, 1899/1900-1969/1970

Year	Tram		Trolley bus		Motor bus		Underground		Total
	%	(N)[*]	%	(N)[*]	%	(N)[*]	%	(N)[*]	(N)[*]
1899/1900	90.3	(127.6)	-	-	-	-	9.7	(13.7)	(141.3)
1904/5	92.3	(195.8)	-	-	-	-	7.7	(16.3)	(212.1)
1909/10	93.7	(222.7)	-	-	-	-	6.3	(15.1)	(237.8)
1914/15	95.8	(336.3)	-	-	-	-	4.2	(14.8)	(351.1)
1919/20	97.9	(509.3)	-	-	-	-	2.1	(11.0)	(520.3)
1924/25	95.4	(439.3)	-	-	0.3	(1.3)	4.3	(20.0)	(460.6)
1929/30	87.4	(470.0)	-	-	8.9	(48.1)	3.7	(19.9)	(538.0)
1934/35	83.6	(449.7)	-	-	13.7	(73.8)	2.7	(14.4)	(537.9)
1940/41	78.5	(478.2)	-	-	18.7	(113.5)	2.8	(17.1)	(608.8)
1946/47	76.6	(587.3)	-	-	18.6	(142.7)	4.8	(36.5)	(766.5)
1949/50	66.8	(537.7)	2.5	(20.1)	26.0	(209.5)	4.7	(37.3)	(804.6)
1956/57	52.5	(327.6)	6.6	(41.4)	35.5	(221.1)	5.4	(33.5)	(623.6)
1964/65	-	-	-	-	95.5[**]	(419.6)	4.5	(20.0)	(439.6)
1969/70	-	-	-	-	92.5	(284.7)	7.5	(23.0)	(307.7)

[*] Millions of passenger journeys. [**] Includes trolley buses. NB: Data only refer to Glasgow Corporation transport and include journeys for all purposes.
Sources: Glasgow Corporation Tramways Committee, Annual Reports, 1900-1928; Glasgow Corporation Transport Committee, Annual Reports, 1929-1970; J. Wright and I Maclean, *Circles under the Clyde* (Glasgow, 1997) p. 221.

Second, because they ran on fixed lines trams were perceived by some as inflexible and unable to respond to changing patterns of demand, and they were blamed for causing congestion amongst other road users because their fixed presence occupied a large portion of urban road space. This argument was put forward especially forcefully both by the proponents of motorbuses – seen as more flexible and responsive to demand – and by car drivers who complained bitterly about the congestion caused by trams. Manchester Corporation established a 'Traffic Congestion Committee' in the 1930s to try to tackle the city's perceived traffic problems, and after the failure of one scheme the chairman of the committee laid the blame wholly on the trams: 'If there was any failure in the scheme today it seems that it was due to tram cars. We should all like to rid ourselves of tram cars, but it will take time' (*Manchester Evening News*, 7th June, 1938). Similar sentiments were expressed in Glasgow in the 1930s where one councillor stated that: 'Traffic congestion in the city centre is aggravated by the existence of tramway turning points ... they add to congestion in the busiest parts of the city ...

providing delays to traffic and increase the dangers to pedestrians' (*Glasgow Herald*, 7th September 1937, p. 7), and in the 1950s, just prior to the closure of the tram network, the General Manager of the Municipal Transport Department stated that: 'It is acknowledged by all highway authorities that tram cars, occupying as they do the crown of the road, contribute to traffic congestion' (*Glasgow Herald*, 25th June, 1957, p. 7).

Third, and increasingly important, trams were seen by municipal authorities as a costly way to provide urban mass transport. They had a high initial capital cost because of the need to construct a fixed route, and by the 1940s and 1950s most tram systems required extensive and costly maintenance to keep them running. Moreover, successive decisions to subsidise fares meant that, especially after the Second World War, they could not cover increasing running costs, but it was deemed politically unacceptable to substantially increase fares that historically had been kept at a low level. It was generally argued that the travelling public would accept higher fares for new motorbuses or trolley buses, but not for trams (GCTC Annual Reports; MCTranspC Annual reports). Thus as early as 1938 the Chairman of Manchester's Transport Committee, concerned about the finances of municipal transport, argued that: 'We believe that the substitution of buses will make it a paying proposition again' (*Daily Despatch*, 12th January 1938). Thus one motive for replacing trams with buses was clearly financial, in that municipal transport managers believed they could run a lower cost service with higher fares, and even in 1946, just before the closure of the tram network in Manchester, average tram fares were 0.94d per mile compared to 0.98d for buses (MCTranspD Annual Report, 1946).

Although most critics of trams argued for their replacement by motorbuses, in both cities there was also a debate about the relative merits of trolley buses and motorbuses. These issues were summarised by a journalist writing for the Glasgow Herald in 1937, in an article entitled 'The motor bus and trolley bus: its advantages and disadvantages'. He compared the two forms of transport and concluded that, although trolley buses did have certain advantages – notably smoothness and absence of noise and smell – at road junctions they would inevitably cause the same problems of congestion to other road users as were created by trams. Because trolley buses ran on a fixed route they had many of the inherent disadvantages of trams and he praised the: 'simplicity and freedom of the motor bus in the city' (*Glasgow Herald*, 22nd June 1937, p. 10). However trolley buses did receive support from some commentators, and later the same year one Glasgow councillor argued for the introduction of a fleet of trolley buses on the grounds that: 'The chaotic conditions of the traffic in the centre of the city makes it imperative that every possible method be explored' (*Glasgow Herald*, 16th December 1937, p. 7). Much the same debate continued on and off for the next 20 years with 'Progressive' city councillors arguing in 1955 that: 'the only satisfactory method of running the transport of a city of Glasgow's size was by a diesel bus', and that they 'would not have another trolley bus on the road' (*Glasgow Herald*, 31st December, 1955, p. 5).

Opponents of the introduction of motorbuses used mainly environmental arguments, and cited the experience of continental cities that were retaining their tram systems. Concern about the environmental and health-related impacts of substituting diesel buses for trams surfaced particularly strongly in Manchester in the 1930s, and was also used as an argument for investing in pollution-free trolley buses. In 1938 the letter page of the *Manchester Guardian* carried a lively correspondence on the issue:

> ... those familiar with the streets of the City of London ... know how the numerous oil-driven buses poison the atmosphere and add to the noise and dirt. In Manchester oil-driven buses to the number of the present trams, would affect the atmosphere to a serious extent ... [and] would be little quieter than the trams (Letter, *The Manchester Guardian*, 15th January 1938).

> The fumes from the exhaust of oil-driven vehicles have always been objectionable, and among such vehicles in the Manchester streets the corporation buses are the worst offenders ... It is not unusual to witness a bus travelling along the streets emitting a thick jet of black smoke a yard long, accompanied by the stench of half-burnt oil. A rapid succession of these vehicles passing along the narrow and crowded streets of the city creates a condition of air pollution which is already extremely offensive, and will become intolerable if the number of buses is further increased (Letter, *The Manchester Guardian*, 4th February 1938).

Correspondents in the Manchester Guardian backed up their views with evidence from other (not necessarily unbiased) commentators, including the Salford Medical Officer of Health who, in his Annual report of 1936, condemned the exhausts of heavy oil engines as: 'a real menace to public health' (Annual Report of the Medical Officer of Health, Salford, 1936) and a speaker at the 1938 meeting of the Electrical Association for Women at Stoke on Trent who noted that:

> It is becoming realised that the large-capacity motor bus in densely populated areas is undesirable because of its slow acceleration, which adds to congestion, and because of the noise and smell (Cited in *Manchester Guardian*, 14th January, 1938).

Although by no means uniformly accepted, such views were locally important in the 1930s, and were influential in the decision of Manchester Corporation to introduce quiet and pollution-free trolley buses on a number of abandoned tram routes (MCTranspD, Annual reports).

A similar debate also surfaced in Glasgow in the 1950s, when the tram network in that city was coming under pressure. The 'Progressive' group on the City Council, supported by the *Glasgow Herald*, argued for the removal of trams from Glasgow's streets, but the Labour group and many correspondents to the Herald put forward contrary views. One letter writer cited the '... unbelievable ignorance of continental and world-wide trends in municipal transport ...' and argued that scrapping the trams would be: '... a grave mistake and one which Glasgow would soon bitterly regret' (*Glasgow Herald*, 31st December 1955 p. 4). Another correspondent, using similar arguments to those cited in Manchester in the

1930s, noted that: 'The diesel bus was a growing cause of air pollution in large towns, also a cause of illness ... [and trams were] ... the only vehicles which do not pollute the air'. The same writer went on to argue that: 'No reason [was] given for scrapping the trams except that other towns have done so' and that if the trams were removed the Corporation would be: 'failing in their duty to provide an efficient system which does not pollute the air' (*Glasgow Herald*, 29th December 1955, p. 8). These arguments had some influence as in 1955 plans to abolish the trams in Glasgow were defeated by the Labour group on the council, though the reprieve was short-lived and a plan to phase trams out was agreed two years later. Again this decision generated opposition, with some 21 letters in support of the trams published in the (largely anti-tram) *Glasgow Herald* between June and October 1957. The last tram eventually ran in Glasgow in 1962. Travellers in Manchester and Glasgow thus had their transport choices reduced by policy decisions that reflected contemporary views of the relative desirability of different forms of urban transport.

From the 1930s, both cities also took other steps to relieve mounting traffic congestion in the city centres, some of which went beyond the simple argument that fixed tram routes were the cause of traffic chaos. Thus in Manchester in the 1930s there were a series of proposals to build an inner ring road to remove traffic from the town centre and to increase the availability of off-street parking to reduce congestion caused by parked vehicles (Simon, 1938). Both proposals foreshadowed later trends as, even in a period when rates of car ownership were low, the Corporation was apparently prioritising motor vehicles over other forms of transport. However, there were some proposals that placed restrictions on motor vehicles in the 1930s, including the introduction of traffic lights, one-way systems and roundabouts (Simon, 1938). Manchester's first one-way system was adopted in February 1936, and attempted to regulate traffic passing through Albert Square (MCTranspD Annual Report, 1936). The following year proposals were put forward to extend the scheme to a further 30 streets in the city centre and, following a period of public consultation – which generated considerable opposition from letter writers to the *Manchester Evening Chronicle* in December 1937 – the scheme was introduced in June 1938 (MCTranspD Annual Report, 1938).

According to reports in the local press the new one-way system was a disaster, producing traffic chaos and widespread criticism from city centre businesses and those who commuted by public and private transport alike. Trams were particularly badly affected and the only beneficiaries were pedestrians who could now move faster than the city traffic. Although walking to work was still the single most important form of commuting in the 1930s, and in 1936 Simon had argued for the provision of separate pedestrian routes in the city (Simon, 1938), it was not the intention of Manchester's Traffic Congestion Committee to prioritise this group. The scheme attracted much critical comment from the local press:

> Pedestrians revelled in the new scheme for it provided them with the exciting game of tram car overtaking. As they speeded past the trams at three miles an hour, the drivers and guards looked on enviously ... Like a

stone in a pool the chaos in Oxford Street went out in an ever-widening circle until almost all tram car traffic coming from the Stockport and Withington sides of the city was involved in the most complete jam that the city has ever known (*Manchester Evening News*, 7th June, 1938).

After six months the one-way scheme was abandoned and most subsequent reports emphasised the creation of new wide roads to allow cars to move freely, though the City of Manchester Plan of 1945 also recommended the removal of all cross-city traffic from the city centre (Nicholas, 1945; Kidd, 1993). In the event only a small proportion of the proposed highway schemes were completed before the 1960s, but the needs of motorbuses and private cars were increasingly prioritised over trams, trolley buses, pedestrians and cyclists in the competition for urban road space.

With lower levels of car ownership, and a larger and more widely used tram network, traffic regulation in Glasgow in the 1930s was more muted than in Manchester. One focus of the debate was on the increasing danger posed to pedestrians by both trams and motorised vehicles, and in 1937 steps were taken to try to reduce road accidents involving pedestrians. New traffic signals were introduced and a local byelaw made it an offence for pedestrians to disobey traffic signals. It was argued that this would both reduce accidents and be fairer to car drivers who had to abide by road traffic regulations (*Glasgow Herald*, 5th January 1937, p. 4; 2nd February 1937, p. 4; 1st April 1937, p. 7). Thus whilst appearing to give some priority to the safety of walkers, the legislation was also attempting to regulate pedestrian use of the streets. By the 1950s, debates about traffic congestion and the need to regulate urban commuter traffic had surfaced again in Glasgow. Although some commentators criticised the growing number of private motorists, one calling them: '... the most selfish of city road users as they often carry only the driver to and from his place of business, and block up the thoroughfare for the remainder of the day' (*Glasgow Herald*, December 29th 1955, p. 8), as in Manchester most post-war transport schemes emphasised highway construction and prioritised the private car (Bruce, 1945; Abercrombie and Matthew, 1946; Scott, Wilson, Kirkpatrick and Partners, 1965; Checkland, 1981; Pacione, 1995).

The Suez crisis of 1957, which brought petrol rationing and a temporary reduction in car use, particularly focused attention on the problems of urban traffic congestion caused by the private car. As traffic volumes built up again when petrol became more widely available, a number of commentators highlighted the issue: 'Take one stretch – the Cheadle Crawl – in the early days of rationing it was quite easy to travel along it, but now it is getting back to the familiar stop-start-stop' (*Manchester Evening News*, 22nd March 1957). Although most, like the Manchester RAC spokesman cited above, were strongly pro-car, there were a number of voices calling for more restrictions to be placed on the private motorist. Thus in a debate about the provision of new multi-storey car parking in the city, one Manchester councillor objected on the grounds of cost and argued for the development of a park and ride scheme:

It would cost the fantastic sum of £2 10s [£2.50] per car per week to provide the parks. I will oppose such spending ... Many of the motorists who drive into Manchester don't even live in the city ... The answer must be to provide surface car parks outside the city centre where motorists can leave their vehicles and finish their journey by bus (*Manchester Evening News*, 26th April, 1957).

Although in 1960 Manchester's Chief Constable stated that he was to make traffic control a priority, and the first parking meters were installed in the city in 1961, in practice such measures had little impact on traffic volumes and the private car continued to dominate urban road space. It is only in the last decade of the twentieth century that urban planners have begun to take serious steps to control the motorcar in British cities. Thus in Manchester the new 'Metrolink' tram system was developed in the 1990s, and in Glasgow subway use has increased and Strathclyde Passenger Transport claims to have one of the most integrated public transport systems in the UK. It is, of course, somewhat ironic that the traffic congestion problems of the twenty-first century are being solved in some cases by a form of public transport that was eliminated from the streets of Glasgow and Manchester half a century earlier because it was perceived to be old fashioned, inflexible and inefficient! New policy decisions are thus beginning to broaden travel choice within these cities though, arguably, the needs of the pedestrian and the cyclist remain neglected.

Travellers' Reactions to Different Forms of Intra-urban Transport

We have so far examined the ways in which policy debates in Manchester and Glasgow changed the structure of urban transport and influenced the travel choices that were available to urban residents. We now use evidence from interviews with respondents in the two cities to examine the ways in which the travelling public responded to these changes. For instance, to what extent did policy changes that removed the trams cause inconvenience for commuters in Manchester and Glasgow, did travellers rapidly accommodate such changes, and how did the experience of everyday mobility for individuals change over the past 60 years?

Interestingly, although respondents who used public transport to commute in Glasgow and Manchester in the 1920s and 1930s were uniformly enthusiastic about the trams, they found the motorbuses that largely replaced the trams equally convenient, and accepted the removal of the tram system with equanimity. As one Glasgow commuter put it:

Well there was widespread news that they were, they were stopping the tram, the trams. We were all in advance by it, well advanced warning about buses taking their place ... Well it was, it was well known that they were going to change trams to buses so it was well publicised (RJ22, Glasgow, male, 1960s).

Attitudes to the use of motorbuses for commuting were remarkably similar to those expressed about trams and the number of people using motorbuses increased rapidly from the 1930s (Tables 10.1 and 10.2). They were seen as quick, relatively cheap, and convenient, and those who chose not to use them usually did not live on a bus route, wished to save money or enjoyed the exercise of cycling or walking. Such views were expressed by a number of respondents:

> Well it was most convenient. Although we had two train stations the bus was nearer me and I just went up the top of the hill, got a bus and right into the Gallowgate in Glasgow. Got off there, walked down three streets, and I was at work. So it was handiness (RJ21, Glasgow, female, 1940s).

> There were so many buses along the main Wilmslow Road, that they came literally every two minutes and never any problem getting into the centre of Manchester (RJ62, Manchester, female, 1960s).

> By that time my only option really was bus, yes. It was a bit far to go to a train station and certainly by that time all the trams had gone (RJ38 Glasgow, male, 1960s).

> There were no buses going that way cause it was across country so ... I would have had to go into the middle of town and then out again, or changed a couple of times on buses, and I hated buses by then so I got my fresh air on the bike (RJ24, Manchester, male, 1940s).

> ... from Cheetham to Chadderton. Yes I would. I would cycle there because of, because of the reason being that I had to get two or three buses in order to get there because it wasn't on one route you see (RJ32, Manchester, male, 1940s).

> Well, the bus didn't go that way. I could take one to George Square and walk back down, but the tram car was much more convenient for me (RJ23, Glasgow, 1950s).

Evidence from respondents who remembered the substitution of trams for motor buses suggests that in Manchester and Glasgow at least this change was relatively straightforward, they were able to swap from one form of public transport to another without difficulty, and were not unduly inconvenienced by the technology change that occurred. Some found both trams and buses inconvenient because they did not go directly to their preferred destination, and these were some of the first commuters to abandon public transport altogether and swap to a bicycle (especially men in the 1930s and 1940s) and then to the car.

We can also examine reactions to the re-introduction of the tram system in Manchester in the 1990s. How have present-day commuters reacted to this? Have those who previously used buses or trains swapped to the tram? And has the tram system encouraged car drivers to leave their vehicles at home? In fact, the reaction to the new tram system from respondents of all ages interviewed in 2002-2003 was mixed. Whilst many welcomed the tram, and found it quick, clean and convenient, others complained that it was crowded, expensive and that, as yet, the routes were not convenient.

> Because it's [the tram] the only way really that we can use because if we go on a bus it takes ages to get there. And if we go by tram it doesn't, yea that's why (R215, Lorna, aged 10/11, born 1991, Salford).

> Yea, it just doesn't really go to many places. I think/it doesn't go to any of the places I want to go really. Just one time I took it from Stretford into town (R219, Nazira, aged 17/18, born 1986, Manchester).

> Tram, tram, it's faster, you get there quicker. Bus, it's never on time, it's running late. So I'd rather get the tram (R230, Sunil, aged 17/18, born 1984, Manchester).

> Um, first thing in the morning it's incredibly packed. And also like about 6, 7-ish. And Friday nights incredibly packed as well. But it's quick, it's cleaner. It's a bit expensive. And it's pretty reliable, it's every 10 minutes. It's reliable (R231, Colin, aged 17/18, born 1984, Manchester).

> By car probably about 30, 35 minutes. If I had to use public transport I should have to get a bus into Stretford and then I could get a tram into Bury, and then I'd have to get another bus from Bury to the office (R372, Sonia, aged 30s, born 1968, Manchester).

> Oh yes. I mean now if we're going to Manchester on Friday afternoon, which we are, I will take my car and park it on an industrial estate. And then I'll walk to the tram station and get the Metrolink ... The Metrolink is fantastic (R369, Barbara, aged 60s, born 1936, Manchester).

One respondent in particular illustrates the way in which the introduction of a new transport technology, or more accurately a reformulated old technology, did not benefit everyone: the new Metrolink fundamentally affected her journey to work and made it both longer and less pleasant. Development of the tram led to the withdrawal of a train service, leading to a previously simple journey to work becoming much more complex. Although convenient for those whose origin and destination are on the tram route, the current tram network does not adequately reflect either the existing city structure or the complex cross-city journeys that commuters take. The tram network is being extended to other parts of Manchester, but for this person at least new transport technologies, designed to speed up everyday mobility in the city, had the opposite effect:

> And then, then they started talking about the Metro and because of the Metro they did away with the through train because the track, the track, part of the track that they used for the Altrincham to Manchester run was where the train went along and now they don't have trains going on that track. So for me the Metro was, was really terrible because you see the train used to go from Stockport into Manchester and then out to Altrincham and now it can't do that because there isn't the line from that, the direct line from

Manchester to Altrincham ... So you've either got to go into Manchester and change onto the Metro or what I ended up doing was from/you can, if you get into Stockport which, which I have to get a lift or a bus or it's a long walk, then there's another train which cuts across but it's only once an hour and it is so unreliable it is unbelievable (RJ67, Female, born 1946, Manchester).

Evidence from interviews with everyday mobility respondents in Manchester and Salford also provides insights into how travellers negotiated the changing transport network. What strategies did they adopt to deal with congestion, delays and other travel problems, and how did feelings about both public and private transport change over time? Again, it is argued that although contexts and travel opportunities have changed, the strategies and ideologies of travellers have remained largely consistent over time. In this section we focus on data from Manchester and Salford rather than Lancaster and Morecambe because the former conurbation has a much larger and more complex transport infrastructure offering much greater choice for the travelling public.

For many children, especially boys, travelling by public transport was an experience that was viewed with excitement. Thus both Harry and Les recalled the novelty of travelling by train or trolley bus in the 1940s and 1950s, and even adolescents such as Beryl in the 1950s were still attracted by travelling upstairs on a bus. Later generations of children gave very similar testimonies. Thus as a 10 year old Warren found travelling upstairs on a bus exciting in the 1970s, and Colin and Alex gave similar accounts relating to both buses and trams for more recent time periods. For these young travellers public transport was an adventure that added something to their life; and travelling by bus, train or tram was an experience in itself and not just a utilitarian means of getting from one place to another:

And my mum and dad sometimes explored east Manchester, Guide Bridge, Debdale Reservoir and that, they had trolleybuses round there. So it was, it was just to me as a kid who knew about these things it was different. We're going on an electric bus today and we're going on, occasionally an electric train out to Dinting or Glossop (R323, Harry, aged 10/11, born 1942, Manchester).

Well it was adventurous wasn't it going on the train. Sometimes we'd go by coach, that used to go to Morecambe mainly, but my dad, my parents would ask him to drop us off at Lancaster (R351, Les, aged 10/11, born 1937, Salford).

I enjoyed it. It was like an adventure for me you know and, and I used to sit, you know I went upstairs, upstairs on on/they were, they were double deckers you see and go upstairs and look into all, all people's windows, yes. And no it was, it was, it was good fun. I enjoyed it, I felt quite, well I suppose grown up really (R353, Beryl, aged 17/18, born 1935, Salford).

Oh I liked it. I always wanted to go upstairs and my mum always wanted to stay downstairs. So yea. For some reason as a child I used to like sitting on the front seats right at the front yea (R380, Warren, aged 10/11, born 1966, Manchester).

Yea. Because it was like a/it was/I was only just starting to use the bus then, so it was like a whole new experience for me, especially like when upstairs, sit on the front row. And I thought it was absolutely brilliant ... Cause you were a bit high up and you can see all the road (R231, Colin, aged 10/11, born 1984, Manchester).

Tram ... Yea. ... It's just more fun. It's more fun. It, it jiggles around on that middle bit ... [buses] They're alright, with them I like the double deckers top ... Yea I go upstairs at the front, cause when you're going down hills you feel like you're going to fall straight forward, so I use it as a ride (R207, Alex, aged 10/11, born 1991, Manchester).

Travellers of all ages and from each time period also recounted both positive and negative feelings about public transport. Some of these have been explored in earlier chapters in relation to the ways in which people made decisions about which transport mode to use. Here we focus on the ways in which people's feelings about travelling affected both their modal choice and their experience of travelling. We are interested particularly in the ways in which the travelling public interacted with different forms of technology, and the extent to which this changed over time as transport technologies and travelling conditions changed. Negative feelings about travelling by bus or tram related mainly to issues of reliability, crowding, cost and problems inherent in mixing with other travellers. Thus as 10 year olds in the 1940s Margaret and her friends felt uncomfortable travelling to school by bus because other commuters made children unwelcome, so they chose to walk and spent their bus fares on treats! Some 30 years later, Susan (aged 10/11 in the 1970s) recalled enjoying the view from the top of a bus, but also recounted that she felt unsafe and disliked the smoky environment:

It was like we were probably given money to go to school, but we didn't use the bus because we could walk it. And if we used the bus we used to get told off by people going to work because we were taking up spaces on the bus. So we all got in a huff and said that's it we won't, you know no matter what the weather we'll walk it. But the outcome of that was that when we were coming out of school we'd go in the greengrocers and get a penny apple or something (R348, Margaret, aged 10/11, born 1934, Manchester).

I still remember buses that didn't have doors on them. And I always remember getting on the bus and feeling a bit unsafe. You know if I was sat on a seat that you could actually see the open doorway and the steps. And I remember that you could smoke upstairs on the buses as well. And I used to like to sit upstairs because you could see, obviously you could see more, and you felt it was more of a treat. But when you got off the bus you always felt a bit sickly because of the smell of the smoke, and your clothes'd smell and so (R371, Susan, aged 10/11, born 1962, Salford).

The range of feelings generated by public transport is probably best illustrated by examining in more detail accounts from a range of respondents about their experiences of travelling by public transport in the Manchester conurbation today. Thus, whilst some informants in their 60s disliked travelling by public transport others saw it as the best option and, in some cases, gained real enjoyment from travelling by bus or tram. Often disapproval was aimed at a particular form of public transport; thus Harry, who enjoyed travelling by train and trolley bus in the 1950s, was typical of some who complained about congestion on the trams (though he admitted that in other respects it was a good system), but he also stated that he enjoyed using the bus to travel to work because it gave him time to read:

> Oh it's packed. In fact it's overused. And there have been cases of tram rage, where people have missed two trams cause they couldn't get on cause they're so crowded, and they actually had fights to get on it. And, and people are now going back to their cars because the tram is so unfaithfully uncomfortably crowded. And I'm convinced that they're operating an unfair system at certain times, because there are 300 and odd people crowding on a tram that's divide/it's life is for 260 or so. And they won't/there's no money to put extra trams on ... But it's a good system, and I use it cause it runs quite late. It runs later than the train used to. Only about half an hour or so. It doesn't do/it's not 24 hour, not 24 hourly ... No [I would not use car] because it's twice the cost of the bus. And I haven't got a car parking space at work, cause there's very few of those. And I don't like paying. Where I leave it actually is not too bad, but I would rather it be left at work. So if I have to leave it I'd rather leave it somewhere where it's officially protected and closed off from public access. But even I, even if I had a parking space well I'd be/I like using the bus because it give me an hour each way to read like magazines, which I wouldn't get otherwise (R323, Harry, aged 60s, born 1942, Manchester).

Others in their 60s also used public transport frequently and valued the freedom and independence that it gave them. Thus Derek was strongly anti-car and felt that public transport in Manchester was cheap, efficient and allowed him to travel as he wished without having to worry about issues such as drinking or parking. However, Beatrice's experience at the same age is very different. She has disabling arthritis and finds it hard to get on and off public transport, especially buses. This has effectively led to a phobia that restricts her independent mobility and associated activities far more than her physical limitations alone:

> To be quite honest with you if I won the lottery today I wouldn't buy car ... Because I don't want one ... Well, well I, I like the freedom of getting about and not being tied down. I like to have a pint and I'm quite willing to do without a car. It is just a nuisance to me. I've worked with 'em all my life and, and I get fed up of people now ... the public in their, in their cars ... I've not a lot of time for. But like I say the public transport to me is fantastic ... like I say I get out nearly every day and it's like I say no matter where I go it's 76 pence return. I can go anywhere I want (R325, Derek, aged 60s, born 1937, Salford).

> Well I can't get on the bus very easily. I, I could do it, but I feel very conscious of holding people up and like being able to get on properly. And um finding a seat I find difficult when the bus is moving. The train I can, I can get on and I've got in a seat by the time it goes off. And it's easier to get on and off the train ... It's just I don't like holding people/I get panic attacks in Tesco if I can't get my, my shopping and bags fast enough cause I know I'm keeping people waiting. I've gone a bit panicky sort of thing (R367, Beatrice, aged 60s, born 1937, Manchester).

Respondents in their 30s at the time of the interview also recorded a range of experiences and feelings about travelling by public transport, with some such as Tim expressing both positive and negative views. Nick avoids buses, much preferring to hire a taxi and only uses public transport if travelling with friends who want to use the bus, but Peta is happy to travel by bus into Manchester. This is partly because she does not have access to a car in the daytime, but also cites the convenience of the bus and the fact that her children still find it a novelty. Thus, for the kids at least, the experience of travelling by public transport becomes part of the outing.

> They're, they're pretty reliable. The main/again it's fairly busy routes that I use, so on, on that you're not waiting too long for one because it's a, it's a busy route. I'm just trying to think what, I must have some complaints about the bus, I'm trying to think ... I suppose my main complaint is some, some sort of talk people are using sometimes. You, you get this on the bus and I don't like foul language in public for instance and stuff like that. And you get a fair amount of that. Mainly with kids really, and especially in a place like Wythenshawe ... But ... it's, it's quite a good service (R373, Tim, aged 30s, born 1963, Manchester).

> To tell you the truth only when I'm going out with friends and they decide to use the bus. I'd never really step on a bus. I've been on the bus about three times in the last 12 months, if that ... Yea definitely convenience. I'd rather a taxi pull up outside my front door than me to have to walk 500 yards to the nearest bus stop. And it's waiting at the bus stop. And then do you know and buses do go a lot slower, obviously they're picking people up. In a taxi you're there in no time and they/and you/they drop you where you want to go as well (R337, Nick, aged 30s, born 1969, Manchester).

> Sometimes if I was going into Manchester now with, probably with the children, it would seem easier to take the bus than look for car parking. And 'cause car parking obviously is quite expensive in the centre of Manchester it would work out cheaper on the bus. And also it's quite a novelty still for the kids on a bus. So I would use the bus in those sort of circumstances. If my husband needs the car, cause we've only got the one car and we've got to share it between us, if he needed the car for work on a particular day then I might get the bus into Manchester or get the bus to work. So yea again it's, it's various, various things really that make me choose which, which method to use (R389, Peta, aged 30s, born 1971, Manchester).

Adolescents aged 17/18 are amongst the largest users of public transport. They have achieved a high degree of independence but often cannot yet drive or, if they have a licence, don't have regular access to a car. Few respondents were totally uncritical of the buses in Manchester, but many respondents aged 17/18 at the time of interview found public transport effective and convenient, allowing them to move freely around the city. Both Tom and Alan are typical of male respondents in this age group who used buses frequently. However, others were more negative. Thus Samuel complained about comfort, Verity finds them unreliable and can't wait to be able to drive, and Sunil finds negotiating new forms of public transport and unfamiliar routes difficult. He prefers to walk because he feels more in control and can be sure that he will get to the right place. Thus whilst for some adolescents travelling by bus or tram is an emancipating experience, for others it generates negative feelings and can become quite restrictive:

> Yea it, it's fine. I mean they do tend to bunch up in groups which like are quite annoying cause you'll get like a gap of like five to ten minutes then four buses come and its like, oh you just swear (R220, Tom, aged 17/18, born 1985, Manchester).

> I think it's [public transport] good. I think/I don't necessarily like the characters you might encounter on them. But yea I think they're/it's good. But I think they're usually, they're usually clean. Usually they're on time. And you usually get where you want very quick. So yea I haven't got a problem with it at all (R238, Alan, aged 17/18, born 1985, Manchester).

> I think they should make them more comfortable. They're not really very comfortable at all. Like I mean you, say you get one of these buses and I think they're disgusting, most of them are anyway. These new ones they did, like the purple ones that they, they do round town, which are, are quite nice. But some of them are just disgusting. They really are bad. You know for 40p there's no, there's no space and you just don't feel comfortable on them. You're, you're only getting them cause they get you where you want to go (R237, Samuel, aged 17/18, born 1986, Manchester).

> Because I hate getting the buses ... They're not reliable at all. I can't wait to drive. My friend's learning. And this boy I went with school he's got a car and I envy him. I want a car. I want to drive. It's just freedom really ... I can get up and go whenever I want, whatever time. I don't have to worry about buses, what time it's coming. I don't have to sit in the cold waiting for it (R228, Verity, aged 17/18, born 1985, Manchester).

> Cause I was really scared, I was really scared to get on the bus, cause I don't know where I had to get off. So I went once with my friend, who showed me where to get off and that. So then I started going and then started meeting him and all that, then I got used to the bus.Then the same as the tram, he took me on the tram one time. I was like really scared, I don't know where to get off. Well then he told me to get off this part, that goes there, this there that, and then I used to like go on it ... Cause um that's why I like, prefer walking, do you get me, cause at least I know where I'm going.

On a, on a bus I won't. They'll take a left here and then they'll take a right and then they'll go straight on, and they'd ended up in town. But I think he's taking a left is he going/you're supposed to go straight down the road. So that, that's why I prefer walking cause it's just one straight direct walk that you can do (R230, Sunil, aged 17/18, born 1984, Manchester).

Some other respondents, especially children aged 10/11 such as Hannah, Christopher and Layla, also stated that they liked walking: for children of this age exercise was still pleasurable. However, other children got a good feeling from travelling by car, either because of its protection and warmth (Laura) or due to the ability to personalise space and interact only with family (Marcus):

Yea. I like walking cause it gives me an exercise. It exercises my legs and my body. It's [the car] pretty boring, cause you're not walking (R217, Chris, aged 10/11, born 1992, Salford).

It's longer, but I like walking ... You get to see more things (R212, Hannah, aged 10/11, born 1992, Salford).

It's, it's, it's good to get you know fresh/because you get fresh air and you know exercise. So it's pretty fit. Cause it, it just like, it/if your muscles are all tensed up it makes them relax, so (R234, Layla, aged 10/11, born 1991, Manchester).

It's like it's really good, cause like you're quite warm in the car and like/I don't know really, but I just like travelling by car cause like you're not cold when you're stood there (R213, Laura, aged 10/11, born 1991, Salford).

No. No I prefer using the car cause it was like personal wasn't it. I mean if you use the bus it was like you had to share with a group of people, but if you were just with your family it was better (R240, Marcus, aged 10/11, born 1985, Manchester).

Attitudes to driving also varied considerably, but with a strong gender divide. Derek, cited above, was an unusual male respondent in not wishing to use a car. Nick's attitude was much more typical: once he had access to a motor vehicle at the age of 18 he tended to use it for all journeys. In contrast several women stated that they found a car inconvenient and difficult to park, or that they were scared of diving. Nazira, talking about her mobility aged 10/11 in the 1990s, clearly highlighted gender differences in attitudes to the car: if she travelled to Manchester with her father they would go by car, but if she was with her mother she would travel by bus because her mother did not like driving in the busy city centre. Carol and Susan, both in their 30s, were also typical of women who can drive but who prefer not to either because of lack of confidence or due to previous experiences. Some ten years earlier two children Carol knew well had been killed on the road, and even though she learned to drive this experience has put her off driving for life. These quotes demonstrate the ways in which attitudes towards different forms of transport can be shaped by previous experiences, and emphasise that travel by car (or at least driving) is not viewed as a preferable or pleasurable activity by all:

> No, I became, like I say I was/I'd/because I was mobile and I had a van or a car it became a chore. Like if I just nipped down to the local shop I'd jump in the car rather than walk. If I was going/if I was going round to see a friend I'd dive in the car and go even if it was only a couple of minutes away ... Yea, it's cause it was easy (R337, Nick, aged 17/18, born 1969, Manchester).

> Because mam didn't want to take the car into the town because you know parking. If my, if my, if my dad ever took us he always took the car cause he can find parking. But you know with the one way streets, and my mum didn't feel comfortable driving in town, so we just used to take the bus (R219, Nazira, aged 10/11, born 1986, Manchester).

> Cause I'm silly. I got my licence about, um let's see, probably about 7 years ago. And I passed on my second attempt. And the first lot of lessons I had was a crash course, so I literally started on the Monday and I took the test on the Friday. And I failed. Then I did another four weeks of reversing round corners and into spaces, cause that's what I'd failed on, so consequently I didn't do an awful lot of on-road driving practice. And it, it just sort of it worried me. And I've only been out probably about 10 times by myself. And in the end I thought well why feel stressed about it when my husband can drive me wherever I want or I can ring my dad up and my dad can take me (R371, Susan, aged 30s, born 1962, Salford).

> It's just because all that seemed to happen like at the time when I was learning to drive and it just put me off. It, it's just the thought of the responsibility, I get behind a wheel and God forbid killing someone. No it's just, no (R332, Carol, aged 30s, born 1970, Salford).

The importance of individuality in everyday mobility is also emphasised by these quotes. Personal experiences and preferences often shape travel behaviour, and individual decisions based on personal factors may be as important as factors such as cost, convenience, or transport technology. Thus as a 10 year old in the 1970s Warren had a bike, but rarely used it because it was the wrong sort of bike. He did not wish to be laughed at by school friends because his parents could not afford to buy him a fashionable bike. For Colin, his desire to be with friends often shapes his travel behaviour and choice of transport mode, and both Vicki and Aisha select particular forms of transport because of a personal desire to be independent. Their parents could run them around town, but as adolescents aged 17/18 they wish to assert their independence. Their choice of independent mobility is one way in which this can be achieved:

> Yea I think to be perfectly honest we wasn't a very well off family, we was quite poor really, so it was 95 per cent out of/from what I can remember was walking. Cycling, I eventually got a bike, a second hand bike, it was like Granville's bike out of *Open All Hours*, so it was a bit of a/I felt like a right

drier, but I mean at the end of the day it was a bike, so ... Yea I didn't use it a lot no because I mean all the other kids had the latest Raleigh Choppers and I had this old butcher's bike, so yea (R380, Warren, aged 10/11 born 1966, Manchester).

I don't really like travelling about on my own that much purely because I do, I just, I, I like social inter/I like people, I like talking, so ... It's not the fear like if I was attacked or whatever or if I was lost, it's purely because I just don't like being on my own that much really. I mean I, I can handle it. But I just like talking to people (R231, Colin, aged 17/18, born 1984, Manchester).

But the bus really gives me independence cause I'm not relying on my mum to take me or use/and because of the late travel I can basically get anywhere quite quickly. So I think really the bus is just, is quite convenient. From Chorlton into town is a long/is a fairly regular bus service, so I think mainly I like using the bus (R221, Vicki, aged 17/18, born 1985, Manchester).

Because I don't drive I think I/I don't depend on as much people as before, so I'd rather be more independent, just go by bus usually most of the time yea. So it's changed, it's like all the time before it's like car and mum or my dad, and now it's just like mostly by bus or walking ... Yea I like to be independent (R224, Aisha, aged 17/18, born 1985, Manchester).

Conclusions

This chapter has focused on interactions between the provision of different transport facilities in urban areas, linked to changes in both transport policies and technologies, and individual experiences of everyday travel. It argues that at the policy level decisions about transport provision have often been based on economics or fashion and have paid relatively little attention to the needs of the travelling public. Pedestrians, in particular, have been marginalised in cities despite the fact that, as demonstrated earlier, travel on foot is the single most important type of trip undertaken for everyday mobility. We also argue that at each time period and in every age group studied there is considerable variety in travel experiences, and that as transport systems changed and evolved most travellers were able easily to adapt their journeys to the new transport infrastructure. Thus the travelling public greeted removal of the well-used trams in Manchester and Glasgow with relative equanimity. The key messages that again emerge from the data are that there is great variety in individual experience and that the structures and forces that shape travel behaviour in towns have changed little over the past century, even though in some cases there have been fundamental shifts in transport infrastructure.

A focus on the everyday experience of travel also emphasises the ways in which for some mobility is more than a utilitarian process of travelling from place to place to fulfil routine needs. We argue that the materiality of mobility is clearly of prime importance for most people, and most movement is undertaken for a clear purpose. However, some travel does involve little more than being seen (for instance hanging around by teenagers considered in Chapter 8), and how travel is undertaken does assume a deeper meaning for some respondents. In this sense everyday mobility becomes a performance that adds deeper meaning to everyday life. These themes have been developed elsewhere by cultural theorists, and are discussed in more detail in Chapter 2 (Bourdieu, 1984; de Certeau, 1984; Bull, 2000). We argue that the accounts provided by respondents to our surveys place most emphasis on the practical aspects of mobility – most everyday mobility was undertaken for a purpose by the most convenient means available – but that there is a secondary subtext in which where, how and with whom you travel begins to add meaning to everyday life. Thus although it can be suggested that much contemporary cultural mobility theory over-privileges performative aspects of movement, and downplays the utilitarian, the extent to which the experience of everyday mobility had meaning for travellers of all ages is a significant secondary theme.

Chapter 11

The Lessons of History:
Mobility Change and Contemporary
Transport Policy

Introduction

The research reported in this volume is primarily an historical study of the ways in which everyday mobility has changed over the past century. Using a variety of research methods, based mainly on the collection of in-depth life histories from respondents in four cities, we have examined changes in the journey to work since circa 1900, and shifts in everyday mobility (especially of children) since the 1940s. We have also demonstrated the ways in which the experience of everyday mobility has changed over the life course of people currently in their 60s, and have explored the changing attitudes of travellers to new transport technologies and infrastructures.

Although transport policy must be based primarily on contemporary conditions and predictions of future transport demands, we firmly believe that analysis of past trends and experiences can help to inform contemporary transport policy. In this final chapter we first outline the key conclusions that have been drawn from this research and, second, relate these to present-day transport policy statements at both the national and local levels. The focus of our research has been firmly on the mobility needs of individuals, rather than on the role of transport in (for instance) generating economic growth. Although most, though not necessarily all, individuals benefit from a healthy regional or national economy, we argue that a key aspect of sustainable transport policies at both national and local levels must be the provision and management of transport and travel in a way that meets the needs of individuals in local communities. In conclusion we suggest a series of priorities for transport policy that reflect this view and that integrate the key findings of this study within transport policy.

Lessons from the Past

We suggest that there are eight key conclusions from this research that have potential relevance for contemporary transport policy. First, our research emphasises the continued variability and individuality of travel demands and experiences over the past century. Although it is possible to make generalisations and to compute broad trends, the life history approach adopted in this study emphasises the ways in which mobility is constructed to suit the needs of individuals and families. At each time period studied it was possible to find examples of a wide variety of mobility experiences, for instance, with some children highly constrained in their movement whilst others had considerable freedom. We should therefore beware of over-generalisation and remember that all statements of trends obscure enormous individual variation.

Second, although most mobility theory and some interpretations of recent aggregate transport trends emphasise change in travel behaviour over the past century, especially an assumed increase in total mobility and a massive increase in car use and consequent decline in other modes of transport, our study begins to modify this view. Although there have clearly been many significant changes, we argue that the degree of stability in everyday mobility is more significant and surprising than the changes that have occurred. For instance, although most people now have much greater opportunities for long-distance travel than they did in the past, and widespread car ownership has provided new and flexible transport for many; most everyday trips remain short distance and focused on the local area, the total distances that children travel have changed little since the 1940s, the time spent on the journey to work has barely changed since the early-twentieth century, and walking remains an important means of everyday travel around town for many people. Although it is possible to see both stability and change in most aggregate data sets, we argue that in the past too much emphasis has been placed on obvious changes and too little emphasis on important elements of stability in everyday mobility.

Third, and underlining the above point, stability in some aspects of the time, distance and mode of everyday travel is underpinned by even greater stability in the underlying structures and constraints that control individual everyday mobility. Thus the factors that people take into account when evaluating journey to work options, or when changing home or workplace, have altered little over the twentieth century. Likewise, the mechanisms that parents use to determine where and when young children can play out are much the same now as they were in the 1940s. In each time period parents set boundaries of space or time, determined companions and prohibited access to certain areas. Equally, in each time period, the degree to which children actually adhered to these rules varied considerably. In each time period, too, everyday mobility was severely affected by life-course factors with the childcare responsibilities of women having a consistent and considerable effect on the mobility of many young mothers.

Fourth, although in much of the research we stress stability over change, there is one key area in which a significant shift in mobility behaviour has occurred. Compared to the past, people today are much more aware of and concerned about risk and these heightened perceptions of risk are having an increasing influence on where and when people travel in their daily lives. This is seen most clearly in the case of children where, although the rules and structures which parents put in place today are broadly similar to those used in the 1940s, these are now applied more rigorously, and children are much more restricted in where and when they can travel and play out without adult supervision. Moreover, such constraints are not only imposed by parents but also are constructed by children themselves who have become more risk aware and restrict their own travel behaviour. This trend does not only affect children. Adults, especially elderly adults, have also become increasingly fearful of travelling around the urban environment and although, overall, many of those in their 60s now experience greater mobility than at any time in their life, some are also restricting where and when they go because of increased perceptions of risk.

Fifth, it is argued that the relatively high degree of stability found in the structure and organisation of everyday mobility is not entirely surprising when it is viewed from the perspective of individuals and families. Most everyday mobility takes place in an instrumental way, designed to allow an individual to fulfil their everyday needs and obligations. At its most basic level the needs of individuals and families have not altered greatly over the past century. Almost everyone is concerned to find work, to have a home, to have access to essential everyday needs, to support family and friends, to belong to a community and to have some recreation and leisure activity. Despite the ability to travel more easily over long distances in the twenty-first century, most of these needs are still fulfilled locally, and it can be argued that the development of virtual mobility through first telephones and then internet communications has reduced the need for physical travel at the same time as some everyday requirements have become more dispersed. Thus, at its most simple, everyday mobility reflects and responds to basic human desires, beliefs and requirements, and as human beings, living in families and communities, we have changed little over the past century.

Sixth, although one of the greatest and most obvious changes in everyday mobility over the past century has been the expansion of car use for many types of trip, it can be argued that this modal shift is also reflecting a deeper stability of mobility desires amongst the travelling public. Thus it is argued that, whenever people have been faced with a choice of how they could travel, when it could be afforded and was feasible, they have opted for that form of transport that offered the greatest flexibility, privacy and individual control. Thus in the 1920s when the bicycle could first be afforded by the majority of ordinary working people, men in particular began to abandon public transport in favour of using a bike for their journey to work. It can be argued that in the 1920s and 1930s the pedal cycle offered many of the perceived advantages that the car does today: it allows the rider to control when and where they travel, there is no need to share or have close contact with others, it can travel relatively quickly and easily through urban streets, and it provides flexibility allowing individuals to alter their travel schedule to suit immediate needs. The bike also has obvious disadvantages including exposure to the elements, the effort required to power the machine and the difficulty of transporting passengers or large quantities of luggage. It is thus not surprising that as cars became cheaper and more widely available they supplanted the bicycle, but the social and cultural constructions of 'automobility' ascribed to the car can also in large part be linked to the bicycle in the interwar period. This desire for individualised transport has also been male dominated with relatively few women cycling to work in the 1920s and 1930s, though many more cycled for pleasure. Likewise, women lagged some 20 years behind men in car use.

Seventh, examination of the testimonies of travellers from different periods throughout the twentieth century emphasises the extent to which, on the one hand, there is considerable inertia built into most people's everyday mobility but, on the other hand, when required to make changes to their travel behaviour most people were able to do so without difficulty. This was demonstrated most clearly in Glasgow and Manchester when the extensive and popular tram systems were replaced by motorbuses in the mid-twentieth century. Although most travellers found the trams cheap and convenient, they adapted very quickly to new motorbuses and integrated them into their everyday travel. More recently, the development of the Metrolink tram system in Manchester has again led people to change transport modes for many everyday journeys. Although some respondents complained about the trams, especially on the grounds of cost, crowding and convenience, many travellers switched from bus, train or car to the tram without difficulty.

Eighth, analysis of individual travel behaviour in the context of the development of urban public transport schemes emphasises the ways in which many people do not have a free choice of everyday mobility, but rather their mobility is structured by decisions well outside their control. At each time period a particular form of transport dominated the urban transport infrastructure: trams in the early-twentieth century, followed by motorbuses and, in the later-twentieth century, the motorcar. Thus many people felt that they had little choice about the form of transport that they used, and the needs of other road users have been marginalised. In particular, traffic management and transport planning has tended to favour those forms of transport, such as trams, buses and cars, which make technical and infrastructural demands on the urban road network. Other forms of transport including cycling and walking have been relatively ignored. However, we have demonstrated that walking continues to be an important means of everyday local travel for many people and that in the 1920s and 1930s cycling was one of the most important means of travelling to work for men. However, transport planners, politicians and others with power within the city, have historically neglected the needs of these users of urban space.

Implications for Transport Policy

Transport policy in Britain is implemented at a variety of different levels. National government provides an overall framework through its transport strategy documents, and intervenes directly in some (mainly national) transport provision, most notably the development of the motorway and rail networks. Regional and local government have responsibility for drawing up and implementing their own transport strategies at the local level. Whilst in general these reflect national policies, they also reflect local priorities and where there are political differences between local and national government there may be conflicts. In addition, individual employers are increasingly taking responsibility, often in conjunction with local government, for implementing workplace traffic management and travel plans, including schemes such as restrictions on parking and encouragements for workers to share cars. Moreover, it can be suggested that since much transport planning and traffic management entails persuading, rather than forcing, people to travel differently, the success or otherwise of different schemes depends very much on the everyday decisions of individuals with respect to their mobility. There is thus not one single transport policy in Britain, but a series of layers of planning, implementation and use that interact with each other to produce the everyday reality of mobility in British cities.

It can be suggested that there is currently a tension within transport policy in Britain. The government White Paper 'A New Deal for Transport' (DETR, 1998a) attempted to set a new agenda for transport planning in Britain with a commitment towards more integrated transport policies that provided more effectively for those who used public transport, cycled and walked and which increasingly managed and restricted car use, especially in urban areas. It stated clearly that priority would be given to 'the maintenance, and management of existing roads before building new ones' (p. 57), and local authorities were required to draw up strategic transport plans that prioritised integrated public transport and regulated car use, including the development of congestion charging, road tolls and workplace parking charges. However, the more recent White Paper 'The Future of Transport' (DfT, 2004a) which updates transport policy, whilst retaining a commitment to sustainable transport and traffic management, gives much greater priority to road building. Indeed, in listing achievements since publication of the 10 year plan for transport (DfT, 2000), the White Paper first highlights improvements to the road system with '18 major strategic road schemes completed since 2002, plus widening of the A2/M2 and the M6 Toll, and five major local road schemes completed since 2000' (p. 28). Elsewhere in the document mention is made of strategies to encourage walking and cycling, and to reduce car use, but the emphasis has changed since 1998 and commitment to radical change seems much more muted. The Department for Transport has published a separate Walking and Cycling Action Plan (DfT, 2004b) and has commissioned independent research on 'soft' transport policy measures designed to change the way we travel (Cairns et al., 2004), but such issues appear to be a secondary concern of national transport policy.

In contrast, local transport plans produced after the publication of 'A New Deal for Transport' and subsequent revisions, have focused much more explicitly on the need to impose controls on motorists in urban areas, and to give greater priority to other forms of transport. Thus Glasgow's Local Transport Strategy proclaims:

> The main thrust of the transport strategy is to alter travel behaviour in the medium to long term and invoke a culture change away from the use of the private car where alternative modes of transport are available. Changing patterns of behaviour, particularly in children, will ensure a more sustainable future for them and for Glasgow (Glasgow City Council, 2000, p. 3).

The Greater Manchester Local Transport Plan also states 'we have developed a strategy to slow the rate of traffic growth and reduce its impact on local areas …

This relies on getting more people and goods around by other means' (GMPTA, 2001 p. 2). The strategies adopted to achieve these aims include: improving public transport; encouraging cycling and walking; reversing decentralisation to improve accessibility; demand-management measures to reduce car trips; improvements to road safety; more sustainable freight transport; improving road maintenance; and highlighting local measures that impact on particular communities. The 2004 Monitoring Report (GMPTA, 2004) lists the measures taken and shows, amongst other things, that the proportion of trips into Manchester between 0730 and 0930 undertaken by public transport rose from 51 per cent in 1999 to 59 per cent in 2002.

Since the creation of the Greater London Authority in 1999 London has probably implemented more radical policies to reduce car use, and to encourage travel on foot, by cycle and on public transport, than any other city in Britain (GLA, 2001). A central plank of this policy was the introduction of congestion charging in February 2003. London was not the first city in Britain to introduce congestion charging as a small scheme covering central Durham was introduced in 2002, and other cities including Edinburgh and Nottingham are actively considering schemes. Schemes are also in operation in a number of other large cities worldwide including Singapore and Oslo. Despite some opposition, congestion charging in London has both been accepted by the majority of Londoners and has led to a 15 per cent reduction in traffic during charging hours within the charging zone (GLA, 2004). The 2004 Transport Strategy Revision proposes a further extension of the congestion-charging zone to the west of London to become operational in 2006. In conjunction with traffic control measures there has been heavy investment in new bus routes, and the development of a strategy to encourage walking and cycling in London designed to meet the declared aim of making London 'one of the world's most walking-friendly cities by 2015' (Transport for London, 2004, p. 5). This is to be achieved by both encouraging walking as the main mode for short trips, and making walking more attractive as a means of accessing an improved public transport network. The action plan produced by Transport for London entails working with individual boroughs at the local level on a variety of schemes that include the promotion of walking, the improvement of street conditions, the enhancement of interchanges for pedestrians accessing public transport, and the improvement of street safety. A recent review by a range of academics and practitioners has strongly endorsed congestion charging and related policies in London (Richardson, 2004). As in Britain's other major cities, local transport planning initiatives place rather more emphasis on restraining traffic growth and on promoting walking, cycling and public transport than seems to be the case with current national policy.

It can be suggested that the different emphases of local urban transport policies and the national strategies reflect the different constituencies and environments in which they have been created. Whereas the 2004 White Paper 'The Future of Transport' reflects a national political perspective in which there is a very strong lobby from road users, the local transport plans in cities such as London, Glasgow and Manchester reflect specific urban conditions in which not only are levels of car ownership lower than those nationally (for instance in

Manchester in 2001 47.8 per cent of households did not have access to a car or van compared to 26.8 per cent nationally), but also the everyday experience of urban traffic congestion is more acute. Where local authorities have consulted their citizens by and large there has been strong support for their transport policies. For instance, in public consultations in Greater Manchester extending the Metrolink and improving public transport was listed as the top priority for some 75 per cent of respondents (GMPTA, 2001). The Metrolink is a good example of current tensions between local and national policies. Although prioritised by planners and politicians in Manchester, and supported by the general public, in July 2004 the government failed to commit funds to this and other urban tram and light rail schemes because of fears about escalating costs, and light rail receives only a brief and rather lukewarm mention in the 2004 White Paper which suggests that 'bus options are likely to offer the most cost-effective solutions on most corridors' (DfT, 2004, p. 62). By December 2004 although some progress had been made, with new costings submitted to Government, funding for the extension had not been secured.

Strategies to prioritise public transport, walking and cycling also gain support from this historical analysis of travel patterns in two urban areas. Five key points can be highlighted. First, this research has emphasised the continued importance of short-distance and local travel for most people in urban areas. Thus it is appropriate that urban transport strategies should focus on the needs of local neighbourhoods and on the everyday movement of people around towns, and not just on longer-distance movement around the country. Local and national transport policy needs to recognise the continued significance of short and local journeys in fulfilling the everyday travel needs of most people. Second, and following from the above point, the research has highlighted the continued importance of walking and public transport in much everyday travel, especially of children and adolescents. The popular assumption that walking is no longer an important means of travel around urban areas is simply wrong, and urban transport policies need to recognise the central role that walking plays both as a mode in its own right and as a means of accessing public transport. Too often transport policies marginalise the pedestrian or assume that walking is a travel mode that does not need special provision. One key implication of this research is that walking continues to be an important element of travel around towns, and that transport policy should place the needs of pedestrians alongside those of other road users.

Third, one of the key changes that the research has highlighted is increased concern about safety, especially for young children, but to some extent affecting all age groups. Although children do still play outside and walk around town, mobility is increasingly restricted and controlled because of fears of, often unspecified, risks. This suggests that one key element of strategies to promote walking and greater use of the urban environment by children must be moves to improve the perceived safety of urban areas and to reduce risks. This could encompass the promotion of more traffic-free areas, safe routes for children to travel to school, safe areas where children may play out and designated cycle and pedestrian routes that are traffic free and well lit. It is impossible to remove all risk in the urban environment, and as this research has shown the negotiation of everyday low-level dangers was for many of our older respondents an important part of the process of growing up. It can be suggested that it should be possible to encourage children to engage in adventurous play, and to learn to cope with challenging environments, without exposing them to undue risk. Adventure holidays and related schemes, sometime promoted by local authorities, can provide access to safe but challenging experiences for a minority of children. But these sorts of activities can never be more than an occasional experience. It can be argued that more attention should be paid not only to the provision of safe travel routes in town, but also to the provision of safe, and if necessary supervised, play areas for children where kids can engage in challenging activities and outdoor play without facing undue risk.

Fourth, the research has shown that, despite significant inertia in the system, over time people have changed their travel behaviour. There have been significant shifts from trams, to buses and, in the case of Manchester, back to trams in the late-twentieth century. Likewise, the success of congestion charging in London has demonstrated that it is possible to persuade people to switch from their cars to public transport, cycling and walking. Accounts of the changeover from (much-liked) trams to motorbuses in Glasgow stressed that this was perceived by most people to go smoothly because the Corporation gave good information and, at the time, people were persuaded of the necessity of the change. It can thus be suggested that any policy to reduce car use in urban areas and to expand walking, cycling and use of public transport must be accompanied by a persuasive campaign of information and education about the reasons for the change, the services that will be available and the benefits to be gained.

Fifth, our research stresses the individual variability of travel experiences with many people changing their travel patterns on a daily basis and with examples of a wide range of travel behaviour shown to exist at all time periods. Moreover, for any individual travel constraints and requirements vary with life-cycle stage. Thus although we can identify general trends, and one of the main trends is relative stability, within this there is a high degree of dispersion around mean experiences. One implication of this for transport policy is that over-arching solutions that provide one dominant form of transport are unlikely to be successful. There is a need to plan to accommodate a variety of different travel options in urban areas. Thus, almost irrespective of restrictions, cars will continue to be used for some journeys because of their convenience. For trips with multiple destinations and large amounts of luggage the car is likely to be the transport of choice for most families. However, the same families may also be keen to use public transport for journeys to work or to school, or to walk or cycle for shorter trips. Rather then privileging one form of transport in urban areas, transport policy must embrace the individual variability of travel demands and enable people to switch between modes and vary their transport with ease within their local area.

In Chapter 2 the ways in which mobility interacted with different aspects of society were outlined. Six discourses of mobility were discussed: mobilities as everyday life; mobilities that construct communities; mobility as performance; the environmental consequences of mobility; mobility and risk; and mobility, leisure and lifestyle. Furthermore, it can be argued that those individuals and families who experience the greatest mobility constraints are likely to be excluded from at least some aspects of society and economy. This has been clearly recognised as an important policy issue by the report of the government's Social Exclusion Unit on transport and social exclusion (Office of the Deputy Prime Minister, 2003). This focuses on the problems that people have gaining access to work, school, local services and facilities as a result of inappropriate transport provision. However, as identified through some of the local case studies included in the report, the solution is not necessarily to enable people to travel more, but rather to provide facilities in such a way that they are accessible with only a minimal amount of travel. To a large extent, the conclusions of this study reinforce this message. Whilst there has been some increase in the total amount of travel undertaken, (especially by adults) and, particularly, in car use, the main message of the research is that today, as 60 years ago, most people undertake most of their travel within a fairly compact area that contains their friends and provides basic services. It can therefore be suggested that in the past too much emphasis has been placed on enabling people to travel easily over relatively long distances, whereas more people would benefit from improvements in travel facilities at the local level and the provision of a wider range of services close to home.

Conclusions

This final chapter has attempted to draw some broader conclusions from the research and to relate it to contemporary transport policy. In general, analysis of everyday travel trends over the past 60 years emphasises the importance of local and sustainable transport options, and suggests that attempts to generate more environmentally-friendly mobility by cities such as London, Glasgow and Manchester are well-rooted in historical travel patterns. However, it is important to remember the limitations of a study such as this. First, we focus mainly on four urban areas (and on only two situated in the north of England for some of the analysis). Travel needs and behaviour in rural areas are certainly different. Second, data are generated by a relatively small sample of respondents. Although in total these people have provided information on a very large number of individual trips it is not possible to break travel patterns down into small sub-groups. Third, and for these reasons, we have not analysed in detail mobility variations by occupation or social class (though there is little evidence of any significant variations) and we have not been able to focus on the mobility needs of special groups, for instance those with restricted personal mobility.

However, despite these caveats we can state some conclusions with confidence. In particular we stress the individuality of mobility experiences over the past 60 years; the relative stability of travel patterns and behaviour; the fact that although walking is clearly less common than it was in the past it remains a very significant element of everyday mobility for most people; and the ways in which children's play and some travel by adults is increasingly restricted due to changed perceptions of risk. The research also clearly shows the ways in which detailed historical analysis can not only show trends over time, but also help to inform and contextualise our understanding of shorter-term trends. Thus, our data are not incompatible with the picture of greater change painted by some statistics in the National Travel Survey, but these need to be put into perspective by both realising the types of travel that are excluded from the survey and by placing the trends in a longer-term historical context. In some ways we have only just begun to understand historical trends in everyday mobility and travel. Our research outlines the bare bones of where, why and how people travelled in the past, but it ignores completely some much more difficult but pressing contemporary questions: for instance the ways in which changes in travel behaviour over the past 60 years have impacted on child health. The resolution of such issues will have to await further research.

Bibliography

Abercrombie, P. and Matthew, R. (1946), *The Clyde Valley Regional Plan*, Edinburgh: HMSO.

Adam, B., Beck, U. and van Loon, J. (2000), *The risk society and beyond: critical issues for social theory*, London: Sage.

Adams, J. (1999), 'The social implications of hypermobility', in OECD, *Project on environmentally sustainable transport: the economic and social implications of sustainable transport*, Paris: ENV/EPOC/PPC/T(99)3/FINAL, pp. 75-113.

Aitken, S. (2001), *Geographies of young people: the morally-contested spaces of identity*, London: Routledge.

Anderson, M. (1980), *Approaches to the history of the Western family*, London: Macmillan.

Anderson, M. (1985), 'The emergence of the modern life cycle in Britain', *Social History*, 10, 69-87.

Anderson, M. (1994), 'What is new about the modern family?', in Drake, M. (ed.) *Time, family and community*, Oxford: Blackwell, pp. 67-90.

Annual Report of the Medical Officer of Health, Salford, 1936.

Association of London Authorities (ALA), (no date), *Keeping London moving: the ALA transport strategy*, London: ALA.

Baker, A., Hamshere, J. and Langton, J. (1970), *Geographical interpretations of historical sources*, Newton Abbot: David and Charles.

Bamberg, S. and Schmidt, P. (1996), 'Changing travel mode choice as rational choice: results from a longitudinal intervention study', *Rationality and Society* 10, 223-52.

Banister, D. (1994), 'Reducing the need to travel through planning', *Town Planning Review*, 65, 349-64.

Barke, M. (1991), 'The middle-class journey to work in Newcastle-upon-Tyne, 1850-1913', *Journal of Transport History*, 12, 107-34.

Barker, T. and Robbins, M. (1963-74), *A history of London Transport. Vols 1 and 2*, London: Allen and Unwin.

Barlow Report (1940), *Report of the Royal Commission on the distribution of the industrial population*, London: HMSO, Command 6153.

Beck, U. (1992) *Risk society: towards a new modernity*, Sage: London.

Beeching, R. (1963), *The reshaping of British railways*, London: HMSO.

Bentley, R. (1998), 'Sustainable transport: the role of the bus in the post-competitive market', *Transport Reviews*, 18, 199-213.

Black, C., Collins, A. and Snell, M. (2001), 'Encouraging walking: the case of journey to school trips in compact urban areas', *Urban Studies*, 38, 1121-41.

Black, R. and Robinson, V. (1993), *Geography and refugees: patterns and processes of change*, London: Belhaven.

Black, W. (2001) 'An unpopular essay on transportation', *Journal of Transport Geography*, 9, 1-11.

Bloomfield, A. and Harris, R. (1997), 'The journey to work: a historical methodology', *Historical Methods*, 30, 97-109.

Bourdieu, P. (1984), *Distinctions: A Social Critique of the Judgement of Taste*, London: Routledge and Kegan Paul.

British Transport Commission (1948-62), *Reports and Accounts*, London: BTC.

Bruce, R. (1945), *First planning report to the Highways and Planning Committee of the Corporation of the City of Glasgow*, Glasgow: Glasgow Corporation.

Bruton, F. (1927), *A short history of Manchester and Salford*, 2nd edn, Manchester: Sherratt.

Buchannan, C. (1963), *Traffic in Towns*, London: HMSO.

Bull P. (2000), *Sounding out the city: personal stereos and the management of everyday life*, Berg: Oxford.

Butlin, R. (1993), *Historical Geography: through the gates of space and time*, London: Arnold.

Cairncross, F. (1997), *The death of distance*, London: Orion.

Cairns, S., Sloman, L., Newson, C., Anable, J., Kirkbride, A. and Goodwin, P. (2004), *Smarter choices – changing the way we travel*, London: DfT.

Caradog Jones, D. (1934), *The social survey of Merseyside*, Liverpool: University of Liverpool Press.

Carlstein, T., Parkes, D. and Thrift, N. (eds) (1978), *Timing Space and Spacing Time, vol 2: Human Activity and Time Geography*, London: Arnold.

Carter, F. (1975), 'C-K-D employees, Prague 1871-1920: some aspects of their geographical distribution', *Journal of Historical Geography*, 1, 69-98.

Castles, S. and Miller, M. (1993), *The age of migration: international population movement in the modern world*, Basingstoke: Macmillan.

Cervero, R. (1995), 'Planned communities, self-containment and commuting: a cross-national perspective', *Urban Studies*, 32, 1135-61.

Champion, A. (ed.) (1989), *Counterurbanization: the changing pace and nature of population deconcentration*, London: Arnold.

Champion, A. and Fielding, A. (eds) (1992), *Migration processes and patterns. Vol. 1. Research progress and prospects*, Belhaven: London.

Checkland, S. (1981), *The Upas Tree: Glasgow 1875-1975, and after 1975-1980*, Glasgow: University of Glasgow Press.

Cherry, G. (1988), *Cities and plans: the shaping of urban Britain in the nineteenth and twentieth centuries*, London: Arnold.

Clay, H. and Brady, K. (eds) (1929), *Manchester at work: a survey*, Manchester, Civic Week Committee.

Constantine, S. and Warde, A. (2000), 'Challenge and change in the twentieth century', in White, A. (ed.), *A history of Lancaster, 1193-1993*, 2nd edn, Edinburgh: Edinburgh University Press, pp. 199-244.

Corporation of Glasgow (1969), *Glasgow Corporation Transport motor buses: an historical survey*, Glasgow: Transport Museum.

Cross, D. (1990), *Counterurbanization in England and Wales*, Aldershot: Avebury.

Daily Despatch (Manchester), 1938.

Daniels, P. (1970), 'Employment decentralization and the journey to work', *Area*, 1, 47-51.

Daniels, P. (1980), *Office location and the journey to work*, Aldershot: Gower.

Daniels, P. and Warnes, A. (1983), *Movement in cities*, London: Methuen.

Davidoff, L. (1990), 'The family in Britain', in Thompson, F.M.L. (ed.) *The Cambridge Social History of Britain, 1750-1950. Volume 2: People and their environment*, Cambridge: Cambridge University Press, pp. 71-130.

Davies, W. and Musson, T. (1978), 'Spatial patterns of commuting in South Wales, 1951-71', *Regional Studies*, 12, 353-66.

de Certeau, M. (1984), *The practice of everyday life*, Berkeley: University of California Press.

Dennis, R. (1984), *English industrial cities of the nineteenth century*, Cambridge: Cambridge University Press.

Department of Environment, Transport and the Regions (DETR), (1998a), *A new deal for transport: better for everyone. The Government White Paper on the future of transport*, London: TSO.

DETR (1998b), *Transport trends*, London: TSO.

DETR (1998c), *Breaking the logjam: The Government's consultation paper on fighting traffic congestion and pollution through road user and workplace parking charges*, London: TSO.

DETR (1999), *From workhorse to thoroughbred: a better role for bus travel*, London: TSO.

DETR (2000), *Factors Leading to Increased School Journey Length: Final Report*, DETR London. [Online], Available at: http://www.local-transport.dtlr.gov.uk/schooltravel/increase/final/index.htm.

DETR (2001), *A strategy for DETR integrated transport research*, London: TSO.

Department of Transport (DoT) (1979), *National Travel Survey*, London: DoT.

DoT,(1988), *National Travel Survey,* London: DoT.

Department for Transport (DfT) (2000), *10 year plan for transport*, London: DfT.

DfT (2001), *National Travel Survey: 1999/2001 Update*, London: National Statistics.

DfT (2004a), *The future of transport*, London: HMSO.

DfT (2004b), *Walking and cycling action plan*, London: DfT.

Department for Transport Web Pages, *Transport Statistics* (accessed 8/10/2004), http://www.dft.gov.uk/stellent/groups/dft_control/documents/contentservertemplate/dft_index.hcst?n=8802&l=4.

Desalvo, J. and Huq, M. (1996), 'Income, residential location and mode choice', *Journal of Urban Economics*, 40, 84-99.

DiGuiseppi, C., Roberts, I., Li, L. and Allen, D. (1998), 'Determinants of car travel on daily journeys to school: cross-sectional survey of primary school children', *British Medical Journal*, 316 (7142), 1426-28.

Dixey, R. (1998), 'Transport modes for the journey to school', *Traffic engineering and control*, 39, 363.

Docherty, I. and Shaw, J. (eds), (2003), *A new deal for transport?*, Oxford: Blackwell.

Dodge, M. and Kitchin, R. (2000), *Mapping cyberspace*, New York: Routledge.

Dora, C. and Phillips, M. (2001), *Transport, environment and health*, Geneva: World Health Organisation.

Dorling, D. (1997), *Death in Britain: how local mortality rates have changed, 1950s-1990s*, York: Rowntree Foundation.

Doyle, B. (2000), 'The changing function of urban government: councillors, officials and pressure groups', in Daunton, M. (ed.) *The Cambridge Urban History of Britain: Volume III*, Cambridge: Cambridge University Press, pp. 287-314.

Dyos, H.J. and Aldcroft, D. (1969), *British transport: an economic survey from the seventeenth century to the twentieth*, Leicester: Leicester University Press.

Eyre, D. (1971), *Manchester's buses 1906-1945*, Manchester: Manchester Transport Museum Society.

Eyles, J. (1989), 'The geography of everyday life', in Gregory, D. and Walford, R. (eds), *Horizons in Human Geography*, London: Macmillan, pp. 102-117.

Farnie, D. (1980), *The Manchester ship canal and the rise of the port of Manchester, 1894-1975*, Manchester: Manchester University Press.

Featherstone, M., Thrift, N., Urry, J., (eds) (2004), 'Automobilities', *Theory, Culture and Society, Special Issue*, 21, 1-284.

Fields, K. (1989), 'What one cannot remember mistakenly', *Oral History*, 17, 44-53.

Fitzpayne, E. (1948), *A report on the future development of passenger traffic in Glasgow*, Glasgow: Glasgow Corporation Transport.

Forrester, H. (1974), *Twopence to cross the Mersey*, London: Cape.

Fotel, T. and Thomsen, T. (2004), 'The surveillance of children's mobility', *Surveillance and Society*, 1, 535-554 (http://www.surveillance-and-society.org)

Frangopulo, N. (1977), *Tradition in action: the historical evolution of the Greater Manchester County*, Wakefield: Manchester Education Committee.

Freeman, M. (1986), 'Transport', in Langton, J. and Morris, R. (eds), *Atlas of industrialising Britain*, London: Methuen, pp. 81-94.

Freeman, M. and Aldcroft, D. (eds) (1988), *Transport in Victorian Britain*, Manchester: Manchester University Press.

Furedi, F. (2001), *Paranoid parenting: abandon your anxieties and be a good parent*, London: Penguin.

Gibb, A. (1983), *Glasgow: the making of a city*, London: Croom Helm.

Gilbert, D. and Southall, H. (2000), 'The urban labour market', in Daunton, M. (ed.), *The Cambridge Urban History of Britain. Volume III*, Cambridge: Cambridge University Press, pp. 593-628.

GLA (2004), *The mayor's transport strategy revision*, London: GLA.

Glasgow City Council (1996), *Glasgow fact sheets, 1995-96*, Glasgow: Glasgow City Council.

Glasgow City Council, (2000), *Local Transport Strategy 2001-2004*, Glasgow: Glasgow City Council.

Glasgow Corporation (1967-75), *Greater Glasgow Transportation Study, volumes I-V*, Glasgow: Glasgow Corporation.

Glasgow Corporation Transport Committee (GCTC) (1929-70), *Annual Reports*, Glasgow: GCTC.

Glasgow Herald (1924; 1937-38; 1955; 1956-57).

GMPTA (2004), *Greater Manchester Local Transport Plan: Monitoring Report, 2004*, Manchester: GMPTA.

Gonzalez, R. (1997), 'The value of time: a theoretical review', *Transport Reviews*, 17, 245-66.

Government Office for London (1996), *A transport strategy for London*, London: HMSO.

Gray, E. (ed.) (1967), *The tramways of Salford*, 2nd edn, Salford: Trustees of Salford Transport Museum Society.

Greater Glasgow Passenger Transport (GGPT) (1980), *Trans-Clyde: Strathclyde Region's transport system*, Glasgow: GGPT.

Greater London Authority (GLA) (2001), *The Mayor's Transport Strategy*, London: GLA.

Greater London Authority (GLA) website, (accessed 12/10/04): http://www.london.gov.uk/.

Greater Manchester Passenger Transport Authority (GMPTA) (2001), *Greater Manchester Local Transport Plan*, Manchester: GMPTA.

Greater Manchester Passenger Transport Executive, web site (accessed 8/10/04), http://www.gmpte.com/.

Green, A., Hogarth, T. and Shackleton, R. (1999), 'Longer distance commuting as a substitute for migration in Britain: A review of trends, issues and implications', *International Journal of Population Geography*, 51, 49-67.

Green, D. (1988), 'Distance to work in Victorian London: a case study of Henry Poole, bespoke tailors', *Business History*, 30, 179-94.

Gregory, D. (1995), 'Between the book and the lamp: imaginative geographies of Egypt, 1849-50', *Transactions of the Institute of British Geographers*, NS20, 29-57.

Hagerstrand, T. (1975), 'Space, time and human conditions', in Karlqvist, A., Lundqvist, L. and Snickars, F. (eds), *Dynamic Allocation of Urban Space*, Farnborough: Saxon House, pp. 3-14.

Halfacree, K. and Boyle, P. (1993), 'The challenge facing migration research: the case for a biographical approach', *Progress in Human Geography*, 17, 333-48.

Hall, P., Gracey, H., Drewett, R. and Thomas, R. (eds) (1973), *The containment of urban England*, London: Allen and Unwin.

Haraven, T. (ed.) (1978), *Transitions: the family and life course in historical perspective*, New York: Academic Press.

Hewitt, W. (1928), *Workplaces and movement of workers in the Merseyside area*, London: Hodder and Stoughton.

Hillman, M., Adams, J. and Whitelegg, J. (1990), *One false move ...:a study of children's independent mobility*, London: Policy Studies Institute.

Hine, J. and Mitchell, F. (2003), Transport disadvantage and social exclusion: exclusionary mechanisms in transport in urban Scotland, Aldershot: Ashgate.

HMSO (1995), *Manchester: 50 years of change. Post-war planning in Manchester*, London: HMSO.

Hodgson, R. and Cullen, J. (1969), 'Recent developments in highway planning in Scotland', *Proceedings of the Institute of Civil Engineering*, 7106, 223-45.

Hoggart, K. and Green, D. (1991), *London: A new metropolitan geography*, London: Arnold.

Holloway, L., and Hubbard, P., (2001), *People and place: the extraordinary geographies of everyday life*, Prentice Hall, Harlow.

Holloway, S. and Valentine, G. (eds) (2000), *Children's Geographies: playing, living, learning*, London: Routledge.

Howell, F. and Bronson, D. (1996), 'The journey to work and gender inequality in earnings: a cross-validation study for the United States', *Sociological Quarterly*, 37, 429-47.

Inglis Report (1951), *Passenger Transport in Glasgow and District*, London: British Transport Commission.

Jackson, J. (1973), *Semi-detached London: Suburban development, life and transport, 1900-39*, London: Allen and Unwin.

Janelle, D. and Hodge, D. (eds) (2000), *Information, place and cyberspace: issues in accessibility*, Berlin: Springer.

Johnson, D. (1990), *Parental choice in education*, London: Unwin Hyman.

Joireman, J., VanLange, P., Kuhlman, D., VanVugt, M. and Shelley, G. (1997), 'An interdependence analysis of commuting decisions', *European Journal of Social Psychology*, 4, 441-63.

Joshi, M. and Maclean, M. (1995), 'Parental attitudes to children's journeys to school', *World Transport Policy and Practice*, 1, 29.

Joyce, J. (1982), *Roads and rails of Manchester, 1900-1950*, Manchester: Ian Allan.

Kearns, R., Collins, D. and Neuwelt, P. (2003), 'The walking school bus: extending children's geographies?', *Area*, 35, 285-92.

Kellett, J. (1979), *The impact of railways on Victorian cities*, London: Routledge and Kegan Paul.

Kidd, A. (1993), *Manchester*, Keele: Ryburn Publishing.

Kidd-Hewitt, D. and Osborne, R. (1995), *Crime and the media: the postmodern spectacle*, London: Pluto.

King, R. (ed.) (1995), *Mass migrations in Europe: the legacy and the future*, Chichester: Wiley.

Kitchin, R. (1998), *The world on the wires*, New York: Wiley.

Klein, T., Wirth, D. and Linas, K. (2003), 'Play: children's context for development', *Young children*, 58, 39-45.

Knowles, R., Law, C. and Senior, M. (1991), 'Recent transport developments in Greater Manchester', *Manchester Geographer*, New Series 12, 2-24.

Knowles, T. (1983), *Morecambe Bay's municipal buses, 1908-1983*, Lancaster: Lancaster City Council Transport Department.

Kok, J. (1997), 'Youth labour migration and its family setting: The Netherlands, 1850-1940', *History of the Family: An International Quarterly*, 2, 507-26.

Lawson, J. and Silver, H. (1973), *A social history of education in England*, London: Methuen.

Lawton, R. (1963), 'The journey to work in England and Wales: forty years of change', *Tijdschrift voor Economische en Sociale Geographie*, 44, 61-9.

Lawton, R. (1968), 'The journey to work in Britain: some trends and problems' *Regional Studies*, 2, 27-40.

Lawton, R. (1978), *The census and social structure*, London: Frank Cass.

Lawton R. and Pooley C.G. (1975), 'David Brindley's Liverpool: An aspect of urban society in the 1880s', *Transactions of the Historic Society of Lancashire and Cheshire*, 126, 149-68.

Liepmann, K. (1944), *The journey to work: its significance for industrial and community life*, London: K. Paul, Trench, Trubner.

Lloyd Jones, R., and Lewis, M. (2000), *Raleigh and the British bicycle industry: an economic and business history 1870-1960*, Aldershot: Ashgate.

London Passenger Transport Board (LPTB) (1934-48), *Annual Reports and Accounts*, London: LPTB.

London Transport Board (1963-69), *Annual Reports*, London: LTB.

London Transport Executive (1970-85), *Annual Reports and Accounts*, London: LTE.

Longworth, B. (1994), *100 years of Glasgow transport*, Glasgow: Cowbrough and McKeracher.

Lucas, K., Grosvenor, T. and Simpson, R. (2002), *Transport, the environment and social exclusion*, York: Rowntree Foundation.

Manchester Corporation Tramways Department (MCTramD) (1902-1928), *Annual Reports*, Manchester: Manchester Corporation Minutes.

Manchester Corporation Transport Department (MCTranspD) (1929-1965), *Annual Reports*, Manchester: Manchester Corporation Minutes.

Manchester Evening News, 1937-38; 1957, Manchester Central Library, transport press cuttings, F388.4M1.

Manchester Guardian, 1938.

Marsden, W. (1977), 'Education and the social geography of nineteenth-century towns and cities', in Reeder, D. (ed.) *Urban education in the nineteenth century*, London: Taylor and Francis.

Marsden, W. (1979), 'Census enumerators' returns, schooling and social areas in the late-Victorian town: a case study of Bootle', in Lowe, R. (ed.) *New approaches to the study of popular education 1851-1902*, Leicester: Leicester University Press.

Matthews, H., Limb, M. and Taylor, M. (2000), 'The street as third space', in Holloway, S. and Valentine, G. (eds), *Children's geographies: playing, living, learning*, Routledge: London, pp. 63-79.

McDowell, L. (1999), *Gender, identity and place: understanding feminist geographies*, Minneapolis: University of Minnesota Press.

McEwan, C. (1996), 'Paradise or pandemonium? West African landscapes in the travel accounts of Victorian women', *Journal of Historical Geography*, 22, 68-83.

MCTranspD (1935), *A hundred years of road passenger transport in Manchester, 1835-1935*, Manchester: MCTranspD.

Mensah, J. (1995), 'Journey to work and job search characteristics of the urban poor: a gender analysis of survey data from Edmonton, Alberta', *Transportation*, 22, 1-19.

Mildner, G., Strathman, J. and Bianco, M. (1997), 'Parking policies and commuting behaviour', *Transportation Quarterly*, 51, 111-25.

Ministry of Transport (1955), *Committee of Enquiry into London Transport*, London: HMSO.

Mumby, D. (1978), *Inland transport statistics: Great Britain, 1900-1970. Vol 1*, Oxford: Clarendon Press.

Naess, P. and Sandberg, S. (1996), 'Workplace location, modal split and energy use for commuting trips', *Urban Studies*, 33, 557-80.

National Statistics (2002), *Social Trends 32*, London: TSO.

National Statistics (2003), *Transport Statistics Bulletin. National Travel Survey: 2003 provisional results*, London: Department for Transport.

National Statistics (2004), *Social Trends 34*, London: TSO.

National Statistics web site, *UK census of population 2001* (accessed 8/10/2004), http://www.statistics.gov.uk/census2001/profiles/UK-A.asp.

Nicholas, R. (1945), *City of Manchester Plan*, Norwich: Jarrold.

Noland, R. (1995), 'Perceived risk and modal choice: risk compensation in transportation systems', *Accident Analysis and Prevention*, 27, 503-21.

O'Brien, M., Jones, D., Sloan, D. and Rustin, M. (2000), 'Children's independent spatial mobility in the urban public realm', *Childhood*, 7, 257-78.

Office of the Deputy Prime Minister (2003), *Making the connections: final report on transport and social exclusion*, London: Social Exclusion Unit.

Pacione, M. (1995), *Glasgow, The socio-spatial development of the city*, London: Wiley.

Pain, R. (1995), 'Elderly women and fear of violent crime: the least likely victims? A reconsideration of the extent and nature of risk', *British Journal of Criminology*, 35, 584-98.

Pain, R. (1997), 'Social geographies of women's fear of crime', *Transactions of the Institute of British Geographers*, 22, 231-44.

Pain, R. (2000) 'Place, social relations and fear of crime: a review', *Progress in Human Geography*, 24, 365-87.

Pain, R. (2001), 'Gender, race, age and fear in the city', *Urban Studies*, 38, 899-913.

Parkhurst, G. (1996), *The economic and modal split impacts of short-range park and ride schemes. Evidence from nine UK cities*, University College London: ESRC Transport Studies Unit, Working Paper 29.

Parsons, E., Chalkley, B. and Jones, A. (2000), 'School catchments and pupil movements: a case study in parental choice', *Educational Studies*, 26, 33-48.

Patmore, J. (1983), *Recreation and resources: leisure patterns and leisure places*, Oxford: Blackwell.

Pearce, G. (1995), *Tourism today: a geographical analysis*, 2nd edn, Harlow and New York: Longman and Wiley.

Peelo, M., Francis, B., Soothill, K., Pearson, J. and Ackerley, E. (2004), 'Newspaper reporting and the Public Construction of Justice', *British Journal of Criminology*, 44, 256-75.

Peplor, D. and Rubin, K. (eds) (1982), *The play of children: current theory and research*, Basel: Karger.

Perkin, H. (1970), *The age of the railway*, London: Panther.

Perks, R. (1992), *Oral history: talking about the past*, London: Historical Association.

Pettitt, T., Frost, P. and Thornthwaite, S. (1995), 'Travel to school: influencing modal choice and encouraging safer journeys', *Transportation Planning Methods*, 394, 249.

Pooley, C. (1999), 'From Londonderry to London: Identity and sense of place for a Protestant Northern Irish woman in the 1930s', *Immigrants and Minorities*, 18, 189-213.

Pooley, C. (2003), 'Mobility in the twentieth century: substituting commuting for migration', in Gilbert, D., Matless, D. and Short, B. (eds) *Geographies of British Modernity*, Oxford: Blackwell, pp. 80-96.

Pooley, C. (2004), 'Getting to know the city: the construction of spatial knowledge in London in the 1930s', *Urban History*, 31.2.

Pooley, C. and Pooley, S. (2004), 'Constructing a suburban identity: the everyday life of a late-Victorian adolescent girl', Unpublished conference paper, Urban History Conference, London.

Pooley, C. and Turnbull, J. (1997), 'Changing home and workplace in Victorian London: the life of Henry Jaques shirtmaker', *Urban History*, 24, 48-78.

Pooley, C. and Turnbull, J. (1998), *Migration and mobility in Britain since the eighteenth century*, London: UCL Press.

Pooley, C. and Turnbull, J. (1999), 'Moving through the city: the changing impact of the journey to work on intra-urban mobility in 20th century Britain', *Annales de Démographie Historique*, 1, 127-49.

Prentice, A. and Jebb, S. (1995), 'Obesity in Britain: gluttony or sloth', *British Medical Journal*, 311, 437-9.

Pritchard, R. (1976), *Housing and the spatial structure of the city*, Cambridge University Press: Cambridge.

Raju, K., Sikdar, P. and Dhingra, S. (1996), 'Modelling mode choice by means of an artificial neural network', *Environment and Planning B: Planning and Design*, 23, 677-83.

Rhind, D. (ed.), (1983), *A census user's handbook*, London: Methuen.

Richardson, T. (ed.), (2004), 'Interface. Planning and the Big C: Challenging Auto Dependence through Conviction Politics in London', *Planning Theory and Practice*, 5, 487-514.

Roberts, R. (1971), *The classic slum: Salford life in the first quarter of the century*, Manchester: Manchester University Press.

Rodgers, B. (1986), 'Manchester: metropolitan planning by collaboration and consent; or civic hope frustrated', in G. Gordon (ed.), *Regional cities in the U.K., 1890-1980*, London: Harper and Row, pp. 41-58.

Rossi, P. (1980), *Why families move*, 2nd edn, Beverly Hills: Sage Publications.

Royle, E. (1997), *Modern Britain: A Social History 1750-1997*, 2nd edn, London: Arnold.

Russell, D. and Walker, G. (1979), *Trafford Park, 1896-1939*, Manchester: Manchester Polytechnic.

Sandberg, A. (2003), 'Play memories and place identity', *Early child development and care*, 173, 207-21.

Schafer, A. and Victor, D. (1997), 'The past and future of global mobility'. *Scientific American*, October, 36-9.

Schivelbusch, W. (1986), *The railway journey. The industrialization of time and space in the nineteenth century*, Berkeley: University of California Press.

Scott, Wilson, Kirkpatrick and Partners (1965) *A highway plan for Glasgow*, Glasgow: Glasgow Corporation.

Shaw, G. and Williams, A. (eds) (1998), *Tourism and economic development: European experiences*, 3rd edn, Chichester: Wiley.

Shaw, G. and Williams, A. (2004), *Tourism and tourism spaces*, London: Sage.

Shaw, M., Dorling, D., Gordon, D. and Davey Smith, G. (1999), *The Widening Gap: health inequalities and policy in Britain*, Bristol: Policy Press.

Shuttleworth, S. (1976), *The Lancaster and Morecambe tramways*, Blandford: The Oakwood Press.

Sibley, D. (1995), *Geographies of exclusion*, London: Routledge.

Simon, S. (1938), *A century of city government*, London: Allen and Unwin.

Simon, E. and Inman, J. (1935), *The rebuilding of Manchester*, London: Longmans.

Simpson, M. (1971-2), 'Urban transport and the development of Glasgow's West End, 1830-1914', *Journal of Transport History*, NS1, 146-60.

Sjolie, A. (2002), 'School journeys and leisure activities in rural and urban adolescents in Norway', *Health Promotion International*, 17, 21-30.

Skelton T. and Valentine, G. (eds), (1998), *Cool places: geographies of youth cultures*, London: Routledge.

Skelton, T. (2000), '"Nothing to do, nowhere to go?" teenage girls and public space in the Rhondda Valleys, South Wales', in Holloway, S. and Valentine, G. (eds) *Children's Geographies: playing, living, learning*, Routledge: London, pp. 80-99.

Slaven, A. (1975), *The development of the West of Scotland, 1750-1960*, London: Routledge and Kegan Paul.

Smith, G., Dorling, D. and Shaw, M. (eds) (2001), *Poverty, inequality and health in Britain, 1800-2000: a reader*, Bristol: Policy Press.

Sneed, R. (1961), *The traffic problem in towns*, Manchester Statistical Society: Manchester.

Soothill, K. (2003) 'Homicide in the media: what you're afraid of is not what's really going on', *Online opinion* http://www.onlineopinion.com.au/2003/feb03/soothill.htm.

Stead, D. (1998), 'Increasing the need to travel? Parental choice and travel to school', *Transportation Planning Methods*, 422 75.

Strathclyde Passenger Transport (SPT) (1974), *Annual Report*, Glasgow: SPT.

Strathclyde Passenger Transport (SPT) website (accessed 12/10/04): http://www.spt.co.uk/.

Tapsell, S., Tunstall, S., House, M., Whomsley, J. and Macnaghten, P. (2001), 'Growing up with rivers? Rivers in London children's worlds', *Area*, 33, 177-89.

Thomson, A., Frisch, M. and Hamilton, P. (1994), 'The memory and history debates: some international perspectives', *Oral History*, 22, 33-43.

Thrift, N. (1990), 'Transport and communications 1730-1914', in Dodgshon, R. and Butlin, R. (eds), *An historical geography of England and Wales*, London: Academic Press, pp. 453-86.

Thrift, N. (1995), 'A hyperactive world', in Johnston, R., Taylor, P. and Watts, M. (eds), *Geographies of global change: remapping the world in the late-twentieth century*, Oxford: Blackwell, pp. 18-35.

Thyssen, S. (2003), 'Child culture, play and child development', *Early child development and care*, 173, 589-612.

Tivers, J. (1985), *Women attached: the daily lives of women with young children*, London: Croom Helm.

Transport for London (2003), *London travel report, 2003*, London: Transport for London, available at: http://www.tfl.gov.uk/tfl/ltr2003/index.shtml.

Transport for London (2004), *Making London a walkable city: the walking plan for London*, London: Transport for London.

Urry, J. (2000), *Sociology beyond societies: mobilities for the twenty-first century*, London: Routledge.

Urry, J. (2002), *The tourist gaze*, 2nd edn, London: Sage.

Urry, J. (2003), *Global complexity*, Cambridge: Polity Press.

Valentine, G. (1989), 'The Geography of women's fear', *Area*, 21, 385-90.

Valentine, G. and McKendrick, J. (1997), 'Children's outdoor play: exploring parental concerns about children's safety and the changing nature of childhood', *Geoforum*, 28, 219-235.

Vance, J. (1966), 'Housing the worker: the employment linkage as a force in urban structure', *Economic Geography*, 42, 294-325.

Vance, J. (1967), 'Housing the worker: determinative and contingent ties in nineteenth-century Birmingham', *Economic Geography*, 43, 95-127.

van Poppel, F., Oris, M. and Lee, J. (eds) (2004), *The road to independence: Leaving home in Western and Eastern societies, 16th-20th centuries*, Bern: Peter Lang.

VanVugt, M., VanLange, P. and Meertens, R. (1996), 'Commuting by car or public transportation – a social dilemma analysis of travel judgements', *European Journal of Social Psychology*, 26, 373-95.

Verhoef, E., Nijkamp, P. and Rietveld, P. (1996), 'Regulatory parking policies at the firm level', *Environment and Planning C: Government and Policy*, 14, 385-406.

Wannup, U. (1986), 'Glasgow/Clydeside: a century of metropolitan evolution', in Gordon, G. (ed.), *Regional cities in the U.K., 1890-1980*, London: Harper and Row, pp. 83-98.

Wardman, M. (1997), *Disaggregate urban mode choice models: a review of British evidence with special reference to cross-elasticity*, University of Leeds: Institute for Transport Studies, Working Paper 505.

Warnes, A. (1972), 'Estimates of journey to work distances from census statistics' *Regional Studies*, 6, 315-26.

Warnes, A. (1975), 'Commuting towards city centres: a study of population and employment density gradients in Liverpool and Manchester', *Transactions of the Institute of British Geographers*, 64, 77-96.

Westergaard, J. (1957), 'Journeys to work in the London region', *Town Planning Review*, 28, 37-62.

White, A. (2003), *Lancaster: a history*, Chichester: Phillimore.

White, P. and Woods, R. (eds) (1980), *The geographical impact of migration*, London: Longman.

Whitelegg, J. (ed.) (1992), *Traffic congestion. Is there a way out?*, Hawes: Leading Edge.

Whitelegg, J. (1997), *Critical mass: transport, environment and society in the twenty-first century*, London: Pluto Press.

Whitelegg, J. (2003), *Earthscan reader on world transport policy and practice*, London: Earthscan.

Whyte, I. (2000), *Migration and society in Britain, 1550-1830*, Basingstoke: Macmillan.

Williams, P. and Dickinson, J. (1993), 'Fear of crime: read all about it? The relationship between newspaper crime reporting and fear of crime', *British Journal of Criminology*, 33, 33-56.

Williams, J. and Larson, J. (1996), 'Promoting bicycle commuting: understanding the customer', *Transportation Quarterly*, 50, 67-78.

Wolpert, J. (1965), 'Behavioural aspects of the decision to migrate', *Papers and Proceedings of the Regional Science Association*, 15, 159-69.

Wrigley, E. (ed.) (1972), *Nineteenth-century society: essays in the use of quantitative data for the study of social data*, Cambridge: Cambridge University Press.

Young, K. and Garside, P. (1982), *Metropolitan London: politics and urban change 1837-1981*, London: Arnold.

Index

A MOBILE CENTURY?

Transport and Mobility Series

Edited by
Professor Brian Graham, Director, Academy for Irish Cultural Heritages,
University of Ulster, UK and Richard Knowles, Reader in Geography, University
of Salford, UK, on behalf of the Royal Geographical Society (with the Institute of
British Geographers) Transport Geography Research Group (TGRG)

The inception of this series marks a major resurgence of geographical research into
transport and mobility. Reflecting the critical importance of the dynamic
relationships between transport and socio-spatial change, this work includes
research on:

The impacts of liberalisation, privatisation, competition and globalisation on
transport policies, networks and strategies;

Traffic generation and diversion and the economic impacts of large-scale
infrastructure projects such as the Channel Tunnel;

The assessment of environmental sustainability concerns about increasing
mobility, dispersal of activity sites and the dependence of transport on fossil fuels
and its associated air pollution;

Transport, gender and welfare issues;

The relationships between transport and leisure;

Congestion and capacity constraints in transport systems.

This monograph series complements the international, quarterly research journal,
Journal of Transport Geography (launched in 1993) and *Modern Transport
Geography* (eds Brian Hoyle and Richard Knowles, 2nd ed 1998 on behalf of the
TGRG). Together, these three outlets act as a forum for cutting-edge research into
transport and mobility, and for innovative and decisive debates on the formulation
and repercussions of transport policy making.

Also in the Series

Rethinking Urban Transport After Modernism
Lessons from South Africa
David Dewar and Fabio Todeschini
ISBN 0 7546 4169 4

A Mobile Century?
Changes in Everyday Mobility in Britain in the Twentieth Century

COLIN G. POOLEY
Lancaster University, UK

JEAN TURNBULL
Lancaster University, UK

MAGS ADAMS
University of Salford, UK

ASHGATE

Published by
Ashgate Publishing Limited
Gower House
Croft Road
Aldershot
Hampshire GU11 3HR
England

Ashgate Publishing Company
Suite 420
101 Cherry Street
Burlington, VT 05401-4405
USA

Ashgate website: http://www.ashgate.com

British Library Cataloguing in Publication Data
Pooley, Colin G.
   A mobile century? : changes in everyday mobility in Britain
   in the twentieth century. - (Transport and mobility series)
   1.Local transit - Great Britain - History - 20th century
   2.Transportation - Great Britain - History - 20th century
   3.Commuting - Great Britain 4.Travel - Social aspects -
   Great Britain 5.Great Britain - Social conditions - 20th
   century
   I.Title. II.Turnbull, Jean III.Adams, Mags
   388.4'0941'0904

Library of Congress Control Number: 2005927751

ISBN 0 7546 4181 3

Printed and bound in Great Britain by MPG Books Ltd. Bodmin, Cornwall.

List of Figures

Contents

List of Tables

List of Text Boxes

Preface

This book has emerged from two research projects that have together spanned much of the last decade. The first project, on the journey to work in Britain in the twentieth century, funded by The Leverhulme Trust (1996-1999), grew out of previous work by Pooley and Turnbull on migration and mobility in Britain since the eighteenth century. Although this research focused primarily on residential migration, it also touched on changes in the journey to work subsequent to relocation and led us to examine the ways in which the relationships between residential migration and everyday mobility have altered over time. The journey to work project allowed us to focus specifically on these themes during the twentieth century. The second project, on everyday mobility in Britain since the 1940s, funded by the ESRC (2000-2004) expanded our mobility research by focusing on all aspects of everyday mobility, especially the ways in which the daily mobility of children has changed over the past 60 years. In both projects we utilised and refined techniques of longitudinal data collection first developed in the migration research.

When starting this research we expected to record substantial changes in the amount and characteristics of everyday mobility since 1900. The main purpose of the projects was to examine the ways in which such changes impacted on people's lives. In practice, although some aspects of mobility have altered substantially, the most striking aspect of the data has been the degree to which, for many people, the pattern and process of everyday mobility has remained much the same for most of the twentieth century. We have thus found ourselves explaining stability rather than change and we have begun to question some established theories and assumptions about mobility in the recent past. Although not the primary purpose of the projects the research has also allowed us to relate our data on mobility change to contemporary debates about transport planning and urban sustainability.

Much of the material presented in this book is not being made available for the first time. We have presented numerous conference papers on our research and have published some ten articles in academic journals arising from different aspects of the projects. However, what this volume does do is to integrate the material in a way that has not been achieved before and to relate it to a broader context of both theoretical literature and practical transport planning. In so doing we hope to have strengthened the key messages of the research and to have communicated them to an audience beyond the small group of like-minded academics who are likely to read journal articles.

We have inevitably accumulated a large number of debts during the process of this research. Hopefully, all those who have assisted us are formally acknowledged elsewhere. If anyone has been missed we apologise and extend our grateful thanks. We have been particularly fortunate in that the research environment at Lancaster University has been especially stimulating and supportive for research on mobility. The Centre for Mobilities Research (CeMoRe), founded by John Urry, draws together academics from many different disciplines with a common interest in mobility in all its manifestations. We have learned much from seminars and other activities within CeMoRe and thank our colleagues for their interest in our work. The imperfections in the research remain, of course, entirely our own responsibility.

As with all research we complete this volume feeling that there remain many things that we do not fully understand about mobility change in the past. Due to the ephemeral and personal nature of much mobility we may never have satisfactory answers to all the questions raised. However, we hope that our research at least stimulates further interest in everyday mobility and begins to raise questions that others may go on to explore.

Colin G. Pooley
Jean Turnbull
Mags Adams
Lancaster, January 2005

Acknowledgements

We wish to thank everyone who has assisted us with the research upon which this book is based. Particular thanks to:

The Leverhulme Trust and the ESRC for funding the research.
All the respondents who completed questionnaires and agreed to be interviewed. This research could not have been completed without them, though due to a guarantee of anonymity they cannot be thanked individually.
Staff and students at the schools and colleges we contacted who assisted with recruitment of respondents.
Cait Griffith for coding and data entry.
Geraldine Byrne for transcription of tapes.
Dr Sue Owen for additional research assistance.
Siân Pooley for additional research assistance and proof reading.
Emma Joughin for additional research assistance.
Chris Beacock for help with the design of recruitment material and questionnaires.
Simon Chew (Cartographic Unit, Department of Geography, Lancaster University) for all the figures in the book.
Gemma Davies for assistance with GIS and, especially production of the figures in Chapter 5.
Mr. G. Brady (Greater Glasgow Passenger Transport Authority) for access to archives on public transport in Glasgow.
Steve Jenkins for assistance with the Access database.
The editors and staff at Ashgate who have dealt with production of the book.